Seasonal Hunger and Public Policies

Seasonal Hunger and Public Policies

Evidence from Northwest Bangladesh

Shahidur R. Khandker and Wahiduddin Mahmud

THE WORLD BANK
Washington, D.C.

Contents

Figures

Foreword

Seasonal hunger is often a characteristic feature of rural poverty in many parts of the developing world. Even though agricultural diversification, made possible through technological breakthroughs and infrastructural investments, has lessened the severity of seasonal hunger, the phenomenon still persists in many agricultural settings of tropical Asia and Sub-Saharan Africa. A crop failure or a poor harvest attributable to natural calamities like flood and drought can intensify seasonal hardships, sometimes taking the proportion of a famine. Seasonal hunger thus remains a routine cycle of food insecurity, a potential contributor to famine, and a trigger for policy responses such as the seasonal employment programs in Bangladesh, China, and India. The seasonality issue also deserves renewed attention because of the new threat of climate change and associated extreme weather conditions that are likely to exacerbate the frequency, severity, and unpredictability of seasonal shocks.

More than four-fifths of the world's poor live in rural areas and depend mostly on agriculture for their livelihoods. A large proportion of them are vulnerable to seasonal food insecurity but are "invisible" in poverty economics because the poverty numbers are usually based on annualized data and, as such, cannot keep track of the extent and severity of seasonal poverty. As a result, policies aimed at reducing poverty may disregard the seasonal poor if the causes of seasonal poverty differ from those that underlie year-round poverty. Moreover, the adverse seasonal effects, when left unattended, may contribute to endemic poverty by causing irreversible damage to health and livelihood sustainability. Even worse, the regions prone to severe seasonal hunger are also often disadvantaged in attracting the public investments required to break the seasonality-poverty cycle through strengthening and diversification of the local economy.

This book provides an exhaustive inquiry of seasonal hunger in rural Bangladesh, with a special emphasis on the country's northwest region. This region is known for its famine history and is particularly vulnerable to seasonal hunger. By combining large data sets from nationally representative household surveys and from surveys conducted specifically for the northwest region, the authors attempt to analyze the extent and causes of seasonal hunger while highlighting the interlocking nature of seasonality and endemic poverty. The book also attempts to assess the impacts of several recently launched policy interventions for mitigating seasonal hunger in the northwest region, thus providing insights into what works and what does not.

Although based on the case study of Bangladesh, the book's findings have far-reaching relevance for today's global efforts in mitigating food insecurity. The concerns for food insecurity have gained renewed importance in the global policy agenda because of the recent crises in the global food markets and also because of the increasing risks to livelihoods arising from environmental degradation and climate change. The problem of seasonal hunger is thus likely to persist or even deepen further because of these increasing threats to food security. This situation calls for an explicit recognition of seasonality in efforts to improve food security. As the book persuasively argues, seasonally targeted programs and policies within a well-coordinated approach to poverty alleviation need to be supported by international development agencies such as the World Bank.

One reason seasonal hunger does not receive enough attention in policy making is lack of seasonal information in the poverty estimates at the country and global levels. The other reason is inadequate appreciation of the complexity of issues surrounding seasonal hunger. On both counts, the book makes valuable contributions. It demonstrates how the same household survey data from which the official poverty estimates are derived can be used to capture seasonality. The book contributes to our understanding of why hunger linked to agricultural seasonality persists and how the problem can be tackled efficiently and cost-effectively, if not eliminated altogether. It also serves as a reminder of the challenges lying ahead for policy makers and practitioners engaged in combating hunger and poverty worldwide. I am sure this book will also be valuable in defining the scope of further research in poverty economics.

Justin Yifu Lin
Senior Vice President and Chief Economist
Development Economics
The World Bank

Preface

Seasonal hunger arising from agricultural seasonality persists as a distinctive feature of rural livelihood across many regions scattered throughout Sub-Saharan Africa and tropical Asia. Yet the subject has not received enough attention in contemporary poverty discourses or in global efforts to combat food insecurity. This lack of attention is partly because of the deficiency of official annualized poverty estimates in capturing seasonality, but partly also because of inadequate understanding of the complex issues surrounding poverty-seasonality links. This book represents a modest effort to remedy this situation by drawing on the case study of Bangladesh.

More than 70 percent of Bangladesh's nearly 150 million people live in the rural areas of Bangladesh, where life revolves around what is called a *rice economy*. Although the rural economy has become increasingly diversified with the growth of nonfarm activities, nearly 60 percent of the rural workers (and about half of the country's entire workforce) are still employed in the agriculture sector. The country is also prone to floods and other natural disasters. In such a setting, one would expect regular occurrences of seasonal stress, which is only made worse by the natural calamities.

This book provides an exhaustive analysis of seasonal hunger in Bangladesh, with a special focus on the country's northwest region of greater Rangpur. Well known in the famine literature, Rangpur was among the worst-hit regions during the Great Bengal Famine of 1942–44 and was at the epicenter of Bangladesh's 1974 famine. The region not only has lagged the rest of the country in poverty reduction, but also has remained particularly vulnerable to seasonal hunger, locally known as *monga*. Studying the phenomenon of monga in Rangpur can thus provide insights into how the interlocking of seasonality and endemic poverty can intensify the severity of seasonal hunger. Moreover, the recently launched policy interventions in the region provide a test case of what works and what does not in combating seasonal hunger. The quasi-experimental designs of some of these interventions are particularly suitable for assessing their effects.

The statistical exercises reported in the book are based on large, seasonally decomposed data sets from both nationally representative household surveys and specially designed surveys for the Rangpur region. The results from these exercises help to identify the causal mechanisms behind seasonal hunger while also providing insights into household responses in terms of, for instance, coping mechanisms, risk management, and livelihood choices. For example, seasonal hunger's relationship is found to be at least as strong with seasonal income as with year-round income. Hence, seasonal hunger is often a combined result of several factors: endemic poverty; a marked seasonality in agricultural income; and the limited ability of the poor households to smooth consumption through savings, borrowing, or food storage. Moreover, depending on the households' coping mechanisms, poverty and its seasonality may lead to an interlocking cycle that needs to be studied as a dynamic process in the context of long-term livelihood strategies of the poor.

Given the famine history of the region, seasonal hunger in Rangpur may be seen as a recurrent famine-like phenomenon; hence, much of the famine analysis in terms of households' "food entitlement failure" is relevant for explaining monga as well. For example, monga does not seem to be caused by lack of food availability, but by the seasonal loss of livelihoods for the poor. Moreover, as in the case of the past famines in this region, it is the agricultural day laborers who are found to be most at risk. The seasonal loss of employment for this group can be seen to be the most proximate cause of monga. Seasonal food price inflation may make monga more severe, but it is not a necessary correlate, whereas most famines are associated with food market failure resulting in food price hikes. Thus, monga may remain unnoticed as a form of silent hunger, because it is the abnormal increases in food prices that usually create public uproar and attract the attention of policy makers. This difference associated with monga also explains why the government's interventions for food price stabilization as a means of ensuring food insecurity have not worked to mitigate monga.

The variety of recent initiatives undertaken to combat monga in Rangpur includes introduction of new crop technology, provision of public works and other safety nets, facilitation of out-migration, asset transfer and skill training, and introduction of specially designed microcredit programs in addition to the regular ones. These initiatives to combat monga in Rangpur have been prompted by widespread public awareness, which in turn has been largely created by media reports and civic activism. The beneficial effects of these initiatives are already visible. Amartya Sen and others have argued that the incentives in democracy are more effective in averting major economic disasters such as famines than in addressing the problem of endemic hunger and poverty. Bangladesh's recent experience in mitigating monga suggests that political incentives can be created for combating severe incidence of seasonal hunger as well, once the phenomenon catches public attention. However, lack of similar awareness may have resulted in neglect of other regions in Bangladesh that are vulnerable to seasonal poverty and hunger.

The recent data show that, in addition to the greater Rangpur region, areas along the southern coastal belt have now emerged as new poverty pockets because of such agroclimatic factors as salinity intrusion and increased frequency, severity, and unpredictability of natural disasters. The pattern of hunger and seasonality in these emerging poverty pockets may be different from that of Rangpur, but lessons can still be drawn from the experience of combating monga in Rangpur. There is no single cure for seasonal hunger, and each type of environment, being unique in some respect, will have its own priorities and will require its own mix of policies. Ultimately, the challenge is how to enhance the ability of the rural poor to cope with the increasing complexity and uncertainty linked to seasonality by making their livelihoods more flexible, adaptable, and resilient.

The book is the outcome of a collaborative research project of the World Bank and the Institute of Microfinance (InM) in Bangladesh. The project is part of the InM's activities under the program called Promoting Financial Services for Poverty Reduction (PROSPER), which is supported by UKaid from the Department for International Development (DFID). Part of the support has also come from the International Growth Centre's country program in Bangladesh.

The book draws heavily on earlier works on a number of topics done jointly by Shahidur Khandker, Baqui Khaliliy, and Hussain Samad. We are indebted to both Baqui Khaliliy and Hussain Samad for their contributions in the data analysis and findings used in this book. We would like to thank the research staff at the InM, especially Syed Badruddoza, Abdul Khaleque, Suburna Barua, and Jabeer Sherazy, for excellent research support. We are indebted to Rashid Faruqee, Md. Mosleh Uddin Sadeque, Abdul Latif, and Atonu Rabbani at the InM for providing institutional support of various kinds as we carried out this study.

The household survey data used in this study have arisen in large part from the InM's impact evaluation of specially designed microcredit programs that are aimed at mitigating seasonal hunger in the Rangpur region and implemented by Palli Karma-Sahayak Foundation (PKSF), a wholesale microcredit lending institution. We are especially indebted to Jashim Uddin and Quazi Mesbahuddin Ahmed at PKSF for helping us understand the modalities of these program interventions and interpret the data.

At the World Bank, we are indebted to Will Martin for helpful comments on an earlier draft of this book. His comments were instrumental in revising the manuscript substantially and increasing its analytical focus. We are also indebted to Peter Lanjouw for his thoughtful comments, which were helpful in revising the manuscript further. We would like to thank Stephen McGroarty and Mary Fisk in the Office of the Publisher of the World Bank for their support in processing the book's publication. We also thank Estella Malayika in the Development Research Group, Agriculture and Rural Development, for production support.

We are, however, solely responsible for any errors or omissions contained in the book. Also, the views expressed in this book are entirely ours and do not reflect the views of the World Bank, InM, PKSF, DFID, or any other concerned organizations.

Shahidur R. Khandker   Wahiduddin Mahmud
World Bank, Washington, D.C.   Institute of Microfinance, Dhaka

About the Authors

Shahidur R. Khandker (PhD, McMaster University, Hamilton, Ontario, 1983) is a lead economist in the Development Research Group of the World Bank. He has authored more than three dozen articles in peer-reviewed journals, including the *Journal of Political Economy*, *Review of Economic Studies*, and *Journal of Development Economics*. He has also written several books, including *Fighting Poverty with Microcredit: Experience in Bangladesh*, published by Oxford University Press; *Handbook on Poverty and Inequality*, coauthored with Jonathan Haughton and published by the World Bank; and *Handbook on Impact Evaluation: Quantitative Methods and Practices*, coauthored with Gayatri Koolwal and Hussain Samad and published by the World Bank. He has written several book chapters and more than 40 discussion papers at the World Bank on poverty, rural finance, microfinance, agriculture, and infrastructure. His work covers about 30 countries. His current research projects include household coping and government response to economic crisis, long-term dynamics of microcredit programs, and evaluation of energy poverty and rural electrification in countries in Africa, Asia, and Latin America.

Wahiduddin Mahmud (PhD, Cambridge University, United Kingdom, 1978) is chairman of the Institute of Microfinance, Dhaka. He is currently a member of the United Nations Committee for Development Policy, chairman of the South Asia Network of Economic Research Institutes, and Coordinator of the International Growth Centre's research program in Bangladesh. He was until recently professor of economics at Dhaka University and has held visiting research appointments at, among other institutions, the World Bank, Institute of Development Studies at Sussex University, United Nations Development Programme at Jakarta, and International Food Policy Research Institute. He is a founder and former chairman of Palli Karma-Sahayak Foundation, a wholesale lending institution for microcredit in Bangladesh. He was a member of the caretaker government of Bangladesh in charge of the ministries of finance and planning. His books include *Adjustment and Beyond: The Reform Experience in South Asia* (Palgrave-Macmillan), *Handbook on the South Asian Economies* (Edward Elgar), and *The Theory and Practice of Microcredit* (Routledge, forthcoming).

Abbreviations

BRAC	Bangladesh Rural Advancement Committee
DFID	Department for International Development
DID	difference-in-differences (method)
EGPP	Employment Generation Program for the Poorest
EP	extreme poverty
EV	vulnerability to extreme poverty
FE	fixed-effects (method)
FFW	Food for Work (program)
GDP	gross domestic product
HIES	Household Income and Expenditure Survey
HYV	high-yield variety
ICRISAT	International Crops Research Institute for the Semi-Arid Tropics
IGVGD-TUP	Income Generation for Vulnerable Group Development–Targeting the Ultra Poor Programme
IIA	independence of irrelevant alternatives
InM	Institute of Microfinance
MDG	Millennium Development Goal
MFI	microfinance institution
MNL	multinomial logit

MP	moderate poverty
NGO	nongovernmental organization
PESP	Primary Education Striped Project
PKSF	Palli Karma-Sahayak Foundation
PRIME	Programmed Initiatives for Monga Eradication
PROSPER	Promoting Financial Services for Poverty Reduction
PSM	propensity-score matching
RERMP	Rural Employment and Road Maintenance Program
RMP	Road Maintenance Project
SNP	social safety-net program
VGD	Vulnerable Group Development
VGF	Vulnerable Group Feeding (program)

CHAPTER 1

Introduction

Seasonal hunger induced by agricultural seasonality is often a character-istic feature of rural poverty. The evidence of seasonal distress in many agrarian societies can be found in the narratives of economic historians.[1] With agricultural diversification made possible through technological breakthroughs in many parts of the developing world, the severity of seasonal stress and adversities has been reduced considerably, if not alto-gether eliminated. In certain agricultural settings, however, the seasonality of poverty and hunger, along with the associated seasonal shortfalls in income and consumption, is still a policy quagmire. The problem gets more complicated when agricultural seasonality is locked into a cycle of endemic poverty, seasonal hunger, and risk of further impoverishment. Poverty and seasonality may also reinforce each other through various other forces that create and sustain both. The thrust of policy needs to be to break this interlocking cycle of poverty and seasonality.

The importance of the seasonal dimension of poverty and hunger derives from the fact that more than 80 percent of the world's poor live in rural areas and depend on agriculture for their livelihoods. Most of the rural poor live in areas with marked seasonal contrasts; these areas cover Southeast Asia and much of Sub-Saharan Africa (besides parts of Central and South America and parts of Southeast Asia). Even in areas with nonseasonal climates, such as equatorial Africa, rural poverty may be linked to distinct crop cycles (see, for example, chapter 8 in Chambers, Longhurst, and Pacey 1981). All major food crops, such as wheat, rice, and maize, are seasonal crops with distinct annual production cycles. The seasonal stress can therefore become particularly acute in the event of a crop failure or a poor harvest.

Economically depressed and ecologically vulnerable areas are particularly likely to experience seasonal hunger. In areas where water or temperature constraints allow only one major crop harvest in a year, food scarcity and lack of employment may sharply deteriorate in the preharvest months. The seasonality of monocrop agriculture dependent on climatic conditions not only leads to large seasonal variations in rural incomes, but also makes such incomes subject to the vagaries of nature and, thus, unpredictable to a large extent. Such regions are also disadvantaged in attracting the investments that are needed to make the local economy more diversified and resilient and, thereby, to break out of the cycle of poverty and seasonality.

Seasonal hunger arising from the regular patterns of the agricultural cycle often escapes the attention of policy makers because of its short duration and endemic nature. As a result, it often remains unchecked and hidden. Yet such hidden hunger sometimes pushes millions of women and children—the most vulnerable in a rural society—to the brink of starvation every year. In Sub-Saharan Africa and other vulnerable regions, children fall prey to deadly diseases, such as diarrhea and malaria, during the period of seasonal hunger because of nutritional deficiency and the weakening of their immune systems. They may even succumb to permanent stunting of physical and cognitive development if they suffer from repeated seasonal undernutrition. In fact, one might reasonably argue that most of the world's acute hunger and undernutrition occur in the annual "hunger season," the time of year when the previous year's harvest stocks have declined, food prices are high, wages are low, jobs are scarce, and poor people are left with very little "entitlement" to food in terms of income, savings, or access to credit.

Although predictable seasonality creates hardship on a regular basis, it also allows some recovery. But irregular occurrences, such as floods or failure of the monsoon rains, can magnify the adverse seasonal effects and can culminate in a faminelike situation. Seasonal hunger has thus been varyingly described as the "cycle of quiet starvation" and the "father of famine," indicating that controlling seasonal hunger is a step toward averting famine (Devereux, Vaitla, and Swan 2008). Seasonal episodes of unusual intensity can also leave irreversible adverse effects on livelihood sustainability. These "ratchet" effects may arise from the various coping strategies poor households adopt to try to survive. Such strategies may include mortgaging or selling their land and other assets and making advance sales of crops and labor. The interlocking of poverty and seasonality is thus a dynamic process and needs to be studied in the context of livelihood strategies extending beyond a season or a year.

In discourses on food insecurity, seasonal hunger has seldom received the attention that it deserves. Yet the costs of ignoring seasonal hunger can be enormous. Lack of public awareness about seasonal hunger may be in part due to the way that poverty is usually measured. Seasonal hunger is, in fact, missing in the system of official data collection and analysis that averages and annualizes poverty numbers (IDS 2009). Consequently, these poverty estimates do not help identify the extent and severity of seasonal poverty. According to estimates made by the Food and Agriculture Organization of the United Nations for the mid-1990s, 1 billion poor people at that time were not food secure in the sense that they did not have at all times access to sufficient food to meet the dietary requirements for maintaining a healthy life. Recent estimates show no significant decline in that number. However, there is no direct account of how many of "the bottom billion," as Paul Collier (2007) calls them, suffer from seasonal hunger. In fact, the findings of several studies indicate that a much larger number of rural households may be vulnerable to food insecurity than the standard poverty statistics imply. In other words, some of the nonpoor measured by annual data may be seasonal poor because they cannot maintain consumption above the poverty line in response to seasonal shocks (see, for example, Dercon and Krishnan 2000).

Ideas about food insecurity, along with the associated policy debates, have changed over time. For example, emphasis has shifted from the deficiency of food availability on an aggregate level to a lack of entitlement to food at the household level as the source of food insecurity and famines (Sen 1981). The conceptualization of food insecurity in terms of household food entitlement can be useful in explaining seasonal hunger as well, particularly when combined with such ideas as livelihood security, risks and vulnerability, and ecological sustainability.

Along with the conceptual changes, the characterization of food insecurity has also changed, with some studies particularly focusing on short-term variability in entitlements (Chisholm and Tyers 1982). Following the lead of the World Bank (1986), researchers now often draw a distinction between chronic and transitory food insecurity. While transitory food insecurity focuses on risk of short-duration variations in household food access, this category has been further divided into cyclical and temporary food insecurity. These categorizations are meant to draw attention to the fact that many households experience large fluctuations in both consumption and income over relatively short periods of time, thereby causing substantial short-run movements of many people in and out of poverty. Although none of these categories particularly focuses on endemic seasonal hunger, they have common features that can help its analysis.

Although seasonality of poverty and hunger has been studied and has figured in policy discussions, the literature on it remains rather unconsolidated. Moreover, there is not enough emphasis on the possibility of seasonal hunger persisting because of policy failures to address the problem adequately and timely. Some early studies on seasonality emphasized the multidimensional nature of the problem, covering such diverse topics as seasonal labor use and energy needs, nutrition, ecology of disease, patterns of vital events, and community responses.[2] More recent studies have focused on income seasonality and constraints to consumption smoothing.[3] Rural households that lack buffer food stocks or past savings, or are credit constrained, or do not have enough access to remittance or public transfer schemes are found to face difficulty in smoothing consumption in the face of income seasonality related to crop cycles. But neither income seasonality nor lack of consumption smoothing necessarily leads to seasonal hunger; it depends on the extent of consumption shortfall relative to the threshold consumption level needed to prevent food deprivation.

Governments across the developing world adopt various policies for ensuring food security, including public food distribution and feeding programs and a variety of social protection schemes. These policies have varying success in combating seasonal hunger. A focus on seasonality is often missing in these policies and in investments in agricultural and rural development. Policies also must respond to the ever-changing complexity of seasonal hunger. The threat of climate change, for example, adds new concerns for food security. The extreme weather conditions associated with climate change may make seasonal shocks more frequent, severe, and unpredictable. It is the poor people in ecologically vulnerable regions who will be most at risk.

Moreover, seasonal hunger is also context specific, meaning that each rural society has its own dynamics of seasonality and seasonal hunger. Rural households experience and cope with seasonality in many diverse ways. A better understanding of this diversity is necessary to formulate policies and programs to strengthen the seasonal coping mechanisms of rural households.

This book draws on the example of Bangladesh in analyzing the nature and diversity of seasonal hunger, its underlying causes, and the effectiveness of mitigating policies and programs. More than 70 percent of the country's nearly 150 million people live in the rural areas, where life revolves around what is called the *rice economy*. Although the rural economy has become increasingly diversified with the growth of nonfarm activities, nearly 60 percent of the rural workers (and about half of the country's entire workforce) are employed in agriculture.[4] The country is also prone to floods and other natural disasters. In such a setting, one would, therefore, expect to find seasonality of income and consumption to be a regular phenomenon, only to be made worse by the occurrence of natural calamities.

To analyze the interlocking nature of seasonality and poverty, the book particularly draws on the experience of rural households from a region in northwest Bangladesh: the greater Rangpur region.[5] The region not only has lagged in poverty reduction compared to other regions, but also has remained particularly vulnerable to seasonal hunger, locally known as *monga* (Elahi and Ara 2008; Narayan, Yoshida, and Zaman 2007; Rahman 1995; Zug 2006). The region is both economically depressed and ecologically vulnerable. It is prone to river erosion and frequent floods, crop yields are low because of the adverse effects of sand deposits caused by floods, infrastructure is poor, agricultural wage rates are considerably lower than in other parts of the country, and few employment opportunities exist outside agriculture. The households in Rangpur thus seem trapped by economic geography in which livelihood opportunities are limited, are vulnerable to natural disasters, and are tied to seasonal crop cycles.

For many reasons, addressing hardcore poverty and seasonality simultaneously is a formidable task for policy makers. When poverty is already rampant and year round, pronounced seasonality of income and consumption only worsens seasonal poverty. Although seasonal poverty may be alleviated to some extent by bolstering safety-net programs, the roots of the problem may lie deeper and must be addressed through long-term investments in human and physical capital (Jalan and Ravallion 2000). A combination of adverse economic geography and agroecological vulnerability underlying the poverty-seasonality nexus can make the problem even more challenging. Rangpur can thus be an ideal test case for judging the effectiveness of policies in dealing with seasonal hunger. In fact, Rangpur is well known in the famine literature: it was among the worst-hit districts in the Great Bengal Famine of 1942–44 and was literally the epicenter of the 1974 famine in Bangladesh (Alamgir 1980; Sen 1977).

Using unique cross-sectional and panel data from Bangladesh, the book presents the findings from quantitative exercises to explain seasonal hunger in Rangpur vis-à-vis other regions and to evaluate the effectiveness of policies. Traditionally, the government of Bangladesh has attempted to contain seasonal hunger or pronounced seasonality of income and consumption through short-term measures such as Food for Work and other safety-net programs. But given the extent of endemic poverty in Bangladesh—particularly in Rangpur—the policy of mitigating seasonal food insecurity through short-term measures may not likely succeed unless it is accompanied by interventions that enhance levels of income and productivity as a long-term cure for poverty. Such a policy mix would involve interventions that affect credit, labor, and commodity markets as well as public investments in infrastructure.

In recent years, a great deal of public awareness has been created regarding the problem of seasonal hunger, or monga, in Rangpur. Both the government and a number of nongovernmental organizations have started various programs of interventions, some of them on a pilot basis. The programs, which are aimed at having both short-term and long-term effects, include cash or food for work, skill training, transfers of assets such as livestock or equipment, and specially designed microcredit programs in addition to the regular ones. Although the projects vary in scope and design, the target group is the same—namely, the poor households that are vulnerable to monga. These recently launched initiatives in the Rangpur region thus provide a test case for determining what works and what does not in combating seasonal hunger in particular and seasonality of income and consumption in general. The quasi-experimental designs of such projects are particularly suitable for assessing their effects.

This book, therefore, has several objectives:

- To understand the nature and the extent of seasonal hunger in Bangladesh in general and the greater Rangpur region in particular
- To examine why seasonality of income and consumption still persists in Rangpur and is more marked than in other parts of Bangladesh
- To identify the reasons traditional policies have failed and to determine the effectiveness of new initiatives
- To draw lessons from these new initiatives for tackling new poverty pockets that are emerging in other areas of the country because of environmental degradation and climatic changes.

Within these broad themes, the book addresses a number of more specific policy concerns. For example, how do variations in local characteristics—economic and agroecological—affect the extent of seasonality? How do policies and programs affect both poverty and seasonality simultaneously? Is seasonal hunger persistent in Rangpur because of the failure of the labor market, the credit market, or both? How much of the severity of seasonal hunger is due to seasonal shortfalls in consumption, and how much is due to chronic poverty? Are the observed coping mechanisms welfare enhancing, or do they carry the risk of further impoverishment? For example, how effective is seasonal migration as a coping strategy? To what extent can short-term measures such as social safety nets alleviate seasonal hunger? What are the mechanisms through which seasonal poverty can be mitigated in a sustainable way? In particular, do microcredit programs—the conventional ones or those specially designed for tackling seasonal hunger—have a role? An analysis of these issues is expected to shed light for policy makers elsewhere as they design and implement programs for combating seasonal hunger.

The analysis of seasonality requires seasonal data. The findings from statistical exercises reported in this book are based on cross-sectional, seasonal, and multiyear panel data. The first set of data comes from the 2000 and 2005 rounds of the nationally representative Household Income and Expenditure Survey (HIES) of the Bangladesh Bureau of Statistics. The HIES data allow the examination of not only the extent of seasonality of income, consumption, and poverty in various regions of Bangladesh, including the greater Rangpur region, but also the role of infrastructure, the safety-net programs, and local area characteristics in affecting the extent of poverty and its seasonality. It may be noted that although the published results of the HIES refer to year-round averages, the survey is designed to capture the effects of seasonality and their variations among regions within the country.

The second data set comes from a baseline household survey conducted by the Institute of Microfinance (InM) in 2006 to assess the situation of monga in the Rangpur region. These data were collected as part of a new initiative of the Palli Karma-Sahayak Foundation (PKSF), a premier wholesale facility of microfinance, to combat extreme and seasonal poverty in that region. The survey was, in fact, a household census in the selected villages that collected information on almost half a million poor households, which represented nearly the bottom 60 percent of all households in the survey villages. The InM survey data also include household panel data from a follow-up survey conducted in 2008 with respect to a subsample of the InM baseline survey of 2006.[6] Together, all these data allowed an in-depth analysis of the policy questions that the book was intended to answer.

The book has nine chapters. Chapter 2 looks at the key conceptual issues and presents a global perspective on the challenge of addressing seasonal hunger. Chapter 3 brings Bangladesh's reality to the fore regarding seasonal poverty and food insecurity and the vulnerability of the northwest region. Chapter 4 analyzes the vulnerability of households to seasonal hunger, their coping strategies, and the extent to which income seasonality affects seasonal poverty and food deprivation. Chapter 5 reports some findings for both the Rangpur region and the country as a whole regarding the effects of policies and programs on poverty and food deprivation. The findings reported in the next three chapters are mainly related to the Rangpur region only. Chapter 6 examines the issue of seasonal migration in the context of mitigating seasonal deprivation. In chapter 7, the impact of the social safety-net programs is tested, whereas the effectiveness of microfinance is assessed in chapter 8. The concluding chapter, chapter 9, looks at the policy implications while also pointing to some emerging challenges.

Notes

1. See, for example, Destombes (2006) for a review of long-term patterns of seasonal hunger and malnutrition in northeastern Ghana. A discussion on agricultural seasonality in South Asia in a historical context can be found in Ludden (1999).

2. For an early study on the subject, see, for example, Chambers, Longhurst, and Pacey (1981).

3. For examples of these later studies, see Chaudhuri and Paxson (2001, 2002); Deaton (1991); Dercon and Krishnan (2000); Rosenzweig (1988); and Rosenzweig and Wolpin (1993).

4. This estimate is based on the Labor Force Survey of 2005/06, the latest year for which official information is available. *Agriculture* includes livestock, fishery, and forestry, in addition to crop agriculture.

5. The greater Rangpur region was one of the old 17 administrative districts of Bangladesh and now comprises five districts: Rangpur, Gaibandha, Kurigram, Lalmonirhat, and Nilphamari. The region accounts for 11 percent of both the land area of Bangladesh and its population, according to the preliminary results of the 2011 population census.

6. The follow-up survey was designed to evaluate PKSF interventions that included targeted microcredit for the poor along with a host of other program inputs. Since then, the InM has conducted two more follow-up surveys, in 2009 and 2010. The final chapter of the book provides a brief overview of the results of those surveys.

References

Alamgir, Mohiuddin. 1980. *Famine in South Asia: Political Economy of Mass Starvation.* Cambridge, MA: Oelgeschlager, Gunn & Hain.

Chambers, Robert, Richard Longhurst, and Arnold Pacey. 1981. *Seasonal Dimensions to Rural Poverty.* London: Frances Pinter.

Chaudhuri, Shubhom, and Christina Paxson. 2001. "Smoothing Consumption under Composition and Profitability of Agricultural Investments." *Economic Journal* 103 (416): 56–78.

———. 2002. "Smoothing Consumption under Income Seasonality: Buffer Stocks vs. Credit Markets." Discussion Paper 0102-54, Department of Economics, Columbia University, New York.

Chisholm, Anthony H., and Rodney Tyers, eds. 1982. *Food Security: Theory, Policy, and Perspectives from Asia and the Pacific Rim.* Lexington, MA: Lexington Books.

Collier, Paul. 2007. *The Bottom Billion: Why the Poorest Countries Are Failing and What Can Be Done about It.* New York: Oxford University Press.

Deaton, Angus. 1991. "Savings and Liquidity Constraints." *Econometrica* 59 (4): 1221–48.

Dercon, Stefan, and Pramila Krishnan. 2000. "Vulnerability, Seasonality, and Poverty in Ethiopia." *Journal of Development Studies* 366 (6): 25–53.

Destombes, Jérôme. 2006. "From Long-Term Patterns of Seasonal Hunger to Changing Experiences of Everyday Poverty: Northeastern Ghana c. 1930–2000." *Journal of African History* 47 (2): 181–205.

Devereux, Stephen, Bapu Vatila, and Samuel Swan. 2008. *Seasons of Hunger: Fighting Cycles of Quiet Starvation among the World's Rural Poor.* London: Pluto Press.

Elahi, K. Maudood, and Iffat Ara. 2008. *Understanding the Monga in Northern Bangladesh.* Dhaka: Academic Press and Publishers Library.

IDS (Institute of Development Studies). 2009. Special issue on the Seasonality Revisited International Conference. *IDS Bulletin* 17 (3).

Jalan, Jyotsna, and Martin Ravallion. 2000. "Is Transient Poverty Different? Evidence for Rural China." *Journal of Development Studies* 36 (6): 82–99.

Ludden, David. 1999. *Agrarian History of South Asia*. Cambridge, U.K.: Cambridge University Press.

Narayan, Ambar, Nobuo Yoshida, and Hassan Zaman. 2007. "Trends and Patterns of Poverty in Bangladesh in Recent Years." World Bank, Washington, DC.

Rahman, Hossain Zillur. 1995. "Mora Kartik: Seasonal Deficits and the Vulnerability of the Rural Poor." In *Rethinking Rural Poverty: Bangladesh as a Case Study*, ed. Hossain Zillur Rahman and Mahabub Hossain, 234–53. New Delhi: Sage.

Rosenzweig, Mark. 1988. "Risk, Implicit Contracts, and the Family in Rural Areas of Low-Income Countries." *Economic Journal* 98 (393): 1148–70.

Rosenzweig, Mark, and Kenneth Wolpin. 1993. "Credit Market Constraints, Consumption Smoothing, and the Accumulation of Durable Production Assets in Low-Income Countries: Investments in Bullocks in India." *Journal of Political Economy* 101 (2): 223–44.

Sen, Amartya K. 1977. "Starvation and Exchange Entitlements: A General Approach and Its Application to the Great Bengal Famine." *Cambridge Journal of Economics* 1 (1): 33–59.

———. 1981. *Poverty and Famines: An Essay on Entitlement and Deprivation*. New York: Oxford University Press.

World Bank. 1986. "Poverty and Hunger: Issues and Options for Food Security in Developing Countries." World Bank, Washington, DC.

Zug, Sebastian. 2006. "Monga: Seasonal Food Insecurity in Bangladesh— Understanding the Problem and Strategies to Combat It." Report prepared for the NETZ Partnership for Development and Justice, Bochum, Bangladesh.

CHAPTER 2

Understanding Seasonal Hunger

Key Issues in a Global Perspective

Key Conceptual Issues

Seasonal food deprivation is essentially an extension and particular manifestation of poverty and food insecurity. Prevalent among rural communities dependent on tropical agriculture, it also may be one of the most persistent and intractable aspects of global food insecurity. Yet as pointed out in chapter 1, the phenomenon has often been bypassed by the way poverty and food insecurity have been commonly characterized or conceptualized.

Before the 1980s, the global initiatives related to food security were concerned with national and global food supplies.[1] Since then, the focus has gradually shifted to questions of access to food at the household and individual levels. At the conceptual level, this shift has been helped by Sen's (1981b) analysis of famine, which emphasized the lack of household "entitlement" to food rather than a deficiency of food availability on the aggregate as the source of food insecurity and famine (see also Ravallion 1987; Sen 1981a). With further elaboration of this concept, food security is now commonly defined as "secure access to enough food all the time." Implicit in this notion of food security are the concepts of (a) sufficient food intake in relation to physical needs; (b) access to food in relation to entitlement through production, purchase, exchange, or assistance; (c) security involving risk and vulnerability; and (d) time, when food insecurity can be chronic, transitory, or cyclical (Maxwell and Smith 1992). Beyond these core concepts, the wider considerations of vulnerable livelihoods, such as those in the context of agroclimatic adversities, have also sometimes been brought into discussions on food security. Although none of these concepts specifically focuses on seasonal hunger, some common features can help its analysis.

Rural households in different agrarian settings experience and cope with seasonal hunger in diverse ways. But essentially, seasonal hunger is a manifestation of agricultural seasonality associated with annual crop cycles. Three distinct sets of factors interact with one another to produce seasonal hunger. First, at particular times of the annual agricultural cycles, some rural households—usually the poorer ones—find their livelihoods falling below a critical threshold for avoiding hunger. Second, those households lack enough capability for year-round smoothing of food consumption. In other words, they are unable to insure themselves against seasonal loss of livelihood. Third, seasonal hunger is mostly an extension of year-round poverty, because the households living at the margin of poverty have less room to maneuver and are therefore more likely to go under at times of seasonal stress. For an understanding of seasonal hunger in more specific contexts, these three basic underlying factors and their interactions need further elaboration.

Seasonal Loss of Livelihoods

Agricultural seasonality arises because of the lag between the planting and harvesting of major food crops, such as rice, wheat, and maize, all of which have distinct seasonal production cycles. As a result, the preharvest period may be characterized by the lack of paid employment for agricultural workers, dwindling food stocks of subsistence farmers, and high food prices. Of course, the production environment is determined by agroclimatic conditions and level of technological development. Seasonal stress will be more severe and more unpredictable in the case of monocrop agriculture dependent on the vagaries of nature than in a more favorable production environment that allows multiple cropping and crop diversification. Moreover, rural communities living in particular poverty pockets will be most at risk because of their limited capacity to deal with income seasonality.

Apart from looking at the effect of varying production environments, tone must break down the analysis of seasonal hunger by socioeconomic group. As with famine analysis, the mechanisms for the loss of entitlement to food can differ substantially among these various household groups and so also can be the remedial measures. For example, having access to off-farm employment and income sources will likely reduce the adverse effects of agricultural seasonality. More important, landless laborers are affected by seasonality because of a decline in the demand for hired labor during the lean season, whereas smallholder subsistence farmers may face starvation when their food stocks are drawn down before the next harvest. Although the time of seasonal stress may coincide for both groups, the sources of their food insecurity differ. Thus, for example, if the crop cultivation activities in a year are disrupted by natural calamities like drought or floods, landless laborers suffer immediate loss of employment and income (provided they are paid in cash), whereas smallholder farmers will be disadvantaged over the following crop cycle because they will begin with lower-than-usual food stocks because of harvest losses.

For both landless laborers and food-deficit marginal farmers, their food entitlement may be further squeezed by possible preharvest increases in food prices. Seasonal hunger is thus related to food market efficiency as well. As discussed in the famine literature, a severe loss of food entitlement may occur for certain household groups even in a year of plentiful food availability if there is a market failure, such as one resulting from irrational price expectations and a buildup of food stocks.[2] But more important for the analysis of recurrent seasonal hunger is the fact that it can occur because of the loss of employment and income alone (linked to the crop cycle), even without seasonal increases in food prices. Consequently, such food deprivation may remain unnoticed as a form of "silent hunger," because the abnormal increases in food prices usually create public outcry and attract the attention of policy makers. This factor also explains why food price stabilization alone as a means of ensuring food security is unlikely to work in mitigating seasonal hunger.

Lack of Self-Insurance and Consumption Smoothing

Seasonal hunger does not result from income seasonality alone; it is typically a particular manifestation of poverty in general. The poor, typically the extremely poor, lack the capacity to maintain their food consumption at the time of a seasonal decline in income; they are even less capable of self-insuring against occasional seasonal stress of unpredictable severity. In other words, seasonal hunger occurs when mechanisms for consumption smoothing fail for poor households. For example, rural households use traditional risk management devices, such as local pooling of resources or mutual support provided by family or friends. Such community-based insurance is more feasible when the risks are idiosyncratic (that is, particular to households) than in the event of aggregate shocks like seasonal ones.

Lack of access to credit or lack of ability to save may prevent rural poor households from smoothing consumption. Even if they would like to save for precautionary reasons, they may not have access to appropriate financial institutions to do so. In the case of self-provisioning smallholder farmers, they might store grains as a buffer stock to smooth consumption; but the cost of storage due to spoilage can be high because of inadequate storage facilities.[3] The unpredictability of the extent of seasonal stress may also be a reason for inadequate self-insurance by poor households, either through savings or through storage of grains. Even in the case of a predictable decline in income, it is difficult for a poor household that lives near subsistence to consciously plan for coping with future hardship. Avoiding severe starvation in the hunger season by undergoing less severe starvation year round may be preferable with regard to the nutritional well-being of family members, but that hardly looks like an option! In other words, immediate food needs may compromise poor households' ability or willingness for smoothing consumption.

The inability to smooth consumption raises some conceptual issues regarding household decisions of intertemporal substitution of food consumption. The problem primarily arises because food contrasts sharply with consumer durables that provide services smoothly over time in line with demand. The human body is able to build up reserves in the form of excess fats that can be used for energy during difficult times. In fact, the effect of seasonal food deprivation can be borne to some extent by drawing on any such bodily reserves; but this is, of course, an extremely inefficient and unhealthy means of coping with seasonal food deprivation. Seasonal hunger also needs to be distinguished from seasonality in food consumption that may arise from preferences related to changes in food prices, labor effort and energy requirements, or seasonal food choices. The seasonal hunger discussed here can hardly be the outcome of this kind of benign preference.

The question still remains whether poor households are incapable of smoothing food consumption in the face of adverse seasonality for some behavioral reasons. Various hypotheses have been offered to explain why poor people may be behaviorally averse to saving, such as the present bias in decision making, lack of self-control, or time-inconsistent preferences reflecting high discount rates (Fafchamps and others 2012; Spears 2009). For example, in discussing "the logic of self-control" for the poor, Banerjee and Duflo (2011, 198–204) point to the use of microcredit (in productive activities rather than for current consumption) as a way of helping the poor think about long-term goals. The fact remains that for those who live at the margin of poverty, the concept of intertemporal consumption substitution that is welfare enhancing is an ambiguous one.

The Nexus between Endemic Poverty and Seasonal Hunger

Seasonal hunger usually occurs when year-round endemic poverty is made worse by seasonal stress. Although predictable seasonality creates hardship regularly, it also allows some recovery. But an irregular occurrence, such as floods or failure of the monsoon rains, can magnify the adverse seasonal effects to an extent that leaves irreversible adverse effects on livelihood sustainability. These "ratchet" effects may arise from the way poor households try to survive by adopting various coping strategies—such as mortgaging or selling land and other assets and making advance sales of crops and labor. Poverty and its seasonality can thus be mutually reinforcing in an interlocking cycle. As such, the phenomenon needs to be studied as a dynamic process in the context of livelihood strategies of the poor extending beyond a season or a year.

Much depends, however, on the way poor households cope with seasonality. Although rural households adopt a variety of coping mechanisms, they may have only limited access to such coping mechanisms and are therefore unable to smooth food consumption year round.[4] Even then, households may take desperate measures, as mentioned earlier, to avoid the direst consequences of seasonality. Those measures are taken under adversity, even at the risk of damaging long-term livelihood sustainability. Some authors, therefore, prefer to distinguish between those "erosive" coping measures and "nonerosive" ones that do not undermine future livelihood (de Waal 1989). Yet others have identified distinct patterns in coping mechanisms that reflect stages of desperation, ranging from insurance mechanisms like savings to destitution behavior such as sale of assets and distress migration (Corbett 1988).

A household's perception of future risk of seasonal hunger is also an important factor in its choice of coping strategies. Several studies have shown how such perceptions, in the absence of adequate insurance mechanisms, can lead households to make inefficient choices, such as when entering into labor contracts, selling assets, or using production inputs.[5] In their efforts to minimize livelihood risks, households are prepared to accept lower but more steady and assured income. Such advance income-smoothing measures are a way for poor households to adapt to seasonality and uncertainty. The result is often a precarious balance between the household's own insurance mechanisms and risks that can be easily disrupted by shocks, triggering a cycle of impoverishment.

Policy Implications: Evidence from Global Experience

What policies can avert or alleviate seasonal poverty and hunger? The foregoing discussions on the key conceptual issues regarding seasonal hunger, together with the available studies on the global experience, suggest that policies need to be context specific.[6] Although global perspectives on the problem are useful, policies and programs derived from any single global template can hardly be the answer.

It is important, for example, to ascertain the sources of seasonal food deprivation that are amenable to policies in specific agrarian and socioeconomic settings. If a country has particular regional pockets of severe poverty and seasonal hunger, policies should focus on strengthening the local economy of those regions. Policy makers also need to take into account that farming systems and households' self-insurance arrangements vary across rural societies. In addition, to the extent that seasonal hunger is caused by seasonal increases in food prices, a policy goal should be to keep such fluctuations within reasonable limits. But if lack of employment in the agricultural lean season is the problem, price stabilization alone will not suffice. In that case, policies to promote rural nonfarm employment could be one way of limiting the effect of agricultural seasonality.

In broad terms, the pattern of seasonal hunger in Sub-Saharan Africa is distinct from that in South Asia. The contrast has been highlighted in the famine analysis as well (Ravallion 1987; Sen 1981a, 1981b). The Sub-Saharan pattern is characterized by the dominance of self-provisioning smallholder farmers in the production and storage of grains. In light of poorly integrated grain markets, local food availability is largely determined by smallholder supply, often resulting in large seasonal and interyear variations in grain prices. Poor farmers face seasonal hunger when their food stocks are depleted, which is also when market prices are high. In any case, they may have little cash to buy food from the market. Strengthening production on smallholder farms, along with improving grain storage facilities, is thus a policy priority for avoiding seasonal hunger.

In contrast, the household groups that are most vulnerable to seasonal hunger in rural South Asia consist of landless agricultural laborers and food-deficit marginal farmers. These household groups are adversely affected by the preharvest increases in food prices, more so if there is also a dip in the wage rates. But the main source of their vulnerability to seasonal hunger is the lack of agricultural employment in the lean season, which alone can result in seasonal hunger. Therefore, providing income-earning opportunities for landless agricultural laborers during the agricultural lean period needs to be a top policy priority.

Policies may also directly address the roots of seasonal hunger by trying to reduce the extent of agricultural seasonality through changes in cropping patterns. The problem is that all major food crops, such as wheat, rice, and maize, are seasonal and have distinct annual production cycles. Replacing numerous traditional crops with high-yielding varieties has no doubt helped increase food production, but it has also increased vulnerability to crop failure from natural calamities, such as drought, flood, salinity, or even pests (Strange and Scott 2005).[7] Public policies supporting research to develop high-yielding crop varieties that are suited to the local environment and are resistant to such natural calamities will benefit farmers, particularly in ecologically vulnerable regions that are prone to seasonal hunger.

Another possibility is to diversify food production and food choices by growing nonseasonal crops like cassava, which can be grown and harvested at any time of the year. For example, it has been suggested that the most promising way to reduce the severity of seasonal hunger in a country like Madagascar is to increase agricultural productivity of the secondary food crops, such as cassava and other roots and tubers (Dostie, Haggblade, and Randriamamony 2002). Not surprisingly, cassava is known as a "famine reserve crop" in Africa. More than 80 percent of cassava produced in the world is consumed by humans, and it is the principal source of energy for 500 million people in the tropical world (Lozano 1986). However, the problem with the production of cassava and similar root crops is a low yield per hectare compared with wheat or maize.

In the monsoon-fed rice agriculture of India and Bangladesh, promoting the production of irrigated winter rice has not only contributed to the growth of rice production but has also significantly reduced the extent of the seasonal agricultural cycle.[8] Crop diversification through a shift from cereals to high-value crops like vegetables and fruits can potentially reduce seasonal hunger by increasing farmers' income and creating more agricultural employment, but it will need government support for marketing and technology promotion (Mahmud, Rahman, and Zohir 2000).

With regard to the various mechanisms that households adopt as insurance against seasonal hunger (for example, buffer stocks, past savings, informal credit markets, or interfamily risk pooling), it is necessary to find out how efficient these mechanisms are and whether there is scope for institutional innovations. Improved storage, for example, has been found to help consumption smoothing in a cost-effective way. Microcredit is also found to have a role in consumption smoothing, both when loans are used directly for consumption and when they are used to support income-generating activities year round (Pitt and Khandker 2002). As noted earlier, ample evidence exists to suggest that lack of access to credit not only is a major constraint to consumption smoothing but also can result in serious efficiency losses for poor households in their effort to diversify livelihood risks.[9] It is worth noting, in this context, that alternatives to formal credit, such as informal lenders, could be costly and susceptible to failing completely in the event of an aggregate shock (Townsend 1995).

Various public programs for targeted income transfer can be a way to reduce the severity of seasonal consumption shortfalls. However, the problem here is often inadequate coverage and extent of assistance, as well as poor program implementation. Innovative programs of nongovernmental organizations can also help (Matin and Hulme 2003). The categories of interventions include emergency assistance; social protection safety nets, such as those provided by public works programs; and rural livelihood development, such as through asset transfer to vulnerable households (Devereux, Vatila, and Swan 2008). When targeted seasonally, these interventions can enhance the welfare of poor households by providing them increased food entitlement when they need it and by preventing them from resorting to desperate coping strategies (for example, Chetty and Looney 2006). The safety nets can thus act as social insurance.

In contrast, the interventions that are not seasonally targeted can affect seasonal hunger by altering year-round income and consumption. But this outcome will then depend in part on the capacity of the beneficiary households to smooth consumption. Targeted public works programs, such as Food for Work, may not always be suitable for seasonal targeting. The optimal timing of public works programs can thus pose a policy dilemma. Much of the rice cultivation in South Asia depends on the monsoon rains so that the preharvest lean season coincides with the late rainy season. This season is not often suitable for public works involving earthwork, although jobs are most needed then. Seasonal hunger aside, social safety-net programs are found to be more effective in arresting transitory poverty than persistent poverty (Ravallion, van de Walle, and Gautam 1995).

Because seasonal hunger is a manifestation of poverty in general, the answer to the problem ultimately lies in promoting poverty-alleviating economic growth. Experiences of countries show that economic growth alone is not enough; growth must be broad based enough to make the rural economies stronger, more diversified, and resilient to shocks— particularly in regions that are prone to seasonal hunger. Because of the interlocking nature of poverty and its seasonality, the two problems need to be addressed simultaneously, which is a formidable task for policy makers. Although seasonal poverty may be alleviated to some extent by bolstering safety-net programs, the roots of the problem may lie deeper and will need to be addressed through long-term investments in human and physical capital (Jalan and Ravallion 2000).

The persistent nature of seasonal hunger is evident from its prevalence across many parts of the developing world. However, in the absence of official data, there is no direct account of how many people actually suffer from seasonal hunger, and one must rely on the available studies. Of the examples from India, Malawi, and Myanmar, one such recent study provides a compelling account of the magnitude of seasonal hunger (Devereux, Vatila, and Swan 2008). The nature of seasonal stress in rural India is also analyzed by Agarwal (1990). In Sub-Saharan Africa, seasonal hunger is found to be a major dimension of declining food availability and increasing instability in food supply (Devereux 2009; Hadley, Mulder, and Fitzherbert 2007; Reardon and Matlon 1989). One might reasonably argue that most of the world's acute hunger and undernutrition occur during what is known in many countries as the annual "hunger season." The findings of several studies indicate that, compared with the standard poverty statistics, a much larger number of rural households may in fact be vulnerable to food insecurity. In other words, some of the nonpoor measured by annual data may be seasonal poor because they cannot maintain consumption above the poverty line in response to seasonal shocks (for example, Dercon and Krishnan 2000).

Policy makers may, however, draw some comfort from the fact that many rural communities successfully cope with income seasonality. For example, in the ICRISAT (International Crops Research Institute for the Semi-Arid Tropics) sample of Indian villages used in Chaudhuri and Paxson's (2001) study, agricultural households received on average 75 percent of their annual income in a three-month period, yet seasonal food consumption is found to be largely unrelated to income seasonality. The study further finds that food consumption may still show seasonality because of other factors, such as seasonal variations in prices, preferences, labor efforts, and precautionary savings motives. But the consumption seasonality of this nature is by choice, not a result of a lack of capacity to tackle the problem of income seasonality. Similarly, in the case of rural Thailand, Paxson's (1993) findings suggest that the observed seasonality in consumption patterns results from seasonal variations in prices or preferences, rather than from an inability of households to use savings or borrowing to smooth consumption. Other studies show that in many rural settings in the developing world, households may be able to smooth consumption (controlling for price and preference) even when they lack access to credit markets (Deaton 1991; Kazianga and Udry 2006). Households may do so using mechanisms such as savings, buffer stocks, or interfamily transfers. These examples show that seasonal food deprivation is not inevitable even with marked agricultural seasonality and that the way households can ensure against such seasonality may vary across diverse agrarian settings.

Fighting Hunger and Its Seasonality: A Global Challenge

From what is known about seasonal hunger, one might look at the roles that governments, international aid agencies, and donor countries could play in fighting this global problem. At the top of the Millennium Development Goals (MDGs) is "eradicating extreme poverty and hunger," and among the indicators for measuring progress toward reducing hunger are prevalence of child malnourishment (the proportion of underweight children younger than five) and the proportion of the population below a minimum level of dietary energy consumption. Thus, the emphasis on food security is not lacking in the goals set by the global community. However, there seems to be insufficient awareness about the seasonal dimension of the problem, which remains, at best, implicit in these goals. Although—following the lead of the World Bank (1986)—global discourse now commonly distinguishes between chronic and transitory food insecurity, seasonal hunger does not figure prominently in its characterization of food insecurity (Maxwell and Smith 1992).

Can Growth Handle Hunger and Its Seasonality?

Significant progress has been made in the past two decades or so in accelerating economic growth and reducing poverty in the developing countries. The world as a whole seems to be on track to reach the poverty reduction target included in the MDGs. Progress, however, has not been uniform with some parts of the developing world; Sub-Saharan

Africa, in particular, lags other regions. The acceleration of economic growth has also been accompanied by a sharp increase in income inequality, thus reducing the extent of the favorable effect of growth on poverty reduction.

It is commonly agreed that raising per capita income will likely reduce poverty and that economic growth can be the route out of poverty even for the poorest segments of the population. Figure 2.1 shows how global poverty has been reduced with growth. As Collier (2007, 11) argues, the problem of the so-called bottom billion of the world's population is that "they have not had any growth" rather than the "wrong type of growth," and "growth usually does benefit ordinary people." But there is also a debate regarding the nexus between poverty, inequality, and growth; that is, the effectiveness of growth in reducing poverty can be compromised if it also increases inequality. Economic growth needs to be inclusive as well as sustainable. For example, the volatile growth history in Sub-Saharan Africa has demonstrated that gains in poverty reduction through commodity boom–based growth are hardly sustainable.

Although growth on average is matched by proportionate reductions in poverty, the incomes of the poorest may increase less than proportionately with growth (Ravallion 2001). The magnitude of the growth

Figure 2.1   Relationship between Growth and Poverty Reduction Worldwide, 1981–2004

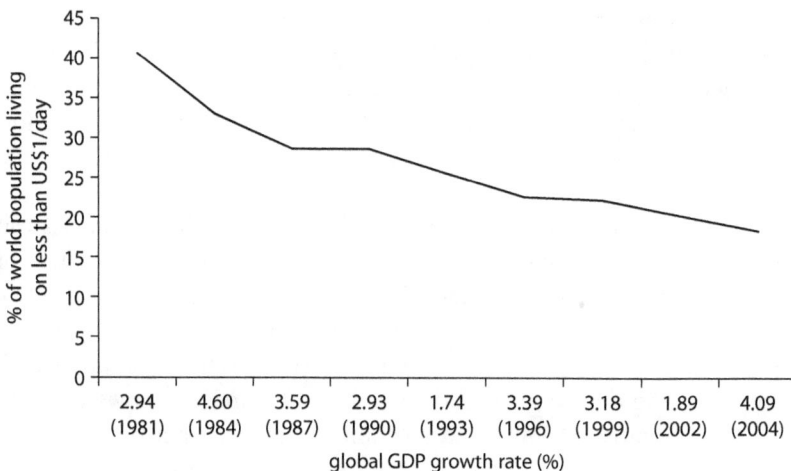

Source: World Bank 2008.
Note: GDP = gross domestic product.

elasticity of poverty is found to be influenced by various factors, such as initial inequality, the distributional pattern of growth, the composition of public expenditure, the level of human development, and the role of labor markets. Governments can intervene in these respects to make growth more pro-poor (Besley and Cord 2007).

But the aspect of poverty reduction that is the focus of this book and that has been rather ignored in policy discourses is the interlocking nature of poverty and its seasonality. As already discussed, extreme poverty makes seasonal poverty more acute, whereas the latter can have ratchet effects on future poverty because of the adoption of "erosive" coping strategies. Moreover, the uncertainty associated with seasonality can lead to serious efficiency losses in the livelihood strategies adopted by the poor. In such delicately balanced livelihood systems, an episode of seasonal distress, particularly of occasional high intensity, can easily trigger a cycle of impoverishment. For that reason, extreme poverty and seasonality need to be addressed simultaneously, a formidable task for policy makers. In agroecologically vulnerable areas, the complexity of the underlying poverty-seasonality nexus can make the problem even more challenging.

Compared with poverty reduction, the global record of reducing hunger and undernourishment is rather disappointing (UN 2011). According to the estimates of the Food and Agriculture Organization of the United Nations, the absolute number of undernourished people has not declined since the early 1990s; the number increased to more than 1 billion in 2009, partly as a result of the global recession during 2008–09 and the food crisis of 2008, and then declined to 925 million in 2010. This number is well above the MDG target for hunger reduction. Micronutrient deficiencies, termed *hidden hunger*, affect 2 billion people worldwide. Unfortunately, there is no official estimate of the people affected by the other hidden hunger, namely, seasonal hunger.

The progress in various hunger-related indicators across countries can be seen from the Global Hunger Index, which is prepared by a trio of think tanks led by the International Food Policy Research Institute. The index combines data on undernourishment in the population, underweight children, and under-five mortality rate to arrive at an overall measure of the degree of food deprivation.[10] Figure 2.2 shows the estimates for the most recent period for some of the worst-performing countries.[11] According to this index, most of the countries where hunger is rife are in South Asia and Sub-Saharan Africa. When compared with similar estimates for the early 1990s, the countries in South Asia are found to

Figure 2.2   The Worst-Performing Countries According to the Selected Factors of the Global Hunger Index, 2004–08

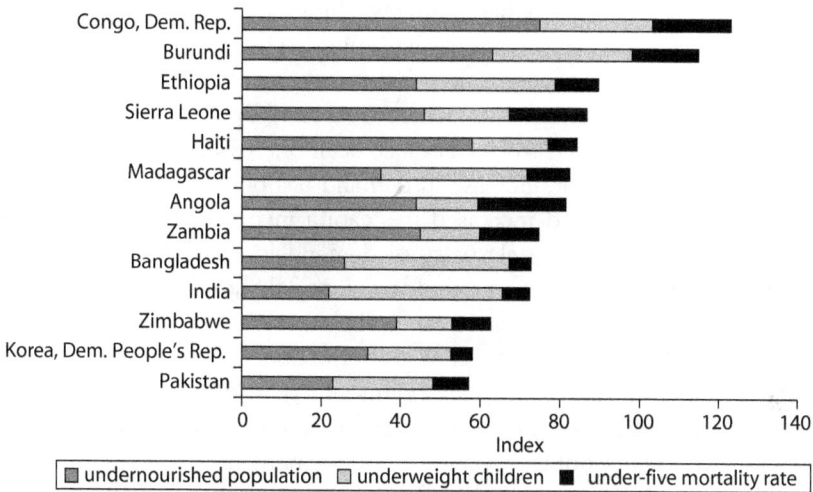

Source: IFPRI 2010.

have made better progress over the past two decades or so compared with the African countries. In some countries during the same period, hunger has worsened—staggeringly so in the Democratic Republic of Congo (with a 66 percent increase in the index), but also in Burundi, the Republic of Korea, and Zimbabwe. In contrast, Angola, Bangladesh, and Ethiopia have each achieved more than a 30 percent reduction in the hunger index.

Although progress has generally been good in reducing the child mortality rate, particularly by adopting such low-cost solutions as child immunization and the use of oral saline for diarrhea treatment, the continuing high prevalence of child malnourishment remains a major concern. The prevalence of underweight children is particularly high in South Asia (figure 2.2). In fact, South Asia's persistent poor ranking in the Global Hunger Index, particularly in the case of Bangladesh and India, is due to the disproportionately high incidence of child malnutrition. Evidence worldwide shows that children in rural areas are twice as likely to be underweight as urban children (UN 2011).

Economic growth in the recent decades appears to have been far less successful in reducing hunger than in reducing income poverty. Household-level food security thus deserves separate attention in the strategies for poverty reduction. The nutritional well-being of children, particularly in rural areas, seems to be most at risk. This finding may be due to intra-household food distribution that discriminates against children, but seasonal hunger that particularly affects child nutrition may also be a contributing factor. Several studies have pointed out the long-run adverse nutritional effect of repeated seasonal stresses, particularly for children (for example, Ferro-Luzzi 1990; Ferro-Luzzi and Branca 1993).

The world's grain production has been increasing in response to increased demand. The increase in demand has been propelled by both population growth and increased per capita income in the developing countries, where income elasticity of demand for staples remains relatively high among poorer households. Figure 2.3 shows how the world's grain production has increased with the reduction in global poverty; there was a 1 percent growth in food production with reduction in poverty at a rate of 1.92 percentage points per year (figure 2.3). One can perhaps conclude from this information that the world's food production has failed to abate hunger because of policy failures, not because of the inability to make enough food available. Consequently, the shift of policy emphasis from aggregate food supply to access to food at the household level makes sense.

Even if the world's food production has not been a constraint thus far in reducing global poverty and hunger, it may yet prove so in the future. Growing population and income in emerging and developing countries will add significantly to the demand for food in the coming decades,

Figure 2.3   Poverty Reduction and Growth in Grain Production (Rice, Wheat, and Maize), 1981–2004

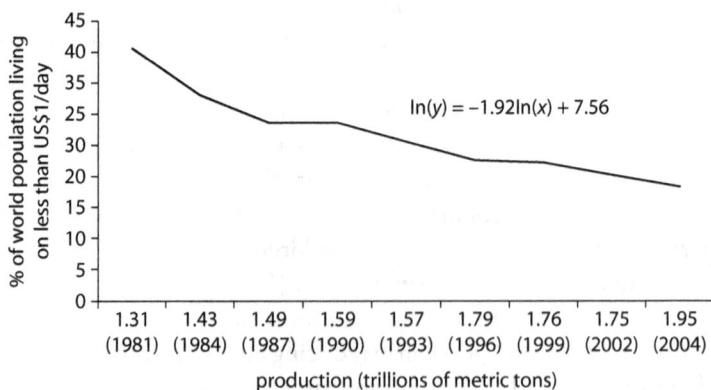

$$\ln(y) = -1.92\ln(x) + 7.56$$

y-axis: % of world population living on less than US$1/day

x-axis: 1.31 (1981)   1.43 (1984)   1.49 (1987)   1.59 (1990)   1.57 (1993)   1.79 (1996)   1.76 (1999)   1.75 (2002)   1.95 (2004)

production (trillions of metric tons)

Source: World Bank 2000.

exerting pressure on food prices. According to the latest medium-term outlook projections of the Food and Agriculture Organization of the United Nations and Organisation for Economic Co-operation and Development (FAO and OECD 2011), prices of crops and most livestock products will be higher in both nominal and real terms during the 2010s than they were during the decade preceding the 2007–08 price spike in the global grain markets. A supply shock in a situation where the supply-demand balance is already tight can easily trigger a serious problem of food insecurity in various parts of the developing world as happened during the 2007–08 food crisis.

The way increased food demand will be met will have implications for food insecurity and its seasonality. In the less developed countries, increasing food production through technological innovations not only is a means of increasing food supply but can also be important for creating rural employment and mitigating the adverse effects of agricultural seasonality. It is noteworthy that the supply response to the price hike of 2007–08 that subsequently helped calm the global grain markets came largely from increased production in the developed countries and not the developing ones. In the case of smallholder farming in Africa, increasing food production will require assisting small farmers with improved technologies and facilities for water and soil management and postharvest processing, storage, and marketing. All these improvements can be the tools for combating seasonal hunger as well.

Toward a Coordinated Policy Approach

The slippage in achieving the global food security targets has created awareness about the complexity of the problem and the need for a coordinated approach. Clearly, addressing the seasonal dimension of the problem needs to be part of such an approach, not only because seasonal hunger is one of the most prevalent forms of food insecurity but also because it is interlocked with extreme poverty and other forms of food insecurity. Moreover, hunger and poverty are recognized as an overall outcome of actions taken by various actors across the globe. Thus, concerns about food insecurity are being increasingly linked with such diverse subjects as the functioning of global markets, the depletion of freshwater resources, management of energy resources, risks to ecosystems, climate change, and so on. Dealing with food insecurity and its seasonality in such multidimensional contexts requires partnerships, at both national and global levels, among government agencies, nongovernmental organizations, the private sector, and research institutions.

A coordinated approach to deal with seasonal hunger will require creating public awareness.[12] Although some interventions have proved their effectiveness in different country contexts around the world, such interventions are rarely formulated and implemented on a large scale in an integrated manner. This deficiency is primarily because nonemergency chronic and seasonal hunger has ranked low on the list of national and global priorities. It has been argued that governments, particularly democratic ones, are more successful in averting dramatic disturbances like famines than in addressing endemic hunger and deprivation (Drèze and Sen 1989). International donors likewise respond more readily with humanitarian assistance in the event of disasters like famines, cyclones, or floods than in dealing with hidden hunger of different forms, like micronutrient deficiency in diet, child malnourishment, and seasonal hunger and food insecurity. Although such action by international donors in dealing with emergency situations is understandable, it is less easy to explain the neglect of seasonal hunger even in the regular aid programs.

One reason for the neglect of seasonal hunger is the lack of information. As mentioned earlier, the seasonal dimension of poverty and food deprivation is missed by the official data collection systems that annualize poverty estimates. There is less information on seasonal hunger than even on the other forms of hidden hunger, such as child malnutrition. The lack of data also makes it difficult to monitor the effect of whatever policies and programs are undertaken to address seasonality. Another reason for inadequate action is a lack of understanding of the phenomenon of seasonality. Seasonal hunger is commonly perceived as part of endemic or chronic poverty, which is only partly true. Although addressing poverty generally will also help reduce seasonal hunger, such an approach will miss many policies that can specifically address seasonality. As discussed earlier, a strategy to break out of the cycle of poverty and its seasonality must address both simultaneously.

An integrated approach needs to be developed to monitor and evaluate actions against seasonal hunger (IDS 2009). According to the Institute of Development Studies, the following actions may be essential ingredients of this approach. First, awareness on seasonality must be increased among development professionals, policy makers, and field workers, including agricultural extension officials. Second, a standard practice must be to include seasonality assessments in the design of rural social protection programs and investment programs for agricultural and rural development. Third, while supporting the growth of annual agricultural production, public policies must also intervene to stabilize intra-annual food consumption of the poor, such as by providing access to credit, weather-indexed insurance schemes, and off-farm employment. Finally, governments need to promote effective seasonally targeted interventions that promote livelihood resilience and that stabilize the effects of seasonal shocks.

Developing such an integrated approach is likely to involve trade-offs and balancing among competing objectives. For example, promoting agricultural growth through technological innovations may sometimes increase rather than decrease the extent of income seasonality. Consequently, there will be a greater need for promoting consumption-smoothing mechanisms. To promote rural diversification in regions that are particularly vulnerable to seasonal hunger, public investments, such as those for infrastructure development, may need to be directed to those regions even if the returns from such investments may be lower than in other regions. As for social security programs, a balance must be achieved between what Drèze and Sen (1989, 60) call the *protection* and *promotion* aspects, that is, between short-run measures that *prevent* immediate hardship and programs that have longer-run effects in *promoting* livelihoods.

Although learning from international experience is important, policies for addressing seasonal hunger need to be locally relevant, socially acceptable, and economically feasible. Because of the multidimensional nature of the problem, these policies need to be harmonized within the general economic, social, and environmental policies of a country. There is no single cure for seasonal hunger; a country may need to implement an array of specific measures with the help of international actors. Meeting the emerging threats of climate change and environmental degradation will need even more innovative solutions. Ultimately, the challenge is how to enhance the ability of the rural poor to cope with the increasing complexity and uncertainty linked to seasonality by making their livelihoods more flexible, adaptable, and resilient. This book addresses some of these questions using data from Bangladesh with the hope that the findings are relevant for policy makers from the governments and international agencies fighting poverty and hunger worldwide.

Notes

1. For a chronological review of global initiatives related to food security from 1943 to 1990, see Maxwell and Smith (1992).
2. For an analysis of the role of price expectation in the functioning of rice markets in Bangladesh during the 1974 famine, see Ravallion (1985).

3. In fact, small subsistence farmers are often forced to sell their produce at bottom prices during harvest and buy food later at high prices. This outcome may occur because they have to repay the loans they take out to meet the production costs. Farmers are thus deprived of entitlement to the food they produce.

4. See, for example, Longhurst (1986) for a discussion of household coping strategies.

5. For evidence on perceptions and choices in various contexts, see Besley (1995); Binswanger, Khandker, and Rosenzweig (1993); Bliss and Stern (1982); Dercon (1998, 2002); Eswaran and Kotwal (1989, 1990); Jalan and Ravallion (1999, 2003); Kochar (1995); Mordoch (1995); Rosenzweig and Binswanger (1993); and Townsend (1995).

6. For a host of policy options for reducing hunger that are practiced in the developing world, see Drèze, Sen, and Hussain (1995).

7. It may be noted that seasonality affects not only the crop cycles but also the prevalence of plant diseases, which sometimes can spell ruin and starvation for farmers (Strange and Scott 2005).

8. In Bangladesh, about 60 percent of total rice production now comes from irrigated dry-season rice, although in India, rain-fed rice production is still dominant.

9. As noted earlier, there is a sizable literature on the lack of access to credit. See also Alderman and Paxson (1992); Behrman, Foster, and Rosenzweig (1997); Chaudhuri and Paxson (2001); Harrower and Hoddinott (2004); Jalan and Ravallion (1999); Rosenzweig (1988); and Rosenzweig and Wolpin (1993).

10. Under-five mortality rate is per 10,000 live births.

11. The index is measured with a maximum of 100, but this scaling down is not shown in figure 2.2 because it does not affect the country rankings.

12. The importance of creating public awareness leading to effective action to combat hunger is discussed by Drèze and Sen (1989).

References

Agarwal, Bina. 1990. "Social Security and the Family: Coping with Seasonality and Calamity in Rural India." *Journal of Peasant Studies* 17 (3): 341–412.

Alderman, Harold, and Christina Paxson. 1992. "Do the Poor Insure? A Synthesis of the Literature on Risk and Consumption in Developing Countries." Policy Research Working Paper 1008, World Bank, Washington, DC.

Banerjee, Abhijit V., and Esther Duflo. 2011. *Poor Economics: A Radical Rethinking of the Way to Fight Global Poverty*. New York: Public Affairs.

Behrman, Jere R., Andrew Foster, and Mark Rosenzweig. 1997. "The Dynamics of Agricultural Production and the Calorie-Income Relationship: Evidence from Pakistan." *Journal of Econometrics* 77 (1): 187–207.

Besley, Timothy. 1995. "Savings, Credit, and Insurance." In *Handbook of Development Economics*, vol. 3B, ed. Jere Behrman and T. N. Srinivasan, 2123–207. Amsterdam: North-Holland.

Besley, Timothy, and Louise J. Cord. 2007. *Delivering on the Promise of Pro-Poor Growth: Insights and Lessons from Country Experiences.* Washington, DC: World Bank.

Binswanger, Hans, Shahidur Khandker, and Mark Rosenzweig. 1993. "How Infrastructure and Financial Institutions Affect Agricultural Output and Investment in India." *Journal of Development Economics* 41 (2): 337–66.

Bliss, C. J., and Nicholas H. Stern. 1982. *Palanpur: The Economy of an Indian Village.* London: Oxford University Press.

Chaudhuri, Shubhom, and Christina Paxson. 2001. "Smoothing Consumption under Composition and Profitability of Agricultural Investments." *Economic Journal* 103 (416): 56–78.

Chetty, Raj, and Adam Looney. 2006. "Consumption Smoothing and the Welfare Consequences of Social Insurance in Developing Economies." *Journal of Public Economics* 90 (12): 2351–56.

Collier, Paul. 2007. *The Bottom Billion: Why the Poorest Countries Are Failing and What Can Be Done about It.* New York: Oxford University Press.

Corbett, Jane E. M. 1988. "Famine and Household Coping Strategies." *World Development* 16 (9): 1099–112.

Deaton, Angus. 1991. "Savings and Liquidity Constraints." *Econometrica* 59 (4): 1221–48.

Dercon, Stefan. 1998. "Wealth, Risk, and Activity Choice: Cattle in Western Tanzania." *Journal of Development Economics* 55 (1): 1–42.

———. 2002. "Income Risk, Coping Strategies, and Safety Nets." *World Bank Research Observer* 17 (2): 141–66.

Dercon, Stefan, and Pramila Krishnan. 2000. "Vulnerability, Seasonality, and Poverty in Ethiopia." *Journal of Development Studies* 366 (6): 25–53.

Devereux, Stephen. 2009. "Seasonality and Social Protection in Africa." FAC Working Paper SP07, Future Agricultures Consortium, University of Sussex, Brighton, U.K.

Devereux, Stephen, Bapu Vatila, and Samuel Swan. 2008. *Seasons of Hunger: Fighting Cycles of Quiet Starvation among the World's Rural Poor.* London: Pluto Press.

de Waal, Alex. 1989. *Famine That Kills.* Oxford, U.K.: Clarendon.

Dostie, Benoit, Steven Haggblade, and Josee Randriamamony. 2002. "Seasonal Poverty in Madagascar: Magnitude and Solutions." *Food Policy* 27 (5): 493–518.

Drèze, Jean, and Amartya Sen. 1989. *Hunger and Public Action*. Oxford, U.K.: Clarendon Press.

Drèze, Jean, Amartya Sen, and Athar Hussain. 1995. *The Political Economy of Hunger: Selected Essays*. Oxford, U.K.: Clarendon Press.

Eswaran, Mukesh, and Ashok Kotwal. 1989. "Credit as Insurance in Agrarian Economies." *Journal of Development Economics* 31 (1): 33–53

———. 1990. "Implications for Credit Constraints for Risk Behaviour in Less Developed Countries." *Oxford Economic Papers* 42 (2): 473–82.

Fafchamps, Marcel, David McKenzie, Simon Quinn, and Christopher Woodruff. 2012. "Using PDA Consistency Checks to Increase the Precision of Profits and Sales Measurement in Panels." *Journal of Development Economics* 98 (1): 51–57.

FAO (Food and Agriculture Organization of the United Nations) and OECD (Organisation for Economic Co-operation and Development). 2011. *Price Volatility in Food and Agricultural Markets: Policy Responses*. Rome: FAO.

Ferro-Luzzi, Anna. 1990. "Social and Public Health Issues in Adaptation to Low Energy Intakes." *American Journal of Clinical Nutrition* 51: 309–15.

Ferro-Luzzi, Anna, and Francesco Branca. 1993. "Nutritional Seasonality and Dimensions of the Problem." In *Seasonality and Human Ecology: Society for the Study of Human Biology Symposium 35*, ed. Stanley J. Ulijaszek and Simon S. Strickland, 149–65. Cambridge, U.K.: Cambridge University Press.

Hadley, Craig, Monique Borgerhoff Mulder, and Emily Fitzherbert. 2007. "Seasonal Food Insecurity and Perceived Social Support in Rural Tanzania." *Public Health Nutrition* 10 (6): 544–51.

Harrower, Sarah, and John Hoddinott. 2004. "Consumption Smoothing and Vulnerability in the Zone Lacustre, Mali." Food Consumption and Nutrition Division Discussion Paper 175, International Food Policy Research Institute, Washington, DC.

IDS (Institute of Development Studies). 2009. Special issue on the Seasonality Revisited International Conference. *IDS Bulletin* 17 (3).

IFPRI (International Food Policy Research Institute). 2010. 2010 *Global Hunger Index: the Challenge of Hunger*. Washington, DC: IFPRI. Focus on the Crisis of Child Undernutrition.

Jalan, Joytsna, and Martin Ravallion. 1999. "Are the Poor Less Well Insured? Evidence on Vulnerability to Income Risk in Rural China." *Journal of Development Economics* 58 (1): 61–81.

————. 2000. "Is Transient Poverty Different? Evidence for Rural China." *Journal of Development Studies* 36 (6): 82–99.

————. 2003. "Behavioural Responses to Risk in Rural China." *Journal of Development Economics* 66 (1): 87–103.

Kazianga, Harounan, and Christopher Udry. 2006. "Consumption Smoothing? Livestock, Insurance, and Drought in Rural Burkina Faso." *Journal of Development Economics* 79 (2): 413–46.

Kochar, Anjini. 1995. "Explaining Household Vulnerability to Idiosyncratic Shocks." *American Economic Review* 85 (2): 159.

Longhurst, Richard. 1986. "Household Food Strategies in Response to Seasonality and Famine." *IDS Bulletin* 17 (3): 27–35.

Lozano, José Carlos. 1986. "Cassava Bacterial Blight: A Manageable Disease." *Plant Disease* 70: 1089–93.

Mahmud, Wahiduddin, Sultan Hafeez Rahman, and Sajjad Zohir. 2000. "Agricultural Diversification: A Strategic Factor for Growth." In *Out of the Shadow of Famine: Evolving Food Markets and Food Policy in Bangladesh*, ed. Raisuddin Ahmed, Steven Haggblade, and Tawfiq-e-Elawi Chowdhury, 232–60. Baltimore, MD: Johns Hopkins University Press.

Matin, Imran, and David Hulme. 2003. "Programs for the Poorest: Learning from the IGVGD Program in Bangladesh." *World Development* 31 (3): 647–65.

Maxwell, Simon, and Marisol Smith. 1992. "Part I: Household Food Security: A Conceptual Review." In *Household Food Security: Concepts, Indicators, and Measurements*, 1–72. New York: United Nations Children's Fund.

Mordoch, Jonathan. 1995. "Income Smoothing and Consumption Smoothing." *Journal of Economic Perspectives* 9 (3): 103–14.

Paxson, Christina. 1993. "Consumption and Income Seasonality in Thailand." *Journal of Political Economy* 101 (1): 39–72.

Pitt, Mark, and Shahidur Khandker. 2002. "Credit Programmes for the Poor and Seasonality in Rural Bangladesh." *Journal of Development Studies* 39 (2): 1–24.

Ravallion, Martin. 1985. "The Performance of Rice Markets in Bangladesh during the 1974 Famine." *Economic Journal* 95 (377): 15–29.

————. 1987. *Markets and Famines*. Oxford, U.K.: Clarendon Press.

————. 2001. *Measuring Aggregate Welfare in Developing Countries: How Well Do National Accounts and Surveys Agree?* Washington, DC: World Bank.

Ravallion, Martin, Dominique van de Walle, and Madhur Gautam. 1995. "Testing a Social Safety Net." *Journal of Public Economics* 57 (2): 175–99.

Reardon, Thomas, and Peter Matlon. 1989. "Seasonal Food Insecurity and Vulnerability in Drought-Affected Burkina Faso." In *Seasonal Variability in*

Third World Agriculture: The Consequences for Food Security, ed. David E. Sahn, 118–36. Baltimore, MD: Johns Hopkins University Press.

Rosenzweig, Mark. 1988. "Risk, Implicit Contracts, and the Family in Rural Areas of Low-Income Countries." *Economic Journal* 98 (393): 1148–70.

Rosenzweig, Mark, and Hans Binswanger. 1993. "Wealth, Weather Risk, and the Composition and Profitability of Agricultural Investments." *Economic Journal* 103 (416): 56–78.

Rosenzweig, Mark, and Kenneth Wolpin. 1993. "Credit Market Constraints, Consumption Smoothing, and the Accumulation of Durable Production Assets in Low-Income Countries: Investments in Bullocks in India." *Journal of Political Economy* 101 (2): 223–44.

Sen, Amartya K. 1981a. "Ingredients of Famine Analysis: Availability and Entitlements." *Quarterly Journal of Economics* 96 (3): 433–64.

———. 1981b. *Poverty and Famines: An Essay on Entitlement and Deprivation.* New York: Oxford University Press.

Spears, Dean. 2009. "Dosas by the Dozen: Theory and Evidence of Present Bias in Microentrepreneurs." Working Paper 27, Institute of Financial Management and Research, Chennai, India.

Strange, Richard N., and Peter R. Scott. 2005. "Plant Disease: A Threat to Global Food Security." *Annual Review of Phytopathology* 43: 83–116.

Townsend, Robert. 1995. "Consumption Insurance: An Evaluation of Risk-Bearing Systems in Low-Income Economies." *Journal of Economic Perspectives* 9 (3): 83–102.

UN (United Nations). 2011. "Accelerating Progress towards the Millennium Development Goals: Options for Sustained and Inclusive Growth and Issues for Advancing the United Nations Development Agenda beyond 2015." Annual Report of the Secretary-General to the Sixty-Sixth Session of the General Assembly." Document A/66/126, United Nations, New York.

World Bank. 1986. "Poverty and Hunger: Issues and Options for Food Security in Developing Countries." World Bank, Washington, DC.

———. 2008. *World Development Report 2008: Agriculture for Development.* Washington, DC: World Bank.

CHAPTER 3

Seasonal Poverty and Hunger in Bangladesh

Vulnerability of the Northwest Region

Country Context

Bangladesh emerged from its 1971 war of independence poor, overpopulated, and reeling from overwhelming war damage to its institutional and physical capital. The country was ravaged by acute food shortages and famines during the early years of its independence. Its income per capita was among the lowest in the world along with dismally low levels of various social development indicators. According to some authors, Bangladesh was designated as a "test case" for development, and Henry Kissinger called it "an international basket case."

In the decades since the 1974 famine, the country has made commendable progress in several development areas. With sustained growth in food production and a good record of disaster management, famines have become a phenomenon of the past. Bangladesh's per capita real gross domestic product (GDP) has more than doubled since the mid-1970s. Life expectancy has risen from 50 years to 63 years; population growth rates of around 3 percent a year have been halved; child mortality rates of 240 per 1,000 live births have been cut by 70 percent; literacy has more than doubled; and the country has achieved gender parity in primary and secondary schools.

Most of these gains have taken place since the early 1990s, when the introduction of wide-ranging economic reforms coincided with the transition to democracy. The growth of per capita GDP was slow in the 1980s, at an annual average of 1.6 percent a year, but it accelerated to 3.0 percent in the 1990s and averaged about 4.0 percent more recently. The acceleration resulted partly from a slowdown in population growth but also from a sustained increase in GDP growth, which averaged 3.7 percent annually during the 1980s, 4.8 percent during the 1990s, and 5.7 percent since then.

Progress in the human development indicators was even more impressive. Bangladesh ranks among the top-performing countries in the extent of improvement in the United Nations Development Programme's Human Development Index since the early 1990s, and it is among the few developing countries that are on target for achieving most of the Millennium Development Goals. As a result, Bangladesh is now clearly an overperformer in many social development indicators in relation to its per capita GDP, whereas two decades or so ago it lagged among countries with similar per capita income levels. These achievements have in fact been dubbed a "development surprise," given the country's desperate initial conditions and allegedly poor record in governance (Ahluwalia and Mahmud 2004; Mahmud 2008; Mahmud, Ahmed, and Mahajan 2010).

Despite these positive changes, pervasive poverty and undernutrition persist. The most disturbing consequence of widespread poverty is that 40 percent of Bangladesh's 150 million people cannot afford an adequate diet. Chronically food insecure and highly vulnerable, many of these people remain without assets (other than their own labor power) to cushion lean-season hunger or the crushing blows of illness, floods, and other natural calamities. The country also has to tackle several growth-retarding factors: (a) poor governance, (b) a low-skilled labor force, (c) extremely high population density and the associated scarcity of land and natural resources, and (d) vulnerability to floods and other natural disasters, including the prospect of being one of the major victims of climate change. One commentator has aptly put Bangladesh's development challenge in the following words: can "the people of one of the poorest and yet resilient and innovative countries transform it from being the world's most famously 'vulnerable' country to being recognised as one of its most 'adaptive' countries?" (Mahmud 2010).

Poverty and Food Security

Trends in Poverty

With the acceleration in the growth of per capita income, considerable progress has been made in poverty reduction. The incidence of poverty has declined from 57 percent in 1991–92 to 32 percent in 2010 and that of extreme poverty from 41 percent to 18 percent (table 3.1). The official estimates of poverty in Bangladesh are derived from the data of the Household Income and Expenditure Survey (HIES) using poverty lines based on the "cost of basic needs," which includes the cost of a minimum food basket and an allowance for nonfood expenditures. Estimates are also made for the incidence of "extreme poverty," which is defined by the household's total consumption expenditure—on food and nonfood combined—falling short of the cost of the food basket included in the cost of basic needs.[1]

In recent years, growth acceleration in many developing countries, including those in South Asia, has been accompanied by increased income inequality (Mahmud and Chowdhury 2008). In contrast, the pattern of economic growth in Bangladesh seems to have been relatively pro-poor—with the main stimulus to economic growth outside agriculture coming from labor-intensive garment export, micro- and small-scale enterprises in manufacturing and services, and remittances from migrants working abroad. All these sectors typically provide scope for upward economic mobility for the poor. Yet inequality tended to increase in the 1990s, for two reasons: (a) even within a generally employment-intensive pattern of growth, the more dynamic parts of the economy happened to be those

Table 3.1   Head-Count Rates of Poverty and Extreme Poverty, 1991/92–2010: Cost-of-Basic-Needs Method

Year	Moderate poverty rate (%)			Extreme poverty rate (%)		
	Rural	Urban	National	Rural	Urban	National
1991/92	58.7	42.7	56.6	43.7	23.6	41.0
1995/96	54.5	27.8	50.1	39.4	13.7	35.1
2000	52.3	35.2	48.9	37.9	20.0	34.3
2005	43.8	28.4	40.0	28.6	14.6	25.1
2010	35.2	21.3	31.5	21.1	7.7	17.6

Source: Household Income and Expenditure Survey (HIES), various rounds.

with relatively unequal income, and (b) growth was not strong enough to increase wages in the vast agricultural and informal labor markets. But since the late 1990s, real wages in the agricultural and other informal labor markets have shown strong upward trends. As shown by the Household Income and Expenditure Survey of 2000 and later years, income inequality in urban and rural areas has not worsened, even if it has not improved; as a result, poverty has been reduced at a much faster rate.

The poverty estimates above may be compared with the estimates of the proportion of the population with calorie-intake deficiency (the so-called direct calorie-intake method of poverty estimation). For this, two cutoff points of per capita daily calorie intake are considered: the higher one is the same as that used in the estimate of the poverty line by the cost-of-basic-needs method and refers to what we call moderate calorie-intake deficiency, whereas the lower one may be considered to represent severe deficiency. In line with the poverty estimates, the proportions of people with deficient calorie intake, both moderate and severe, can be seen to have declined steadily since the early 1990s (table 3.2).[2] It may be noted, however, that the extent of this decline is less than the decline in the rate of poverty estimated by the cost-of-basic-needs method, although the latter relates to the same level of per capita calorie intake as that used for defining moderate calorie-intake deficiency. Although this inconsistency may be explained by the way poverty estimates differ depending on the estimation methodology (Ravallion and Sen 1996), the point to note is that the improvements in calorie-intake deficiency seem to have been far less encouraging compared with the official poverty estimates.

Particularly since the early 1990s, Bangladesh has achieved rapid improvements in many human development indicators, such as female

Table 3.2   Percentage of Population with Moderate and Severe Deficiency in Calorie Intake, 1991/92–2005

Year	Moderate deficiency (< 2,122 kilocalories/person/day)			Severe deficiency (< 1,805 kilocalories/person/day)		
	Rural	Urban	National	Rural	Urban	National
1991/92	47.6	46.7	47.5	28.3	26.3	28.0
1995/96	47.1	49.7	47.5	24.6	27.3	25.1
2000	42.3	52.5	44.3	18.7	25.0	20.0
2005	39.5	43.2	40.4	17.9	24.4	19.5

Source: HIES, various rounds.

school enrollment, child mortality, and contraceptive adoption rates. These achievements have been possible in spite of widespread poverty, low per capita public social spending, and the poor governance of service delivery systems in Bangladesh. Much of this progress has resulted from the adoption of low-cost solutions, such as the use of oral rehydration saline for diarrhea treatment, leading to a decrease in child mortality. More progress has come from increased public awareness created by effective social mobilization campaigns, such as those for child immunization, contraception, or female child enrollment in school.[3] But as the gains from low-cost easy solutions are reaped, further progress will increasingly depend on the amount of public social spending, quality of services, and synergies with poverty reduction. Also, in spite of the achievements cited, child malnutrition rates in Bangladesh remain among the highest in the world, with an estimated 46 percent of children under five suffering from malnourishment compared with 27 percent in Sub-Saharan Africa (UNICEF 2011).[4] As discussed in chapter 2, this problem is common in other South Asian countries as well, especially India.

Food Production and Availability

Since the 1970s, the growth of domestic production of food grains—rice and wheat combined—has kept pace with or even surpassed population growth. Yet the government's avowed goal of achieving national self-sufficiency in food grains has remained elusive. Toward the late 1990s, the acceleration in rice production led to predictions of achieving the goal of self-sufficiency within a short period, but those predictions turned out to be too optimistic (figure 3.1).

Food grain supply and price stabilization remain central to the government's policy of ensuring food security. The policy has changed significantly since the early 1990s. As part of market-oriented economic reforms, the public food-rationing system was dismantled and the grain trade was liberalized to allow private grain import. The emphasis of public procurement and distribution of food grain shifted from supporting and stabilizing prices to strengthening social safety nets and disaster mitigation programs. Private grain imports helped stabilize prices in the domestic grain market by meeting the shortfalls in domestic production and preventing the risk of speculative price hikes in the preharvest periods (Dorosh 2001). The increased domestic production along with the liberal import policy also led to a secular decline in real rice prices in the domestic market, thus benefiting the consumers. The sense of urgency regarding national food security was thus eliminated in spite of

Figure 3.1   Production and Import of Rice and Wheat in Bangladesh, 1980/81–2009/10

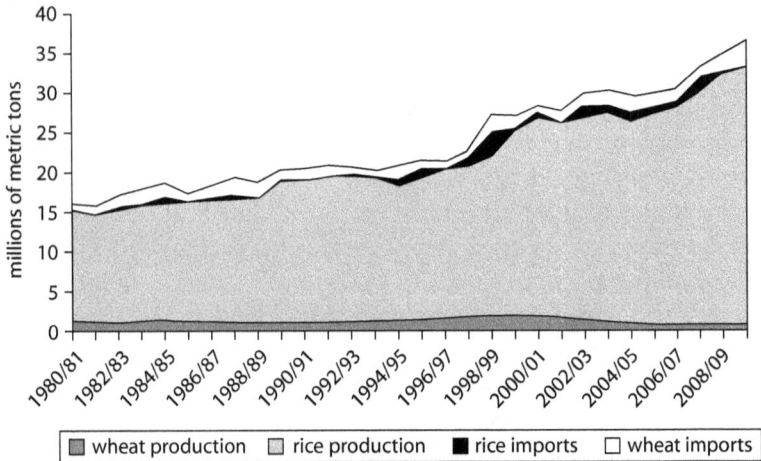

Source: Government of Bangladesh, food grain statistics.

the continuation of chronic food insecurity reflected by the large numbers of undernourished people cited earlier.

The global food crisis of 2007–08 has changed all that. Bangladesh was severely affected by the food crisis with regard to large grain import bills and price volatility in the domestic grain markets. The experience of the crisis and its likely repetition has brought the issue of food self-sufficiency to the fore again. Although Bangladesh has little prospect of eliminating dependence on imported wheat, self-sufficiency in rice is possible given the decline in population growth and the fact that, with the increase in income, the average diet is likely to become more diversified. But as the benefit from the modern high-yield variety (HYV) technology in rice production has largely been reaped, maintaining growth in rice production will become increasingly difficult. Bangladesh's vulnerability to the adverse effects of climate change will pose an additional challenge.

According to the official food statistics, per capita availability of food grains has shown an upward trend since the mid-1990s, after having remained stagnant during the preceding decade or so (figure 3.2).[5] The increase in per capita income seems to have led to increased demand for food grains, which is explained by the fact that a large segment of the population still remains calorie deficient and food grains are the cheapest source of calories in the diet.

Figure 3.2   Per Capita Availability of Rice and Wheat, 1980/81–2009/10

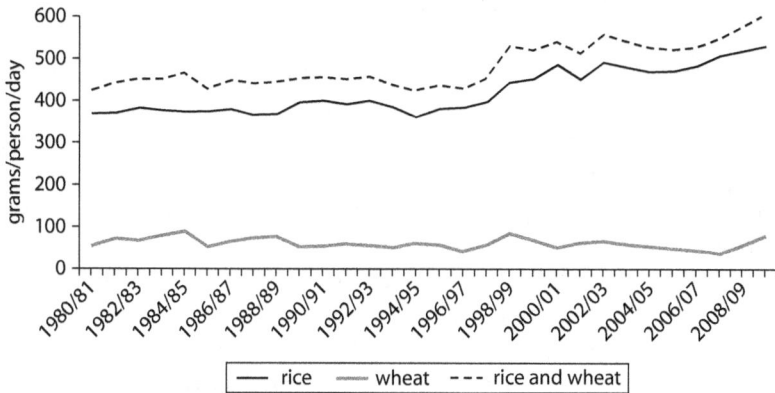

Source: Food Policy Monitoring Unit, Ministry of Food, Government of Bangladesh.

It is noteworthy that the per capita availability of rice increased even during the food crisis of 2007–08. The domestic prices of both wheat and rice nearly doubled during that time, keeping pace with prices in the international markets. The real wages of agricultural day laborers did not fall, in spite of this sharp price spike (see figure 3.5 later in this section). Although poverty rates were predicted to have been adversely affected by the food price increases, not much evidence of that could be found in the subsequent poverty estimates, with the poverty head-count rates falling more rapidly than ever between 2005 and 2010 (table 3.1). Unlike many food-importing low-income countries, Bangladesh thus seems to be an exception in demonstrating that poverty can be reduced even in the face of sharp increases in essential-food prices, provided that adequate food supply can be ensured, economic growth remains robust, and enough employment opportunities can be created to keep real wages from falling.

Agricultural Seasonality

Because of the predominance of rice in crop production, agricultural seasonality in Bangladesh is mainly determined by the timing of planting and harvesting of the three seasonal rice crops: early monsoon *aus*, late monsoon *aman*, and the dry season *boro*. Over the years, the relative importance of these three rice crops has changed significantly with the introduction of modern irrigation along with the HYVs. Although trans-plant aman rice was previously the main rice crop, the HYV boro rice now accounts for the largest share of rice output, about 60 percent. The spread of HYV boro rice has also diminished the importance of aus rice because of the overlapping growing period.

An important outcome of the change in the seasonal pattern of rice output is a more even year-round availability of rice from domestic production and the consequent changes in the rice price seasonality. The preharvest price peaks seem to have become bimodal and less marked, thus reducing the extent of the seasonal price spread (see Dorosh, Ninno, and Shahabuddin 2004, 61). This change can be seen from the average annual cyclical pattern of rice prices estimated for the late 1970s, the 1980s, and the 1990s (figure 3.3). The monthly price indexes for each period are calculated as annual averages of the ratios of the monthly price to the 12-month lagged moving average; estimates are based on the national average wholesale price of coarse rice. No further systematic changes can be detected in the more recent years, except for occasional volatility related to changes in prices in the global markets.

Although the change in the rice crop cycle has helped reduce the seasonal spread in rice prices, the traditional lean season preceding the aman harvest and spreading from September to November has changed little in its characteristics. It is the season of the least crop-related activity with no major crops planted or harvested, as can be seen from the crop

Figure 3.3   Seasonal Price Indexes of Coarse Rice, 1977/78–1979/80, 1980/81–1989/90, and 1990/91–2001/02

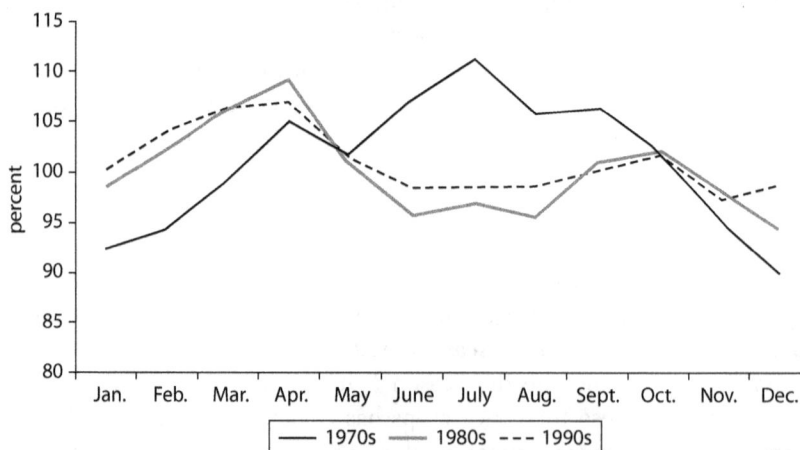

Figure 3.4   Crop Calendar of Major Crops

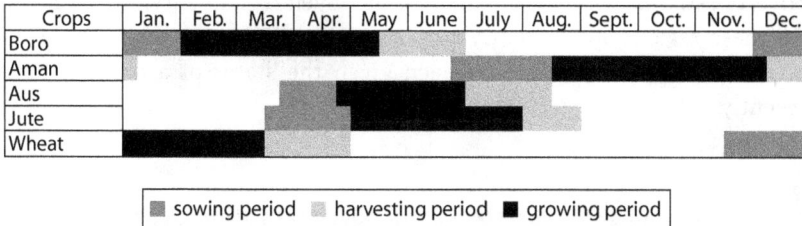

Crops	Jan.	Feb.	Mar.	Apr.	May	June	July	Aug.	Sept.	Oct.	Nov.	Dec.
Boro												
Aman												
Aus												
Jute												
Wheat												

■ sowing period   ▩ harvesting period   ■ growing period

Source: Estimated from the data reported by Bangladesh Bureau of Statistics (various years).

calendar shown in figure 3.4. Although the wheat-growing season starts in November, the crop is grown in only about 5 percent of the cultivated land area. Moreover, the aftermaths of natural disasters like floods, drought, or excessive rains are usually felt most severely in this season.

The cropping patterns in Bangladesh are delicately balanced within the natural cycles of rains and annual floods. Thus, farmers' production options and perception of risk are often determined by the physical environment: the degree of seasonal flooding, the timing and quantity of rainfall, and the soil characteristics (Mahmud, Rahman, and Zohir 1994, 2000). Investment in irrigation and flood control as well as improvement in crop production technology can change the cropping patterns by influencing the physical constraints. Some regions may thus be disadvantaged relative to others because of a lack of investment and adverse agroclimatic factors.

Regional Disparity in Poverty: Rangpur and the Rest of Bangladesh

The main focus of this book is seasonal hunger—locally known as *monga*—in the Rangpur region of northwestern Bangladesh. As mentioned in chapter 1, the region not only has lagged in poverty reduction compared with other regions, but also has remained particularly vulnerable to seasonal hunger (Elahi and Ara 2008; Rahman 1995; Zug 2006). The phenomenon of monga in Rangpur needs to be understood in the context of how a certain region can be disadvantaged because of its adverse economic geography and agroecological vulnerability—a recurrent theme of this book.

Bangladesh's impressive performance in poverty reduction, discussed earlier, has not been uniform across the country; although overall poverty has declined, the incidence of poverty is much higher in lagging regions than in others (Khandker 2012; Narayan, Yoshida, and Zaman 2007).

Map 3.1 shows the incidence of extreme poverty, as defined in the official poverty estimates discussed earlier, in the seven regions surveyed in 2005. All these regions are currently administrative divisions (each comprising several districts). Rangpur has been given the status of a division only recently.

Map 3.1   Bangladesh: Regional Disparity in Poverty at a Glance, 2005

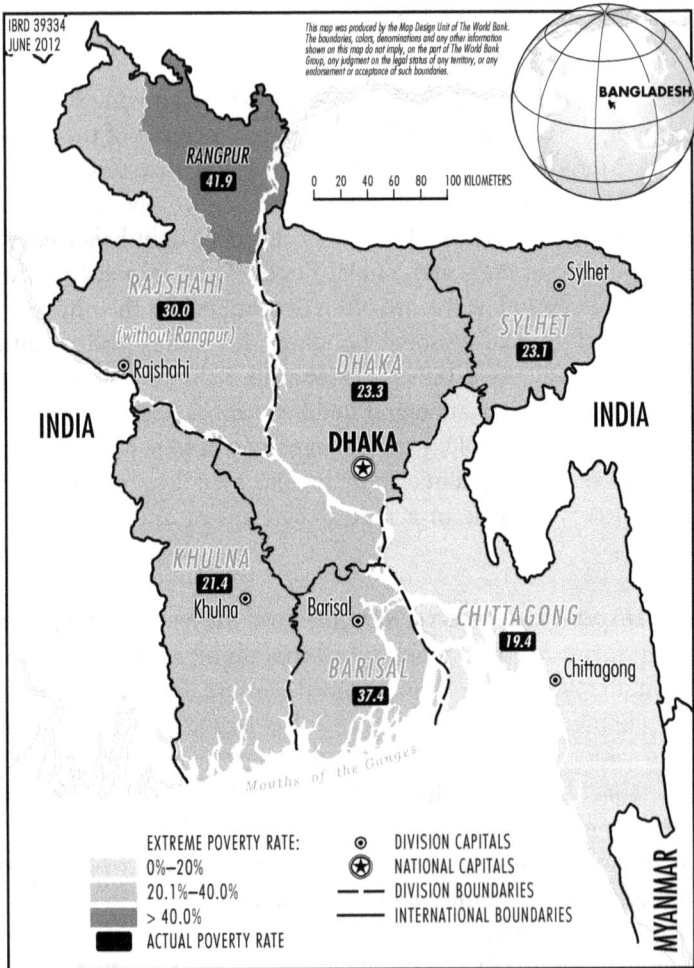

Source: Authors' estimates based on HIES, 2005.
Note: Extreme poverty rate of the divisions is as follows: division 1 = 41.9 percent, division 2 = 37.4 percent, division 3 = 30.0 percent, division 4 = 23.3 percent, division 5 = 23.1 percent, division 6 = 21.4 percent, and division 7 = 19.4 percent.

Table 3.3   Moderate and Extreme Poverty in Rural Areas of Bangladesh and the Rangpur Region, 2000–10

Country or region	Moderate poverty head count (%)			Extreme poverty head count (%)		
	2000	2005	2010	2000	2005	2010
Bangladesh	52.3	43.8	35.2	37.9	28.6	21.1
Rangpur	70.9	61.0	44.5	55.5	44.2	29.4

Source: HIES, 2000, 2005, and 2010.

Note: The estimates are based on the rural sample of households. The national estimates (that is, for Bangladesh) are the official ones; for Rangpur, the authors' estimates are based on the HIES data.

Table 3.3 shows the estimates of poverty incidence among the rural households in Rangpur compared with the national estimates. The persistently higher incidence of poverty in Rangpur is evident from the estimates. However, along with a fairly rapid decline in the poverty levels generally over this period, the relative disadvantage of Rangpur with regard to the gaps in the poverty levels has also substantially declined. Of course, these estimates do not show how poverty incidence varies among other regions of the country or how such disparities are changing over time. Besides Rangpur, there are other poverty pockets as well, and new ones may be emerging with increasing environmental degradation and climatic risks; this topic is discussed in the final chapter of this book.

Earlier in this chapter, the trends in real wages were mentioned in the context of Bangladesh's record of ensuring food security in the face of the price volatility in the global food markets in recent years. The disadvantage of the Rangpur region is evident from these wage trends as well. Figure 3.5 shows that the agricultural wage rates in real terms have generally showed an upward trend, but the wage rates in Rangpur have consistently remained lower compared with the country as a whole.[6]

Seasonality of Income, Consumption, and Poverty: Rangpur and the Rest of Bangladesh

Given that the rural economy of Bangladesh is predominantly a "rice economy," the important policy question is the following: How much does agricultural seasonality matter to the consumption and income patterns of the rural households? And if seasonal poverty or monga is pronounced in the Rangpur region, does it mean that other regions of Bangladesh do not experience seasonality in agriculture? As stated in chapter 1, more than 70 percent of the population in Bangladesh lives in rural areas and nearly 60 percent of the rural workers (and about half the

Figure 3.5   Monthly Trend in Agricultural Wage Rates of Males (without Meals), 2007–10

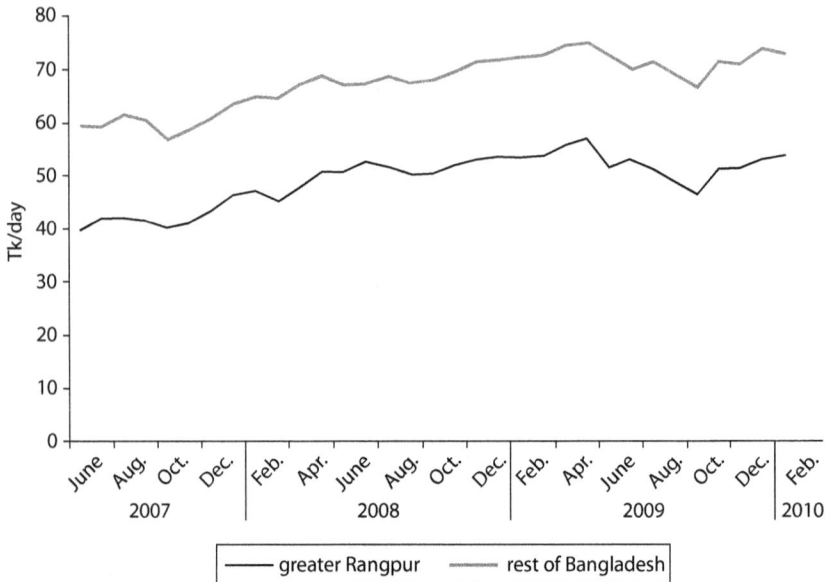

Source: Authors' estimates based on the official data of the Bangladesh Bureau of Statistics.
Note: Figures are deflated by monthly rural consumer price index (1995–96 = 100).

country's entire workforce) are employed in agriculture as their main occupation.

The extent of seasonality in income and consumption can be shown through a disaggregate analysis of income and consumption data by season. As mentioned in chapter 1, it is possible to derive estimates by region and by season from the data of the HIES because the HIES collects data at various times of the year across the different regions of the country.[7] For most of our analysis, we divide the country into two regions: Rangpur (representing the greater Rangpur region) and the rest of Bangladesh. Further, in view of the cropping cycle, four seasons are distinguished for the estimates: (a) the boro (winter rice) season of March–May, (b) the aus (early rain-fed rice) season of June–August, (c) the preharvest aman (the main rain-fed rice) season of September–November, and (d) the postharvest aman season of December–February. It may be noted that, in addition to the three cropping seasons in Bangladesh, we create another season as the pre-aman or monga period to examine whether household circumstances and their response behavior differ in this season compared with other seasons.

Because the seasonality of poverty and hunger is a rural phenomenon, we use data from the rural samples of the HIES of 2000 and 2005.[8] Rural areas, as defined in the HIES, include semi-urban areas that are outside the municipalities. This inclusion is in fact helpful in capturing the seasonality of nonfarm activities in these areas that are often tied with the rhythm of the annual agricultural cycle.

The HIES data on household consumption can be estimated by season because the information on food intake was collected daily for one month for each surveyed household, whereas that on most nonfood consumption expenditures was collected at the end of the month for a reference period of one month. For only some items of durable nature like clothing, the data refer to one year preceding the interview so that the estimates of seasonal consumption will capture only the annualized estimates for these items. These latter expenditures may have seasonality arising from the fact that rural households usually spend more on such items in the postharvest seasons or at the time of annual religious festivals. Nevertheless, it is the seasonality of recurrent types of expenditure for current consumption that is relevant for analyzing seasonal poverty and hunger. The HIES data on consumption are therefore particularly suitable for showing the kind of seasonality in household consumption that is relevant for our analysis.

The estimation of seasonal income from the HIES data is somewhat problematic, because for all the income data collected, the reference period is one year preceding the date of interviews. However, the income from crop production can be sorted by season because we know which crop is harvested during which months of the year.[9] This estimate omits income from all other sources, including all wage employment as well as employment in noncrop agriculture and off-farm activities. The estimates of seasonal income used in this study therefore do not capture the seasonality that may exist in these sources of income. The estimates may still be taken as reasonable approximations, given that the annual crop cycle is the predominant source of seasonality in rural incomes.

The poverty lines used in the official poverty estimates are estimated in a disaggregated way to reflect price variations across the rural and urban areas of various regions.[10] Also, for the poverty estimates of 2000 and 2005, the poverty lines and consumption expenditures were estimated at 2000 prices. Because we have used these same price deflators, all monetary figures in this book relating to the HIES for these two years are at 2000 prices.

The seasonal patterns of household food expenditure in Rangpur compared with the rest of the country for 2000 and 2005 are shown in figure 3.6.[11] For both years, monthly food consumption per household is much lower in Rangpur than in the rest of the country, although the difference appears to have decreased because of the increase in the level of food consumption in Rangpur in 2005 compared with 2000. It appears that there is marked seasonality in food consumption for the country as a whole, but it is more pronounced in Rangpur. The generally lower level of food consumption in Rangpur, along with its sharp seasonality, seems to explain the severe food deprivation in this region during monga (the third period in figure 3.6). Moreover, as can be seen in figure 3.6, households in Rangpur seem to recover from the dip in seasonal consumption more slowly than in the rest of the country.

If the dip in food consumption expenditure during monga were to be accompanied by a seasonal rise in food prices, an even larger decline in

Figure 3.6   Seasonal Pattern of Household Food Expenditure by Region, 2000 and 2005

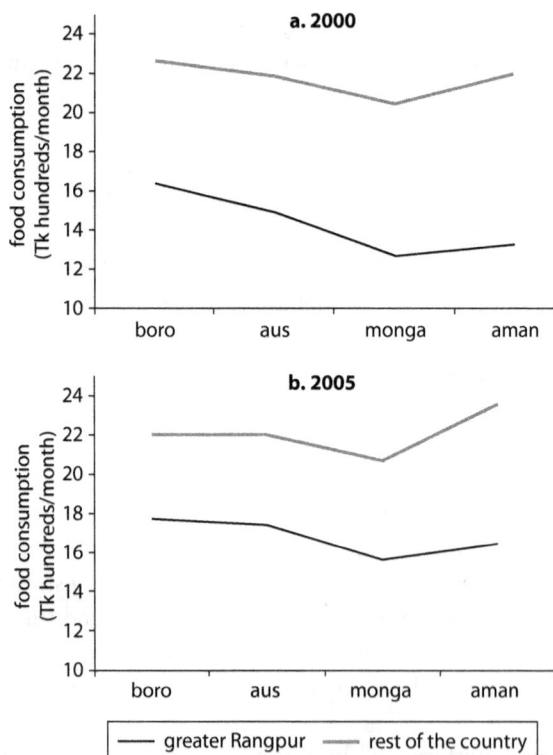

food intakes would have occurred, and such price increases would have been a further cause for seasonal food deprivation. Using the HIES data, we examined the seasonal price movements for rice, which accounts for half the food expenditure in Rangpur and two-fifths in the rest of the country. Although a seasonal peak in rice price during the (preharvest) boro season is observed for all regions and for both years, the monga season prices were not found to be very different from those of the other two seasons. This finding is in line with our earlier analysis about the changing patterns of rice price seasonality in Bangladesh (figure 3.4). Thus, the income seasonality seems to be the primary reason for seasonal food deprivation.

To disentangle food expenditure from prices, we also estimated actual food content for per capita calorie intake.[12] Figure 3.7 shows the seasonal patterns of calorie intake in Rangpur and the rest of the country in 2005. As expected, calorie-intake levels are generally lower in Rangpur than in the rest of the country. There is also a clear decline in calorie intake in all regions during the monga season, but there is also a similar decline in the boro season in Rangpur. Two additional points may be noted, particularly in the case of Rangpur. First, the seesaw pattern observed in Rangpur suggests that the seasonality in food intake extends beyond monga—with a

Figure 3.7   Seasonal Pattern of Calorie Intake by Region, 2005

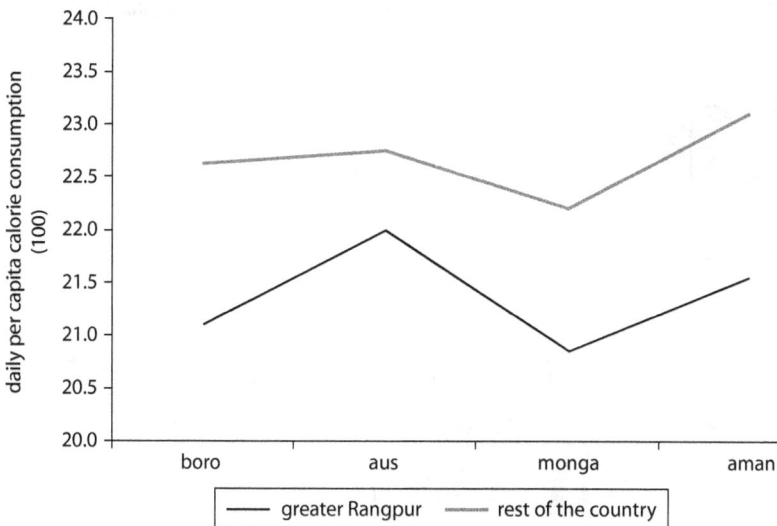

Source: Khandker 2012.

fall in the (preharvest) boro season as well, and a rise in both the (post-harvest) aman season as well as in the aus season (which is the posthar-vest season of boro rice). Second, for the relatively poorer households, the extent of seasonal fall in calorie intake must be much higher than that shown in figure 3.7, which depicts the average for all households.

It is also useful to see how the seasonality in food consumption varies across regions in the country. Figure 3.8 shows seasonal variations in per capita monthly food consumption for the seven regions of Bangladesh, estimated on the basis of the 2005 HIES. The seven regions are adminis-trative divisions of the country: Barisal, Chittagong, Dhaka, Khulna, Rajshahi, Rangpur, and Sylhet (among which Rangpur has been given the status of a division only recently and was previously a part of Rajshahi division). The estimates show some variations in the patterns of seasonal-ity in food consumption across regions, which is explained by regional variations in the cropping patterns and the resulting income seasonality. But a dip in food consumption during monga or the pre-aman season, along with a subsequent recovery after the aman harvest, is common to most regions. As expected, the food consumption curve for Rangpur lies at the bottom of those for other regions.

The consumption expenditure of rural households is cyclical in response to income seasonality arising from the crop cycle. In figure 3.9,

Figure 3.8   Seasonal Pattern of Per Capita Food Consumption by Division, 2005

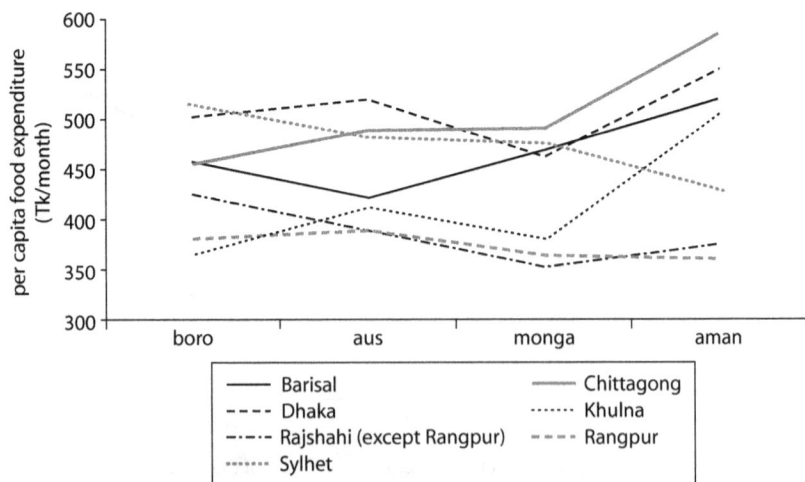

Figure 3.9   Seasonal Pattern of Income, Food Consumption, and Total Consumption by Region, 2005

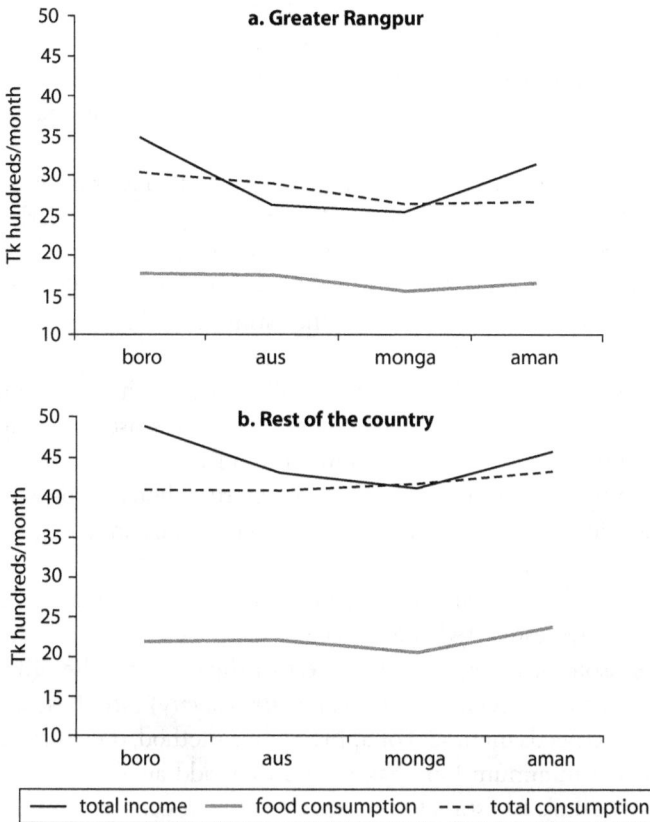

a. Greater Rangpur

b. Rest of the country

— total income   — food consumption   - - - total consumption

Source: Authors' estimates based on HIES 2005 data, rural sample.

the estimates of seasonal monthly household income, food consumption, and total consumption are shown together for both Rangpur and the rest of the country for 2005. As noted earlier, the estimates of seasonal income reflect the seasonality of crop income only, estimated on the basis of the timing of the crop harvests. If the incomes from other sources are also linked to the crop cycle to some extent, then the extent of seasonality in total income has been underestimated. However, the estimates of food consumption and total consumption fully capture seasonality, except for some nonrecurrent expenditure, such as on durables.

A distinct pattern of income and consumption seasonality occurs in Rangpur and other regions, as shown in figure 3.9. Although the monthly expenditure on food is clearly less than monthly income, total income falls short of total consumption during the monga period in both regions. But this shortfall in income is strikingly more pronounced in Rangpur than in the rest of the economy. The problem lies in the fact that the households in Rangpur not only have lower income than households in other regions, but also are more dependent on farm income, making them more vulnerable to agricultural seasonality.

The fact that seasonality influences household consumption does not mean that seasonal poverty will result as a consequence. Similarly, even if consumption smoothing varies by region, it does not indicate how much poverty is actually caused by seasonality (through either idiosyncratic or aggregate shocks). More specifically, the estimates in figure 3.9 cannot tell us how many households fall into seasonal hunger or poverty owing to seasonality combined with a lack of ability to smooth consumption. To gauge that number requires an examination of how seasonality affects the ability of households to maintain a minimum livelihood during particular times of the year. In other words, how many rural households experience a decrease in seasonal income that lowers consumption enough to force them below the poverty line?

Following the official methodology for poverty estimates discussed earlier, we have estimated the incidence of moderate and extreme poverty by season for Rangpur and the rest of the country. The official estimates of poverty (called here *moderate poverty*) are based on the cost-of-basic-needs method. For applying this method, one must establish the cost of a minimum food basket and then add an allowance for nonfood expenditure to estimate the poverty line. In contrast, extreme poverty is defined as a situation in which a household, with combined expenditure on food and nonfood, cannot match the cost of the minimum food basket, let alone remain above the total poverty line. We have used the appropriately disaggregated and price-deflated poverty lines to derive the respective poverty estimates by season and by region.

Figure 3.10 presents the estimates of seasonal incidence of moderate and extreme poverty by region (Rangpur compared with the rest of the country) based on the HIES data of 2000 and 2005. The seasonal variations in poverty incidence are clearly demonstrated by these estimates, with poverty generally peaking toward the monga period. However, in contrast to the rest of the country, seasonal poverty in Rangpur seems to persist even beyond the monga period. The higher incidence of poverty in Rangpur than in other regions is also clearly shown, particularly with respect to the estimates of extreme poverty.

Figure 3.10   Seasonal Pattern of Moderate and Extreme Poverty by Region, 2000 and 2005

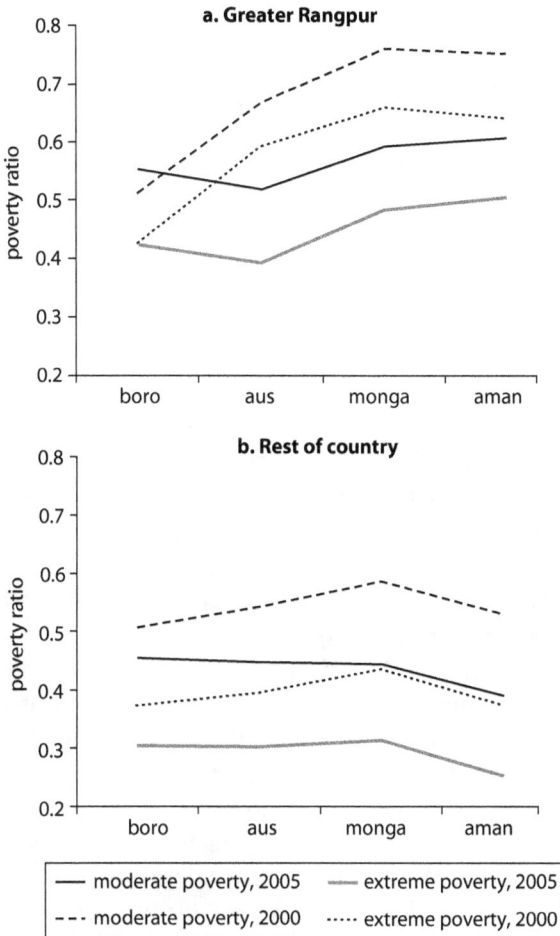

a. Greater Rangpur

b. Rest of country

— moderate poverty, 2005   — extreme poverty, 2005
--- moderate poverty, 2000   ..... extreme poverty, 2000

Source: Authors' estimates based on HIES 2000 and 2005 data, rural samples.

Table 3.4 reports the distribution of moderate and extreme poverty for rural households, disaggregated by region and season, for 2000 and 2005. Three basic trends are observed from these poverty figures. First, the poverty situation is worse in the Rangpur region than in the rest of the country. Second, the poverty situation is generally worse during the monga season than during the non-monga season. And third, the poverty situation improves from 2000 to 2005. All these findings conform to our earlier findings.

Table 3.4   Head-Count Rates of Moderate Poverty and Extreme Poverty by Season and Region, 2000 and 2005

percent

Period	Greater Rangpur		Rest of the country	
	2000	*2005*	*2000*	*2005*
Monga season	MP = 76.0	MP = 59.2	MP = 59.0	MP = 44.6
	EP = 66.0	EP = 48.3	EP = 43.9	EP = 31.6
Non-monga season	MP = 69.4	MP = 61.5	MP = 53.1	MP = 43.1
	EP = 59.4	EP = 43.0	EP = 38.4	EP = 28.6
Number of households	440	520	4,600	5,520

Source: Adapted from Khandker 2012.
Note: EP = extreme poverty, MP = moderate poverty.

Nature and Extent of Seasonal Hunger in Rangpur

Estimates of Seasonal Hunger from the InM Baseline Survey, 2006

Besides the HIES data, another data set used for the analyses in this book is much more directly focused on seasonal hunger in Rangpur. The baseline survey administered in 2006 by the Institute of Microfinance (InM) covered nearly half a million rural households from 23 *upazilas* (subdistricts) and some 2,300 villages (after data cleaning, 480,918 households are retained for our analysis). These households constitute roughly 60 percent of all households in the survey villages. The survey covered the greater Rangpur region, comprising five administrative districts—Gaibandha, Kurigram, Lalmonirhat, Nilphamari, and Rangpur.[13]

The InM survey was carried out as part of an effort by the Palli Karma-Sahayak Foundation, the only wholesale outlet of microfinance in Bangladesh, to identify the extreme poor who are vulnerable to monga and to design and implement appropriate interventions to mitigate monga. The extreme poor in the InM survey are identified as those households that satisfy at least one of the following criteria: (a) having less than 50 decimals (0.5 acre) of land, (b) having a monthly income of Tk 1,500 (equivalent to US$22) or less, or (c) selling labor for daily wage. Of the three criteria, the one relating to landownership was found to be pervasive, applying to 98 percent of the surveyed households. Although the HIES data contain detailed questionnaires about living conditions, the InM survey contains limited information, with a focus on the extent of seasonal food deprivation and the coping mechanisms adopted by the households. We have also used data from a much more intensive follow-up survey conducted in 2008 with respect to a subsample of households covered in the InM baseline survey of 2006.[14]

The InM survey categorizes households in three groups by their food deprivation status: starvation (having no meals on some days), meal rationing (skipping of one or two meals or having half meals each time on some days), and full meals (having full meals usually three times a day). This information was recorded for both monga and non-monga periods for all households. Figure 3.11 shows the extent of seasonal hunger in the Rangpur region as a whole, and table 3.5 provides a breakdown by the five administrative districts.

Both the extent and the seasonality of hunger become strikingly evident from the estimates presented here, particularly if one takes into account the fact that the lean season of 2006 was no different from that of a normal agricultural year in Rangpur. The situation would of course have been much worse if it were a year of abnormal floods or other natural calamities. Some 47.0 percent of the households experienced starvation during the monga season, whereas only 4.4 percent had full meals. About half the population had to ration meals in both seasons, indicating a persistent form of food insecurity among the poor households in the Rangpur region. Even during the non-monga season, about 9 percent of households experienced starvation—an indication of the dire situation among the very poor in that region. The extent of seasonality is evident from the very large changes in the category of starvation and full meals between the seasons.

Although the entire region appears to suffer from severe forms of food insecurity, there are some intraregional differences. The incidence of starvation varies from 26 percent to 58 percent across the districts during the

Figure 3.11   Distribution of Rural Households by Food Deprivation Status in Monga and Non-monga Seasons in the Greater Rangpur Region, 2006

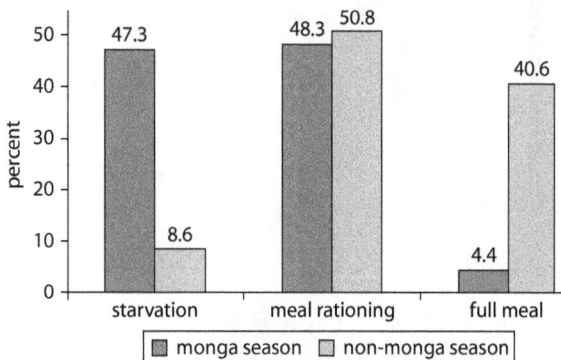

Source: Institute of Microfinance baseline survey, 2006.

Table 3.5   Distribution of Poor Households by Food Deprivation Status in the Rangpur Region, 2006

percent

Consumption status	Kurigram district	Gaibandha district	Nilphamari district	Lalmonirhat district	Rangpur district	Rangpur region
Non-monga period						
Starvation	2.08	12.18	2.32	14.36	17.10	8.53
Meal rationing	49.36	63.44	32.89	54.78	53.33	50.85
Full meals	48.56	24.38	64.79	30.86	29.57	40.62
Monga period						
Starvation	48.47	57.62	26.16	47.95	56.34	47.27
Meal rationing	50.14	40.79	60.37	49.54	40.35	48.29
Full meals	1.39	1.59	13.47	2.51	3.31	4.44
Overall						
Starvation	49.68	62.69	27.13	52.07	60.35	50.22
Meal rationing	49.03	36.22	60.11	46.73	37.50	45.97
Full meals	1.29	1.09	12.76	1.20	2.15	3.81
Number of observations	120,426	128,987	102,866	56,772	71,867	480,918

Source: InM baseline survey, 2006.

monga period and from 2 to 17 percent in the non-monga period. Again, the extent of full meals varies from 1 to 13 percent during the monga period and from 30 to 60 percent in the non-monga period. The Nilphamari district seems to be relatively better off, whereas Rangpur and Gaibandha are the most disadvantaged districts.

The InM survey data also allow us to construct the distribution of the households by defining their overall or year-round meal intake status as follows: (a) starvation means experiencing starvation during any period of the year (that is, during either the monga or the non-monga period); (b) meal rationing means having to ration meals during at least one period but avoiding starvation in all periods; and (c) the rest of the households have full meals during both monga and non-monga seasons. As table 3.5 shows, about 50 percent of households experience starvation in at least one period; 46 percent ration meals year round without experiencing starvation in any period; and only 4 percent have year-round full meals. Again, the Nilphamari district seems to be better off than the other districts.

One indirect implication of these estimates of the overall or year-round meal intake status compared with those for the monga and non-monga seasons separately is that most households experience a worsening of their situation during monga. In other words, monga represents an aggregate seasonal shock. For example, the proportion of households that experience starvation in any season of the year (50 percent) is not much higher than the proportion that experience starvation in the monga period only (48 percent). Thus, about 2 percent of the households undergo starvation in the non-monga period only—presumably as a result of some idiosyncratic or household-specific reasons.

Why Seasonal Hunger Persists in the Rangpur Region: Some Proximate Causes

The severe and persistent seasonal hunger that is observed in Rangpur can hardly occur unless there is a confluence of many adverse factors. Some of the factors that put the region at a disadvantage in this respect compared with other regions of the country can be readily identified. The following are some proximate causes:

- A generally high level poverty, particularly extreme poverty
- Inadequate investments in infrastructure, including electricity, resulting in a lack of diversification of the rural economy and limited off-farm employment opportunities
- Low crop yields because of poor soil quality (for example, sandy soil)

- A high proportion of households that are landless and depend on income from daily wages
- Low wage rates for both male and female agricultural day laborers
- Risk of floods and river erosion
- Livelihood vulnerability of the people living in the *char* areas consisting of land reclaimed from rivers, including tiny island-like land fragments
- Low inflows of remittances from migrant family members working within or outside the country.

This list is not necessarily exhaustive, but it is based on the evidence that is readily available. We have already discussed the relatively high incidence of poverty in Rangpur as estimated from the various rounds of the HIES. Evidence has also been presented regarding the relatively low wage rates in Rangpur (figure 3.5). According to the baseline survey, households owned on average only 8.2 decimals (100 decimals make an acre) of land, meaning they are virtually landless.[15] Among the households surveyed, 19 percent lived in the ecologically vulnerable char areas—presumably compelled by poverty and land scarcity. According to the population census of 2001, the proportion of rural households with access to electricity varied from 4 to 13 percent among the districts in Rangpur compared with 20 percent among all rural households in Bangladesh. The official crop statistics show that the yield of aman rice in Rangpur is considerably lower than the national average.

Looking at the pattern of income of rural households in Rangpur compared with the rest of the country provides further insights into the sources of their vulnerability to seasonal hardship. Table 3.6 provides such a comparison based on the HIES data of 2000 and 2005 (see also figure 3.12).

It can be seen that household per capita income in Rangpur was nearly about 70 percent of that in the rest of the country in both years. In addition, the households in Rangpur draw a higher proportion of their income from farming (about 50 percent compared with about 28 percent for the rest of the country in 2005). Moreover, the share of crop income in total income is also higher in Rangpur.[16]

Although remittance income is a significant proportion of income in other areas, it is negligibly low in Rangpur (table 3.6). In many areas of rural Bangladesh, remittances from family members working abroad is now a substantial source of inflow of funds into the local economy, but Rangpur is not one of those areas. It is also noteworthy that the receipts from the safety-net programs not only are a negligible proportion of total household income for all areas, but also are lower in Rangpur than elsewhere on a per

Table 3.6   Selected Welfare Indicators of Rural Households, 2000 and 2005

Indicator	Rangpur region		Rest of the country		Whole sample	
	2000	2005	2000	2005	2000	2005
Per capita farm income (A) (Tk/month)	269.9	318.3	288.2	256.3	286.5	262.2
Per capita nonfarm income (B) (Tk/month)	216.1	258.0	378.2	376.5	363.4	365.2
Per capita nonearned income (C) (Tk/month)	130.3	72.0	235.8	294.5	226.2	273.4
Per capita total income (A + B + C) (Tk/month)	616.3	648.3	902.2	927.3	876.1	900.8
Share of crop income in total income	0.168	0.177	0.110	0.123	0.115	0.128
Per capita receipt from remittance (Tk/month)	17.9	17.1	106.7	132.6	98.6	121.7
Per capita receipt from safety-net programs (Tk/month)	1.8	1.5	2.4	2.6	2.3	3.2
Per capita total expenditure (Tk/month)	541.6	630.4	740.5	875.7	722.4	890.2

Sources: Estimated from HIES 2000 and 2005 data, rural samples.
Note: Per capita total income includes farm and nonfarm income (which are receipts from active employment) as well as all nonearned income such as receipts from investments, assets, pensions, remittances, gifts/charities, and safety-net programs. Safety-net programs are VGD, VGF, IFS, FFW (money), Test Relief, GR, Money for Education, RMP, Old Age Pension, Freedom Fighters Pension, and so on. Monetary figures are deflated by the consumer price index with base year 2000.

capita basis. Finally, by comparing total household income and expenditure, one can see that the households in Rangpur have less surplus cash; consequently, they have less room to maneuver against any adversities, including seasonal stress.

Another concern is that the rural households in Rangpur depend more on the agricultural labor market, thereby making wage income from agriculture a higher share of total income compared with the rest of the country (figure 3.12). The high dependence of the poor households in Rangpur on wage income is also evident from the InM survey, with 54 percent depending on wage employment and only 16 percent on self-employment as the main source of income.[17] However, agricultural wage workers fare worse in Rangpur than do their counterparts in the rest of the country in daily wage rates (see figure 3.5).

The lower wage observed in Rangpur compared with other regions does not resolve the problem of lack of employment during the monga season, because the observed wage rates are hardly market clearing. The wage rates in the informal labor markets in Bangladesh seem to be determined by

Figure 3.12   Breakdown of Household Income by Source in Rangpur and the Rest of Bangladesh, 2005

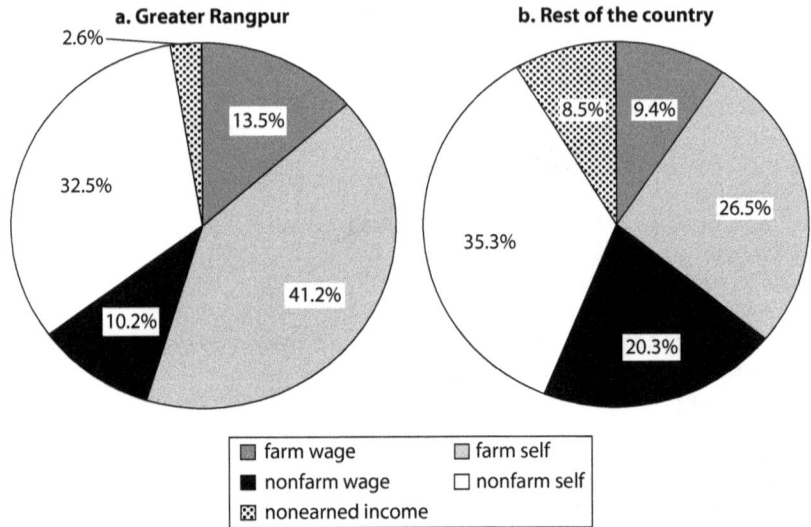

a. Greater Rangpur

2.6%
13.5%
32.5%
41.2%
10.2%

b. Rest of the country

8.5% 9.4%
26.5%
35.3%
20.3%

■ farm wage   ☐ farm self
■ nonfarm wage   ☐ nonfarm self
▨ nonearned income

Source: HIES, 2005.

social norms established in relation to a variety of factors such as subsistence needs, the average living conditions of the locality, and the degree of interregional integration of labor markets. The supply-demand situation in the local labor market is only part of the story. This can also be seen from the relatively low degree of seasonal variation in agricultural wages as shown in figure 3.13. The wage rates decline slightly during the monga months of September to November both in Rangpur and in Bangladesh as a whole, but this decline is unlikely to reflect the extent of the fall in agricultural employment in that season.

As noted earlier, the seasonal variations in rice prices relative to the rice harvesting seasons have been reduced over time (figure 3.3). Moreover, the rice market has also become more spatially integrated over time so that the higher incidence of poverty in Rangpur cannot be attributed to higher food prices.[18] The poverty line income used in the official poverty estimates based on the HIES is in fact slightly lower for Rangpur than for the rest of the country for both 2000 and 2005.

If agricultural wages and food prices are not the reasons for the seasonality of food deprivation in Rangpur, what could then explain it? We

Figure 3.13   Monthly Trend in Agricultural Wage Rates of Males (without Meals), Average for 2003–09

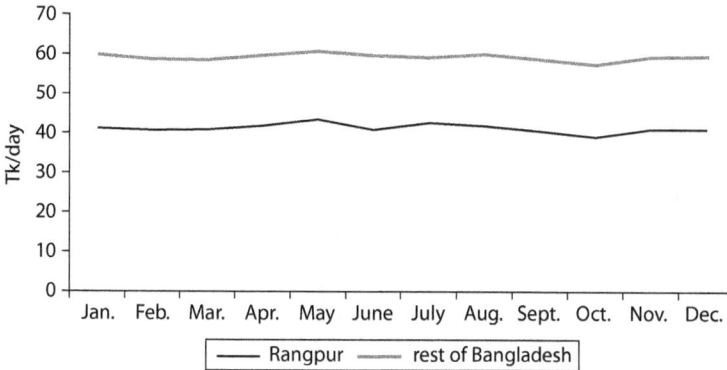

Source: Authors' estimates based on the official data of the Bangladesh Bureau of Statistics.
Note: Figures are deflated by monthly rural consumer price index (1995–96 = 100).

argue that the source of seasonality lies mainly in the lack of employment and income-earning opportunities during the monga season. The seasonal distribution of employment among poor households in Rangpur can be estimated from the InM follow-up survey conducted in 2008 with respect to a subsample of households covered in the InM baseline survey of 2006. Figure 3.14 shows the estimates of monthly days worked in farm and nonfarm sectors by season. The estimates are averages for the entire sample of households, whereas the employment patterns will obviously be different for different occupational groups within those poor households. Nevertheless, the results are quite revealing.

The major source of employment seasonality is the strikingly large decline in farm wage employment during the monga season. Moreover, within farm employment, wage employment is far more dominant than self-employment, which is expected because the survey covered households with meager amounts of land. Compared with the wage laborers, the self-employed in the farm sector can better protect themselves from lack of employment; even then, farm self-employment declines in the monga season as well. Employment in the nonfarm sector—wage or self-employment—shows only small seasonal variations with no fall in the monga season. However, because of the lack of diversification of the rural economy, the rural nonfarm sector is not large enough to provide employment to many farmworkers during a particular season.

Figure 3.14   Seasonal Pattern of Employment of Poor Households of Rangpur by Sector, 2008

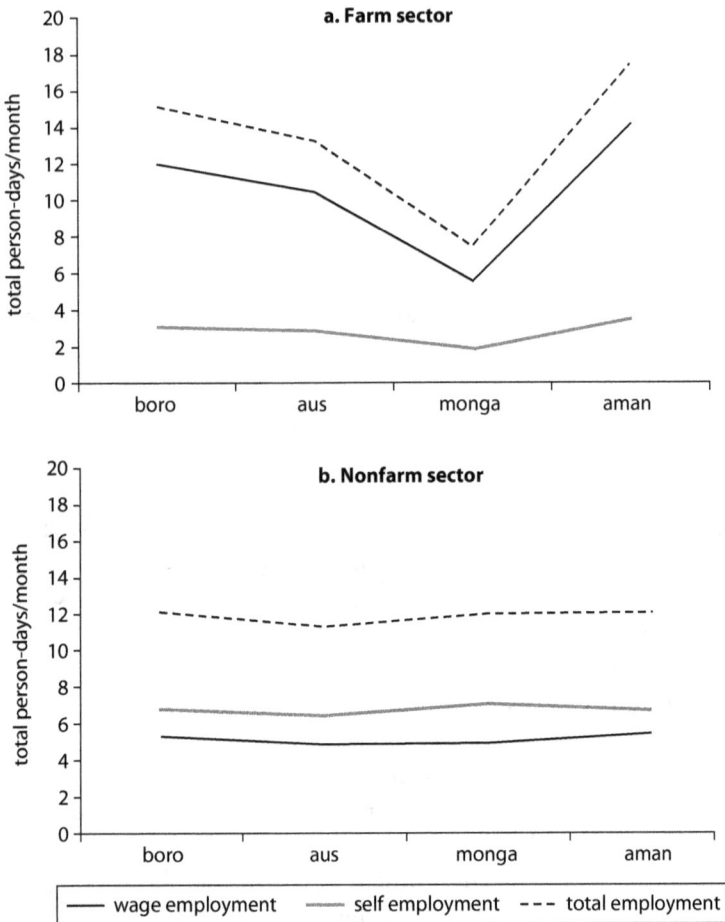

Source: InM follow-up survey, 2008.

Concluding Remarks

The seasonality of income, consumption, and poverty is a common feature of entire rural Bangladesh, but it is more marked in the Rangpur region, where the interlocking of seasonality and endemic poverty results in severe seasonal hunger.[19] The persistent phenomenon of seasonal hunger in Rangpur is explained by the adverse economic geography and agroecological vulnerability of the region that are reflected in the pattern of employment and income-earning opportunities of the poor households.

As noted earlier, Rangpur in fact features prominently in the famine literature; it was among the worst-hit districts in the Great Bengal Famine of 1942–44 and was literally the epicenter of the 1974 famine in Bangladesh (Alamgir 1980; Sen 1977). Although famine is epochal, seasonal hunger or monga is a recurrent phenomenon; yet famine can be seen as the extreme manifestation of the monga phenomenon. The explanation of famines with regard to a lack of entitlement can thus be relevant for explaining seasonal hunger as well. For example, monga does not seem to be caused by the lack of food availability, but by the failure of the income-earning opportunities for the poor.[20] Moreover, as in the case of past famines in this region, it is the landless agricultural laborers who are found to be most at risk.

But unlike in the case of famine, failure of income-earning opportunities need not be accompanied by food price inflation to cause monga. That is why monga may remain unnoticed as a form of silent hunger, because it is the abnormal increases in food prices that usually create public uproar and attract the attention of policy makers. This situation also explains why the government's interventions for food price stabilization as a means of ensuring food insecurity have not worked to mitigate monga. However, poverty reduction generally, along with more integration of labor and food markets, is likely to have helped to some extent in reducing the adverse effects of seasonality in the country as well as in Rangpur. These factors may explain why, since 1974, seasonal hunger in Rangpur has never taken on the proportions of famine in spite of the much more severe intensity of floods and crop damage than happened in that year.

Notes

1. This definition of extreme poverty suggests that even if the entire household expenditure is on food, it will meet only the minimum food needs, let alone the needs of nonfood consumption.

2. The estimates for 2010 are not yet available from the published results.

3. In Bangladesh, the scaling up of programs through the spread of new ideas is helped by a strong presence of nongovernmental organizations and by the density of settlements and their lack of remoteness (see Ahluwalia and Mahmud 2004; Mahmud 2008).

4. *Malnourishment* is defined as moderate to severe underweight (weight for age).

5. The estimates are based on domestic production net of wastage and uses for seed and feed, offtakes from public stocks net of domestic procurement, and

private imports. The population estimates since 2001 are the official pro-
jected ones.

6. These trends are the same for the wage rates of female agricultural laborers as
well, although wages for females are much lower than those for males across
all regions.

7. The HIES divides Bangladesh into 23 statistical regions, one of which is the
Rangpur region. Although different households were interviewed at various
times of the year, the data can be used for both interseasonal and cross-
regional comparisons because of the random sampling of households by seasonal and regional strata.

8. The HIES of 2000 included a total sample of 7,440 households, of which
5,040 were drawn from rural areas. In 2005, the rural sample was 6,040 out
of a total sample of 10,080 households.

9. Because the HIES collected households' crop income by specific crop, the
income can be distributed by season. Incomes from nonseasonal crops were
excluded in the estimating of the seasonal crop income in this way.

10. Food prices are derived from the household-level information on quantity
and expenditure, and nonfood price deflators are based on official cost-of-
living indexes.

11. The figures on seasonal patterns of consumption and poverty shown in this
chapter are based on HIES data and are taken from Khandker (2012).

12. The methodology of converting food quantities into calories is the same as
that used in the official poverty estimates based on the direct calorie-intake
method. The HIES reports food consumption by both quantities and
expenditures.

13. The survey covered all the upazilas in the Kurigram and Lalmonirhat districts;
in the other three districts, selected numbers of monga-prone upazilas were
covered.

14. Since then, the InM has conducted two more follow-up surveys, in 2009 and
2010, the overview results of which will be briefly mentioned in the final
chapter of this book.

15. This finding about landownership was not unexpected given that the amount
of land owned was used as a criterion for being defined as poor and included
in the survey. The significant factor to note is that these households constituted about 60 percent of all households in the survey villages.

16. Crop income does not include wage income in crop production.

17. These estimates include employment in both farm and nonfarm sectors.
Households earning income from certain sources such as begging, remittances, or safety-net programs are not included in the estimates.

18. For rice market integration, see Mahmud, Rahman, and Zohir (1994).

19. Ahmed (2000) presents survey-based evidence of seasonal poverty and food deprivation in some economically depressed areas in the country, including Rangpur.

20. Note that the word *monga* does not necessarily mean shortage of food in this part of the country; rather, it connotes a lack of purchasing power, income, and employment for a large section of people.

References

Ahluwalia, Isher J., and Wahiduddin Mahmud. 2004. "Economic Transformation and Social Development in Bangladesh." *Economic and Political Weekly* 39 (36): 4009–11.

Ahmed, Akhter. 2000. "Trends in Consumption, Nutrition, and Poverty." In *Out of the Shadow of Famine: Evolving Food Markets and Food Policy in Bangladesh*, ed. Raisuddin Ahmed, Steven Haggblade, and Tawfiq-e-Elawi Chowdhury, 101–18. Baltimore, MD: Johns Hopkins University Press.

Alamgir, Mohiuddin. 1980. *Famine in South Asia: Political Economy of Mass Starvation*. Cambridge, MA: Oelgeschlager, Gunn & Hain.

Bangladesh Bureau of Statistics. Various years. *Statistical Yearbook of Bangladesh*. Dhaka: Bangladesh Bureau of Statistics.

Dorosh, Paul A. 2001. "Trade Liberalization and National Food Security: Rice Trade between Bangladesh and India." *World Development* 29 (4): 673–89.

Dorosh, Paul A., Carlo del Ninno, and Quazi Shahabuddin. 2004. *The 1998 Floods and Beyond: Towards Comprehensive Food Security in Bangladesh*. Dhaka: University Press and International Food Policy Research Institute.

Elahi, K. Maudood, and Iffat Ara. 2008. *Understanding the Monga in Northern Bangladesh*. Dhaka: Academic Press and Publishers Library.

Khandker, Shahidur R. 2009. "Poverty and Income Seasonality in Bangladesh." Policy Research Working Paper 4923, World Bank, Washington, DC.

———. 2012. "Seasonality of Income and Poverty in Bangladesh." *Journal of Development Economics* 97 (2): 244–56.

Mahmud, Wahiduddin. 2008. "Social Development: Pathways, Surprises, and Challenges." *Indian Journal of Human Development* 2 (1): 79–92.

———. 2010. "Country Strategy Note: IGC-Bangladesh Growth Research Programme." International Growth Centre, London School of Economics, London.

Mahmud, Wahiduddin, Sadiq Ahmed, and Sandeep Mahajan. 2010. "Economic Reforms, Growth, and Governance: The Political Economy Aspects of Bangladesh's Development Surprise." In *Leadership and Growth*, ed. Michael Spence and David Brady, 227–54. Washington, DC: World Bank.

Mahmud, Wahiduddin, and Anis Chowdhury. 2008. "South Asian Economic Development: Impressive Achievements but Continuing Challenges." In *Handbook on the South Asian Economies,* ed. Wahiduddin Mahmud and Anis Chowdhury, 1–24. Cheltenham, U.K.: Edward Elgar.

Mahmud, Wahiduddin, Sultan Hafeez Rahman, and Sajjad Zohir. 1994. "Agricultural Growth through Crop Diversification in Bangladesh." Working Paper 7, International Food Policy Research Institute, Washington, DC.

———. 2000. "Agricultural Diversification: A Strategic Factor for Growth." In *Out of the Shadow of Famine: Evolving Food Markets and Food Policy in Bangladesh,* ed. Raisuddin Ahmed, Steven Haggblade, and Tawfiq-e-Elawi Chowdhury, 232–60. Baltimore, MD: Johns Hopkins University Press.

Narayan, Ambar, Nobuo Yoshida, and Hassan Zaman. 2007. "Trends and Patterns of Poverty in Bangladesh in Recent Years." World Bank, Washington, DC.

Rahman, Hossain Zillur. 1995. "Mora Kartik: Seasonal Deficits and the Vulnerability of the Rural Poor." In *Rethinking Rural Poverty: Bangladesh as a Case Study,* ed. Hossain Zillur Rahman and Mahabub Hossain, 234–53. New Delhi: Sage.

Ravallion, Martin, and Binayak Sen. 1996. "When Method Matters: Monitoring Poverty in Bangladesh." *Economic Development and Cultural Change* 44 (4): 761–92.

Sen, Amartya. 1977. "Starvation and Exchange Entitlements: A General Approach and Its Application to the Great Bengal Famine." *Cambridge Journal of Economics* 1 (1): 33–59.

UNICEF (United Nations Children's Fund). 2011. *The State of the World's Children 2011.* New York: UNICEF.

Zug, Sebastian. 2006. "Monga: Seasonal Food Insecurity in Bangladesh— Understanding the Problem and Strategies to Combat It." Report prepared for the NETZ Partnership for Development and Justice, Bochum, Bangladesh.

CHAPTER 4

Household Vulnerability and Coping Strategies

For a proper understanding of the phenomena of seasonal poverty and food deprivation, a number of issues relating to the circumstances of vulnerable households and their behavioral responses need to be analyzed. This chapter addresses questions about three such issues. The first issue concerns household vulnerability to seasonal food deprivation, which in turn is related to the question of to what extent is such deprivation predictable and therefore structural in nature. A second issue refers to the capacity of poor households to self-insure against seasonal income shortfalls. In other words, to what extent is seasonal hunger caused by the inability of poor households to smooth consumption year round in the face of income seasonality? Yet a third issue relates to the coping strategies households may adopt when they actually face seasonal hunger—an issue that is also related to wider livelihood considerations for the poor.

Household Vulnerability to Food Deprivation

The phenomenon of household poverty and hunger can be considered in either the ex post or the ex ante sense, that is, either as actual outcomes or as future probability. The various measures of household well-being (such as food deprivation of various extents or moderate and extreme poverty) presented in the last chapter are actual or ex post measures. In contrast, vulnerability refers to the ex ante measure of future probability that takes into account the current characteristics of a household and the likely fluctuations in its consumption or income (Chaudhuri 2003; Chaudhuri, Jalan, and Suryahadi 2002; Pritchett, Suryahadi, and Sumarto 2000).

The analysis of vulnerability can be helpful in many ways. For policy-making purposes, it is important to know who is likely to be poor or food insecure in the future. How far poverty or food insecurity is structural in nature can be judged by the extent to which the characteristics of the poor are found to coincide with those of the vulnerable. In the same way, one can also look at whether vulnerability to aggregate shocks such as seasonal hunger has the same correlates as those of poverty, in which case, seasonal hunger can be said to be structurally determined by poverty in general. It can also be seen that the main difference between poverty and vulnerability is the risk or uncertainty related to future well-being. As such, the analysis of vulnerability is related to the key defining characteristics of household food security (see the earlier discussion in chapter 2 of this book).

Seasonal Transition in Household Food Deprivation Status in Rangpur

Looking at the movements of households with respect to food deprivation status from one season to another can be a way of determining ex ante vulnerability to seasonal hunger (Dercon 2002). For such an analysis of vulnerability, data can be used from the Institute of Microfinance (InM) baseline survey of 2006, discussed in chapter 3. The survey has information on household meal consumption patterns at two times—during the *monga* (seasonal hunger) period (September–November) of 2006 and the following non-monga period (December–February) of 2006/07. Because of this time span, a transition matrix can be used to observe households' movements among various food deprivation statuses from one period to another. Such a transition matrix can indicate vulnerability to seasonal hunger. Because the InM survey is representative of the bottom 60 percent of households in the Rangpur region, the analysis based on this data set helps focus directly on the poor and food-vulnerable households.

Table 4.1 presents a transition matrix of household food consumption patterns across seasons. It was found that 58.8 percent of the sample households (shaded in dark gray) were subjected to what we can call a perpetual

Table 4.1   Transition of Poor Households in Rangpur between Monga and Non-monga Periods

| Non-monga period | Monga period | | | |
	Starvation	Meal rationing	Full meals	Total
Starvation	0.056	0.029	0.001	0.086
Meal rationing	0.366	0.137	0.005	0.508
Full meals	0.051	0.317	0.038	0.406
Total	0.473	0.483	0.044	1.000

Source: Authors' estimates based on Institute of Microfinance baseline survey data, 2006.
Note: Number of observations is 480,918.

shortfall in food consumption because these households experienced some form of food deprivation in both monga and non-monga seasons. Among this group, 5.6 percent of all households faced the most severe form of food deprivation because they experienced starvation during both periods. In addition, 36.8 percent of the sample households (shaded in light gray) experienced occasional shortfall in consumption because they experienced meal rationing or starvation during the lean season only.

It is remarkable that out of the 47.3 percent of households who suffered starvation during monga, the majority (36.6 percent of all households) experienced meal rationing, if not starvation, during the non-monga season. Only less than 5 percent of the households experienced a transition from the full meals status in the non-monga season to starvation in the monga seasons. This is a clear demonstration that the phenomenon of monga largely represents an extension of perpetual food deprivation and is therefore strongly linked to structural poverty that is aggravated by seasonal factors.

The InM survey data also allow us to look at the households' own perceptions about the perpetuity of consumption shortfall during a future monga, which is a subjective way to look at vulnerability. Households were asked about the likelihood of their falling into food deprivation during the following monga season. Table 4.2 reports this likelihood, grouped by the households' food consumption patterns during the most recent monga, that is, by their anticipated future deprivation against their current deprivation.

Among those that face starvation during monga (47.3 percent of all households), a large majority (81.6 percent as calculated from table 4.2) anticipated that they were very likely to face seasonal food deprivation during the following monga, while only 6.8 percent were of the opinion that food deprivation was somewhat likely, and 11.6 percent did not

Table 4.2   Household Perception of Suffering in a Future Monga by Food Deprivation Status during Monga Period

	Exposure of last monga			
Perception about future monga	Starvation	Meal rationing	Full meals	Total
Suffering is very likely	0.386	0.142	0.002	0.530
Suffering is somewhat likely	0.032	0.222	0.030	0.284
Suffering is not likely	0.055	0.119	0.012	0.186
Total	0.473	0.483	0.044	1.000

Source: Authors' estimates based on Institute of Microfinance baseline survey data, 2006.
Note: Number of observations is 480,918.

foresee food deprivation during a future monga. Again, of all households that were food deprived during the monga (95.6 percent of all households), most of them (78.2 percentage points, shaded in dark gray in table 4.2) feared possible food deprivation in a future monga, and only the remaining 17.4 percent of households (shaded in light gray) did not anticipate so. This again is an indication of the perpetuity of food deprivation as a structural feature of poverty. As discussed in chapter 2 of this book, such perceptions about future risk of seasonal hunger are important determinants of how poor households adapt their livelihood systems to an environment of risk and uncertainty. And this can be part of a poverty cycle.

Estimation of Vulnerability to Extreme Poverty from the Household Income and Expenditure Survey Data

Vulnerability can be analyzed by using the statistical methods of estimation (for example, Chaudhuri 2003). This is done by using data from the nationally representative official Household Income and Expenditure Survey (HIES) discussed in chapter 3 in this book. The vulnerability estimates presented here relate to what we call extreme poverty. As may be recalled from the discussion in chapter 3, a household is considered extremely poor if its per capita consumption expenditure falls short of the cost of the minimum food basket as incorporated in the official poverty line estimates. Such a household cannot meet its minimum food requirements, even if its entire consumption expenditure is only on food, and is therefore likely to experience severe food deprivation.

The vulnerability estimates are made in a way to reflect both the predicted level and the volatility of a household's per capita total expenditure (see the annex of this chapter for the detailed estimation methodology).

The predictions are based on the determining factors at the household level (household head's gender, age, education, employment type, land and nonland assets, availability of electricity, and so forth) and at the village level (prices of consumer goods, wage, infrastructure, and agroclimatic characteristics). Estimates are made separately for Rangpur and the rest of the country and, in each case, separately for the monga season and for all other (non-monga) seasons combined. Thus, instead of looking at the risk of change in poverty status between seasons (as in the earlier exercise), we look at the risk in each season separately.

Table 4.3 shows the estimates of the proportion of households that were vulnerable to extreme poverty (EV) in 2000 and 2005, along with the proportion of households that actually experienced extreme poverty (EP) in those years. The extent of correspondence of the estimates of vulnerability to what is actually observed at any time (that is, between EV and EP) is an indication of how well the factors considered can predict extreme poverty, or in other words, how much of the extreme poverty is structurally determined. A divergence between the two estimates, however, results from the unpredictable volatility of consumption, and thus, some nonvulnerable households may currently fall into extreme poverty while some vulnerable ones may escape it.

The estimates in table 4.3 show a much higher incidence of vulnerability to extreme poverty in Rangpur than in other areas of Bangladesh in both seasons. As in the case of actual incidence of poverty, the estimates of vulnerability clearly show the disadvantage of Rangpur compared with the rest of the country. Moreover, vulnerability to extreme poverty is higher in the monga season compared with other seasons, except for Rangpur in 2005. The estimates also show that vulnerability to extreme poverty declined in all regions between 2000 and 2005.

Table 4.3   Incidence of Extreme Poverty and Vulnerability to Extreme Poverty by Season, Rangpur and the Rest of Bangladesh, 2000 and 2005

Period	Rangpur		Rest of the country	
	2000	2005	2000	2005
Monga season (% of households)	EP = 66.0	EP = 48.3	EP = 43.9	EP = 31.6
	EV = 75.0	EV = 35.8	EV = 38.0	EV = 19.8
Non-monga season (% of households)	EP = 59.4	EP = 43.0	EP = 38.4	EP = 28.6
	EV = 50.6	EV = 37.8	EV = 30.2	EV = 16.5
Number of observations	440	520	4,600	5,520

Source: Authors' estimates based on Household Income and Expenditure Survey data, 2000 and 2005, rural samples.
Note: EP = extreme poverty, EV = vulnerability to extreme poverty.

The overall picture emerging from the estimates in table 4.3 is that the estimated vulnerability index can track actual extreme poverty quite well, as can be seen from the close correspondence between the two sets of estimates. This implies that extreme poverty in large part is structurally determined by household and area characteristics and is therefore predictable to a large extent. The other notable aspect of these estimates is that the proportions of households in extreme poverty are higher than the proportions that are vulnerable (with the exception of Rangpur during the monga season in 2000). This suggests that because of the unpredictable volatility in income and consumption, households are more likely to fall into extreme poverty rather than escape it at any time. Thus, although extreme poverty is mainly structural, the consumption volatility associated with the risk-prone nature of rural livelihood is also an important determining factor.

Impact of Income Seasonality on Consumption and Poverty

One of the main factors responsible for seasonal poverty and food deprivation among rural households is their lack of capacity for smoothing consumption in the face of income seasonality tied to the crop production cycle. The evidence discussed in chapter 3 clearly suggests that this is indeed the case for large numbers of poor rural households in Bangladesh, especially in the Rangpur region. In this section, this hypothesis is put to a more rigorous statistical test to try to gain more insight into the relationships among income seasonality, poverty, and food deprivation.

Test of Household Capability for Consumption Smoothing: The Estimation Model

Following the standard model used to estimate the effect of income seasonality on consumption, we consider that the outcome variable C_{ijs} (the per capita consumption expenditure of household i in village j in season s) would depend on total per capita annual income (Y) as well as its seasonal shares (y) along with other variables such as prices, preferences, and local area characteristics (for example, Deaton 1997; Kazianga and Udry 2006; Khandker 2012; Paxson 1993). Consider the following consumption equation in semi-logarithm form in which seasonal consumption is determined, among other variables, by per capita annual income (Y) and its seasonal shares (y):

$$\ln C_{ijs} = \alpha\tau_s + \beta_1 \ln Y_{ij} + \beta_2 y_{ijs} + \gamma X_{ij} + \mu_{ij} + \mu_{sj} + \eta_j + \varepsilon_{ijs}, \qquad (4.1)$$

where X_{ij} is a vector of household-and village-level characteristics (including prices) influencing consumption and income; τ_s is a dummy variable representing the seasons; $\alpha, \beta,$ and γ are unknown parameters to be estimated; and ε_{ijs} is a zero-mean disturbance term representing the unmeasured determinants of C_{ijs} that vary across households. Note also that household consumption is affected by unobserved household hetero-geneity and village heterogeneity represented by the error terms μ_{ij} and η_j, respectively, as well as unobserved season-specific heterogeneity (μ_{sj}).

Because poverty is defined in terms of a poverty line of consumption expenditure, the relationship above can be extended to explain the effect of income seasonality on poverty as well. For this, equation (4.1) can be converted to a linear probit model of the following form:

$$\Pr(C_{ijs} < Z) = \alpha\tau_s + \beta_1 \ln Y_{ij} + \beta_2 y_{ijs} + \gamma X_{ij} + \mu_{ij} + \mu_{sj} + \eta_j + \varepsilon_{ijs}. \qquad (4.2)$$

Here, *Pr* measures the probability of consumption falling below the pov-erty threshold (Z). Note that in both equations, β_1 measures the response of seasonal consumption and poverty to total income, while β_2 measures the response to seasonal income.

Thus, if $\beta_2 = 0$, seasonality is not an issue, and seasonal income does not track seasonal consumption and poverty, perhaps because a household has the ability to smooth consumption through self-insurance and other means to compensate for losses in income, if any, during a particular season. That is, seasonal consumption depends entirely on year-long income and not on seasonal income. This is a case of a perfect consumption-smoothing model. In respect to poverty, this means that a household is poor because its annual income falls short of the threshold level necessary to be above the poverty line and thus does not experience seasonal deprivation as dis-tinct from chronic or year-round poverty. In other words, the level of pov-erty observed for this household in the lean season is not related to seasonal income but is a reflection of a shortfall in overall annual income.

In contrast, when $\beta_2 > 0$, there is a lack of perfect consumption smoothing and a possibility of seasonality of poverty determined by sea-sonality of income, above and beyond the poverty caused by annual income. That is, a household that is poor chronically or year round may become much poorer during a particular season, and even if a household is not poor based on average year-round consumption, it may become seasonally poor. However, this situation does not preclude the possibility that even the chronically poor may be able to save to manage consump-tion smoothing, although imperfectly (Deaton 1997). In contrast, it is also possible that households veer from the average consumption path that can be supported by their regular income; in such a case, to avoid severe seasonal shortfalls in consumption, they may need to rely on additional sources of funds such as remittances, government handouts, or a distress sale of assets.

Estimation of equation (4.1) or (4.2) is problematic because both income and consumption may be jointly affected by unobserved factors (such as the household and village heterogeneity represented by the error terms μ and η, respectively). There is substantial evidence for joint dependence of income and consumption (Strauss 1986; Strauss and Thomas 1995). More specifically, measurement errors in consumption are likely to be correlated with measurement errors in income, which may seriously bias the estimated coefficients (Deaton 1997; Ravallion and Chaudhuri 1997).

As a way out, we use the instrumental variable method to estimate the income variables, both total annual income (Y) and seasonal income. The instrumental variables used relate to aspects of the production environment, such as community infrastructure (the distance to district and *upazila* [subdistrict] headquarters, and the presence of schools, banks, nongovernmental organizations, and safety net programs) and agroclimatic characteristics (rainfall, land elevation, average number of sunny months, share of flood-prone areas, and the amount of excess rain per month). The local wage rates are also included among the instrumental variables on the basis of the assumption that these influence only income and not consumption directly.[1]

The focus of this analysis is to estimate a consumption or poverty model to demonstrate the extent of the net effect of income seasonality on consumption and poverty. To do this, we need to introduce a model with common seasonal effects using seasonal panel data (that is, repeated observations across seasons for more than one year). For this model, we use the combined data of the two rounds of the HIES of 2000 and 2005, which provide a cross-section of households and villages surveyed across seasons over the two years. Because the upazila is the lowest common sampling unit for collecting HIES data, we can create the panel at this level and estimate an upazila-level fixed-effects regression model.[2] This model thus can control for upazila-specific unobserved seasonal bias (μ_{sj}).[3]

Interpreting the Results: How Income Seasonality Matters for Seasonal Deprivation

This section discusses the results obtained from the estimation of equations (4.1) and (4.2) regarding the effect of income seasonality on consumption and poverty. As before, the country is divided into two regions—greater Rangpur and the rest of the country—and two seasons are considered, namely, monga and non-monga.[4] It was noted in chapter 3 that because of data limitations, seasonal crop income is used to reflect income seasonality. Taking into account the seasonal variations in crop income, seasonal income share (y) is thus expressed as the ratio of monthly seasonal income to monthly year-round income.[5]

The estimated coefficients of the consumption equation (4.1) showing the effects of overall and seasonal income are presented in table 4.4. The consumption equation was estimated separately for seasonal food consumption and total consumption. The results confirm that crop income seasonality does in fact affect the seasonality of consumption. As expected, per capita seasonal consumption (estimated on a monthly basis) is strongly related to per capita year-round income (also estimated as the monthly average). For example, a 10.0 percent increase in per capita annual income increases per capita seasonal consumption by 6.8 percent and food consumption by 5.7 percent.

What is more significant for this analysis is that the seasonal variation in income (represented by the ratio of monthly income in a season to the

Table 4.4 Estimates of Log Per Capita Seasonal Consumption

Selected explanatory variables	Total consumption (Tk per month)	Food consumption (Tk per month)
Log per capita year-round income (Tk per month)	0.687** (0.111)	0.574** (0.085)
Ratio of monthly seasonal income to monthly year-round income	1.042** (0.427)	0.600* (0.311)
Year (0 = 2000, 1 = 2005)	0.267** (0.085)	0.209** (0.079)
Year × Greater Rangpur region	−0.034 (0.097)	0.108** (0.053)
R^2	0.339	0.232
Hausman F test for endogeneity	$F_{(3,7426)} = 65.677$, $p = 0.000$	$F_{(3,7426)} = 51.07$, $p = 0.000$
Number of observations	7,640	7,640

Source: Authors' estimates based on Household Income and Expenditure Survey data, 2002 and 2005, rural samples.
Note: Based on upazila-level fixed-effect regression with panel data. Regressions include other household variables (for example, household head's gender, age, education, and land and nonland assets) and community-level variables (for example, prices of consumer goods and daily wage). Income variables are treated as endogenous and so instrumented. Instrumental variables are community infrastructure (for example, distance to district- and thana-level headquarters, and presence of schools, banks, nongovernmental organizations, and safety net programs) and agroclimatic characteristics (for example, rainfall, land elevation, and average number of sunny months). Figures in parentheses are robust/bootstrapped standard error. * and ** refer to a statistical significance of 10 percent and 5 percent or better, respectively.

year-round monthly income) is also found to be a significant determinant of seasonal food and total consumption. If, for example, this ratio increases from 1 (suggesting no income seasonality) to 2 (suggesting a doubling of the income in that season) in a season, the estimated coefficients suggest that seasonal food consumption will increase by 60 percent and total seasonal consumption by 104 percent.[6] That increase implies a very strong relation between seasonal income and seasonal consumption, including food consumption.

The statistically significant coefficient of the year dummy in table 4.4 indicates that seasonal consumption grew autonomously by more than 20 to 27 percent in real terms between 2000 and 2005. The coefficient of the interaction between the Rangpur dummy and the year dummy suggests that this increase was higher for Rangpur compared with the rest of the economy for seasonal food consumption, although not for seasonal total consumption.[7]

Overall, the evidence suggests that changes in seasonal consumption track seasonal income, indicating that households are unable to smooth consumption with crop income across seasons. This contradicts the null hypothesis of perfect consumption smoothing. The evidence is consistent with findings from other countries (for example, Jalan and Ravallion 1999; Kazianga and Udry 2006).[8]

The analysis so far does not, however, deal with the question of whether income seasonality affects poverty itself. If a lack of consumption smoothing is a major hurdle for many households, particularly among the poor, it is expected that income seasonality would also affect the incidence of poverty. As already observed in chapter 3, just as consumption is sensitive to income seasonality, so is poverty. To estimate the effect of seasonality on poverty, we simulate the effects on poverty using the estimates of the consumption equation (4.1), as presented in table 4.4, instead of directly estimating the probit model represented by equation (4.2).

The results presented in table 4.5 clearly confirm that there is a negative effect of income seasonality on all measures of seasonal poverty, meaning that a decrease in seasonal income in relation to year-round income will increase seasonal poverty, and the reverse is true for an increase in seasonal income. This is true for all types of poverty: moderate and extreme poverty and food poverty. For example, an increase in the ratio of seasonal monthly income to year-round monthly income by 10.0 percentage points will decrease seasonal extreme poverty by 9.6 percentage points and moderate poverty by 9.5 percentage points. However, with respect to a 10.0 percent increase in year-round monthly

Table 4.5   Simulated Seasonal Poverty Effects Using the Estimates of Consumption Equation Reported in Table 4.4

Income variable	Moderate poverty	Extreme poverty
Log per capita year-round income	–0.064[**]	–0.061[**]
(Tk per month)	(0.010)	(0.010)
Ratio of monthly seasonal income	–0.095[**]	–0.096[**]
to monthly year-round income	(0.039)	(0.039)

Source: Authors' estimates based on Household Income and Expenditure Survey data, 2002 and 2005, rural samples.
Note: Based on upazila-level fixed-effect regression with panel data. Regressions include other household variables (for example, household head's gender, age, education, and land and nonland assets) and community-level variables (for example, prices of consumer goods and daily wage). Income variables are treated as endogenous and so instrumented. Instrumental variables are community infrastructure (for example, distance to district- and *thana*-level headquarters, and presence of schools, banks, nongovernmental organizations, and safety net programs) and agroclimatic characteristics (for example, rainfall, land elevation, and average number of sunny months). Figures in parentheses are robust/bootstrapped standard errors. * and ** refer to a statistical significance of 10 percent and 5 percent or better, respectively.

income, the estimates of seasonal poverty reduction are 6.1 and 6.4 percentage points, respectively (table 4.5). Thus, seasonal income has a strong effect on seasonal poverty, even though year-round income is also an important determinant.

An incidental but important finding arising from the estimation of the seasonal consumption equation (4.1) relates to the levels of per capita income estimated by using the instrumental variables. For the estimation of the consumption equation, the instrumental variable method had to be used to estimate the income variables.[9] The instrumental variables used relate to the local production environment, including agroclimatic characteristics. The estimated per capita year-round monthly income, averaged over the households, was about 30 percent lower in Rangpur than in the rest of the country for both 2000 and 2005, which is nearly the same as the actual observed income disparity between the regions.[10] It is thus remarkable that the economic disadvantage of the households in the Rangpur region can be captured by their adverse economic and agroecological environment, even when their household-specific endowments are not considered.

Household Coping Strategies

The Pattern of Coping Mechanisms

With limited ability to smooth consumption in the face of income seasonality, poor households adopt many coping strategies to meet seasonal deprivation. Given the severity of seasonal hunger in Rangpur, an analysis of the coping strategies of poor households in that region is of particular interest in understanding household behavior under extreme conditions of seasonal stress. Such an understanding is also important in the design of appropriate policy interventions.

Based on the data of the InM baseline survey, table 4.6 provides a summary of coping mechanisms adopted by the poor during the monga of 2006 in various districts of the greater Rangpur region. These data represent approximately the bottom 60 percent of households in the region, nearly all of which experienced some form of food deprivation during monga. The information on coping mechanisms was gathered through the responses to a set of survey questions that referred to the monga period only. Thus, although 36 percent of the households in the Rangpur region had membership in microcredit programs at the time of the survey, less than 6 percent reported taking loans from formal sources, mostly consisting of microcredit, during the monga period (table 4.6).

It can be seen that about 65 percent of the poor households in the greater Rangpur region managed to adopt one or more coping methods to mitigate the adversity of monga. That means that 35 percent did not, or could not, resort to any coping strategy. The coping measures vary considerably among the households. About 30 percent received some support (mostly food) during the lean season from government and nongovernment sources (safety net programs). Less than 6 percent obtained loans from formal sources (mainly microcredit), and about 12 percent from informal sources.[11] It is worth noting that a large majority (36 percent) sought seasonal out-migration to cope with monga. About 16 percent also resorted to the sale of assets or the advance sale of labor and crops.

The coping mechanisms may also be in part area specific, as can be seen from the considerable variations among the five administrative districts in the Rangpur region. The variations are quite marked in the incidence of seasonal migration, which is the major coping mechanism for the entire region. As will be seen from the discussion on this topic in chapter 6 in this book, the determinants of seasonal migration can be quite context specific, involving a range of household-level and area characteristics as well as labor market networks. Another noticeable aspect of these interdistrict variations is that the access to formal means of coping, including both formal loans and a safety-net type of support, is much higher in the Nilphamari district compared with all other districts, and Nilphamari was also found to have the least incidence of starvation (see table 3.5 in chapter 3 in this book). This raises the question of appropriate area targeting of programs, a problem that will

Table 4.6 Distribution of Households by Coping Measure during Monga in the Districts of Rangpur Region

percent

Coping measures	Kurigram district	Gaibandha district	Nilphamari district	Lalmonirhat district	Rangpur district	Greater Rangpur region
Coping households	63.93	65.34	68.99	72.38	56.35	65.25
Informal coping	49.63	50.40	44.26	63.06	40.96	48.91
Advance labor sale	1.60	1.96	6.28	10.50	5.70	4.36
Advance crop sale	0.45	0.23	0.00	1.09	1.59	0.54
Asset sale	12.11	17.03	0.00	18.50	10.51	11.35
Migration	41.82	37.96	24.75	50.37	27.44	35.99
Informal loan	4.73	7.46	25.28	17.34	11.69	12.38
Formal coping	31.00	35.58	47.12	27.70	31.87	35.42
Government and nongovernment support	29.17	32.55	41.59	22.96	26.97	31.67
Formal loan	2.28	4.26	9.90	7.46	7.21	5.79
Noncoping households	36.07	34.66	31.01	27.62	43.65	34.75
Number of observations	120,426	128,987	102,866	56,772	71,867	480,918

Source: Authors' estimates based on Institute of Microfinance baseline survey data, 2006.

Note: Sum of percentage figures is more than 100 because households adopt multiple coping mechanisms. Most of the formal loans are microcredit.

be more closely looked at in subsequent chapters of this book. Another noticeable aspect of these estimates is that the proportion of households resorting to no means of coping is highest in Rangpur, which is among the two most monga-affected districts in the region (see table 3.5 in chapter 3 in this book). This proportion suggests that a lower adoption of coping measures on the whole may indicate more, and not less, need for such measures.

Table 4.7 shows the distribution of households by coping mechanisms when the households are categorized by their food deprivation status during monga. This gives some idea about the effectiveness of these coping mechanisms in reducing the incidence of starvation. Among the households who either starve or ration meals during the monga period, a large percentage (more than 30 percent) did not adopt any coping, which suggests that they probably did not have access to any coping mechanism. For example, the proportion of households resorting to asset sale was the lowest among households experiencing starvation, perhaps because they had very little assets to sell. Another possible explanation is that the coping options available to the very poor households are likely to be only the so-called erosive ones that undermine future livelihood. These households are often found to be prepared to endure a considerable degree of hunger before resorting to such desperate measures (de Waal 1989).

Table 4.7   Distribution of Households by Coping Measures According to Food Deprivation Status during Monga
percent

Coping measures	Starvation	Meal rationing	Full meals
Coping households	66.36	66.34	63.42
Informal coping	50.32	48.08	44.13
Advance labor sale	4.52	4.22	4.18
Advance crop sale	0.48	0.59	0.58
Advance asset sale	4.52	9.57	6.89
Migration	37.46	35.23	28.67
Informal loan	12.26	12.24	15.23
Formal coping	36.53	34.31	35.59
Support from safety net programs	33.41	30.26	28.63
Formal loan	4.94	6.21	10.20
Noncoping households	33.64	35.66	8.58
Number of observations	227,307	232,225	21,386

Source: Author's estimates based on Institute of Microfinance data, 2006.
Note: Sum of percentage figures is more than 100 because households adopt multiple coping mechanisms.

It is true that among the households who had three meals a day during the monga season, a relatively larger proportion (about 39 percent) did not adopt any coping; but many of these households would not probably need to adopt any coping measure to mitigate seasonal deprivation. In any case, this category of households accounts for only 4 to 5 percent of all the households surveyed. The overall picture that emerges from these estimates therefore is that the vast majority of the poor households in Rangpur adopt some monga coping mechanism and are still unable to avoid food deprivation of one form or another during monga.

Factors That Determine the Choice of Coping Mechanisms

It is not easy to determine what factors influence a household's decision to select a coping strategy to reduce the severity of seasonal starvation. For example, not adopting a coping mechanism may reflect that the households either did not need any coping mechanism or had no means to adopt any. Again, among the coping mechanisms, some are adopted only under extreme distress at the risk of erosion of future income, such as the sale of assets or informal borrowing from moneylenders at high rates of interest. In contrast, other coping mechanisms such as access to institutional credit or government and nongovernment support programs may be clearly welfare augmenting, but the choice here may lie less with the beneficiary households than with the institutions that provide such support.

From data on the coping patterns of households discussed earlier, four major categories of households can be identified by coping strategy: informal (27 percent), formal (19 percent), both formal and informal (20 percent), and none (34 percent). One can assume that decision making by the households relating to these four categories of coping is conditioned by their endowments of physical and human capital along with community characteristics. If we assume further that these four categories of choice are mutually exclusive, a multinomial logit model of the determinants of such choice can be estimated.

The results of this multinomial logit model are presented in table 4.8, showing the effects of various factors on household decisions regarding the choice of one of the three options of coping as opposed to not coping. The essence of this framework is to determine how these factors influence the choice of coping options compared with not coping.

The results show that some of the socioeconomic factors are important determinants of this choice structure. For example, age of household head, a measure of experience, increases the probability of adopting

Table 4.8   Estimates of Marginal MNL Effect of Coping Measures Adopted during Monga

Explanatory variables	Informal coping	Formal coping	Both
Age of household head	−0.003**	0.003**	0.0001**
	(0.0001)	(0.0001)	(0.00001)
Self-employed head	−0.013**	−0.004**	−0.003*
	(0.002)	(0.002)	(0.002)
Dependency ratio	0.142**	−0.102**	0.106**
	(0.004)	(0.003)	(0.003)
Log of landholdings	0.011**	−0.011**	−0.010**
	(0.001)	(0.001)	(0.001)
Household that has agricultural	0.033**	−0.027**	0.057**
equipment	(0.001)	(0.001)	(0.001)
Household that has transport	−0.020**	0.029**	−0.008**
equipment	(0.002)	(0.002)	(0.002)
Household that has savings	−0.031**	0.059**	0.044**
	(0.001)	(0.001)	(0.001)
Household that has a cow	−0.013**	0.009**	0.027**
	(0.001)	(0.001)	(0.001)
Village that has access to safety	−0.026**	0.053**	0.045**
net program	(0.002)	(0.001)	(0.001)
Presence of char land	0.058**	−0.047**	0.131**
	(0.002)	(0.001)	(0.002)
Presence of microfinance institutions	0.032**	−0.004	−0.106**
	(0.003)	(0.003)	(0.004)
Percentage of high land in district	−0.374**	0.353**	0.055**
	(0.009)	(0.008)	(0.008)
Long-term average yearly rainfall in	0.007**	−0.002**	0.001**
district (mm)	(0.0001)	(0.0001)	(0.0002)
N	129,965	91,513	94,775

Source: Authors' estimates based on Institute of Microfinance baseline survey data, 2006.
Note: Noncoping households (N = 164,665) constitute the base category. Figures in parentheses are standard errors.
* and ** refer to a statistical significance of 10 percent and 5 percent or better, respectively; mm = millimeter;
MNL = multinomial logit.

either a formal or a combination of formal and informal methods but negatively affects the adoption of an informal coping method. The self-employed are less likely to adopt any method compared with those who are wage employed. Those who have a large number of dependents in their families are more likely to adopt an informal method—separately or along with a formal method—than those who have fewer dependents. The size of landholding has a negative effect on either strategy of coping, that is, formal alone or formal and informal combined. This may reflect the fact that even among the poor households, those with more land may be averse to adopting a distress type of informal mechanism, while they are also less likely to be included in the various safety net programs. Other assets and savings can also be seen to substantially influence the coping decision, although in various ways.

When a village has access to a safety net program, households living in such a village are more likely to adopt a formal method over an informal method to cope with monga. This suggests that the beneficiaries of safety net programs are better able than other poor households to avoid adopting any informal mechanism under distress. However, the presence of microfinance institutions in the village seems to work in the opposite direction by making the households more likely to adopt either of the coping strategies.

Households living in a village that has *char* land (land fragments within rivers) are more vulnerable and more likely to adopt all measures available to cope with monga. Better agroclimatic conditions, such as a high percentage of highland, have a favorable effect on adopting a formal rather than an informal method of coping. Rainfall seems to have the opposite effect.

Without going into a detailed discussion of the possible implications of all the estimates presented in table 4.8, we can draw some broad conclusions. An important finding from these estimates is that there are significant variations in the way household coping decisions are made, even though the households are all generally poor and happen to live in the ecologically vulnerable and economically depressed region of Rangpur. Such decisions are significantly influenced by household-specific factors combined with socioeconomic and policy variables, resulting in the question: How effective are these various coping mechanisms in redressing the seasonality of hunger? The evidence so far suggests that the vast majority of the poor households in Rangpur remain monga stricken even after adopting one or the other coping strategy. For policy making, it is therefore important to know how to facilitate the coping mechanisms that have relatively more beneficial effects.

It is not, however, easy to determine the effectiveness of various coping mechanisms in mitigating seasonal hunger simply by looking at the data as discussed in this section. Because the adoption of various coping mechanisms and the outcomes in terms of the household food deprivation status are likely to be jointly determined by the same set of underlying factors, there is a problem in separating cause from effect. This problem will be addressed more rigorously in the later chapters of this book, which discuss to what extent seasonal migration, microcredit, safety net programs, and other government policies and programs can address the problem of seasonal poverty and food deprivation.

Concluding Remarks

The analyses in this chapter shed light on several features of food deprivation and its seasonality as observed among rural households in Bangladesh.
Seasonal hunger, or monga, in Rangpur can be seen as part of endemic
extreme poverty and an extension of year-round food deprivation. The
households that undergo starvation during monga are also likely to experience food deprivation, although in a milder from, in non-monga seasons.
And those who are exposed to starvation during a monga season expect
to suffer hardship in the next monga season as well.

The statistical estimates of vulnerability are found to track the actual
incidence of extreme poverty quite well, suggesting that such poverty,
whether seasonal or year round, is determined by structural factors and is
therefore largely predictable. But the estimates also suggest that there is
considerable volatility in income and consumption, reflecting risks to
rural livelihoods. Because of such risks, many rural households that
are not otherwise vulnerable may be pushed into extreme poverty at
any given time.

The results of the statistical exercises suggest that there is a strong
relationship between seasonal income and seasonal consumption, including food consumption. Thus, the seasonality of poverty and food deprivation can result from marked income seasonality combined with the
failure of poor households to smooth consumption year round. The
analysis of how the poor households in Rangpur cope with seasonal
hunger provides further insights into the livelihood strategies of the
poor. The vast majority of the poor households are found to adopt a
variety of monga coping mechanisms; some of these may be welfare
enhancing (such as access to social security provided by the government
and nongovernmental organizations), but others are adopted only under
distress at the risk of undermining future livelihood. In spite of such
widespread adoption of coping mechanisms, most of the poor households cannot avoid experiencing some form of food deprivation during
the monga season.

The implications for public policies are threefold: there is a need for
(a) combining seasonally targeted policies with those aimed at removing
the underlying structural causes of endemic poverty, (b) reducing income
seasonality through agricultural and rural diversification and enhancing
the ability of poor households to insure against seasonality, and (c) helping poor households cope with seasonal hunger so that they can avoid
taking extreme coping measures under distress.

Annex 4A: Estimation of Rural Households' Vulnerability to Extreme Poverty in the Monga and Non-monga Seasons in Rangpur and the Rest of Bangladesh

Vulnerability of a household is formally defined by the future probability of having a shortfall from a measure of well-being such as the poverty line consumption expenditure. In practice, it is often measured by the cumulative distribution function of consumption shortfalls, normalized by the variance of the error term of the consumption equation. More formally, if c_{it} represents the consumption level of household i during time t against the poverty line z_{it}, its vulnerability (V) is given by

$$V_{it} = \Pr[c_{it} < z_{it}] = \Pr[\ln(c_{it}) < \ln(z_{it})], \qquad (4A.1)$$

and the index of such vulnerability is given by

$$\hat{v}_{it} = \Pr\left[\xi_{it} < \frac{\ln(z_{it}) - X_{it}\hat{\beta}}{\sqrt{X_{it}\hat{\theta}}}\right] = \phi_{it}\left[\frac{\ln(z_{it}) - X_{it}\hat{\beta}}{\sqrt{X_{it}\hat{\theta}}}\right], \qquad (4A.2)$$

where X is a vector of household and community characteristics used in the consumption equation, $\hat{\beta}$ is an estimate of the vector of parameters influencing consumption, $\hat{\theta}$ is the estimate of the variance of the error term of the consumption equation, $\phi_{it}(.)$ is the cumulative normal distribution function, and ξ_{it} is given by

$$\xi_{it} < \frac{\ln(c_{it}) - X_{it}\hat{\beta}}{\sqrt{X_{it}\hat{\theta}}}. \qquad (4A.3)$$

Here, it is assumed that $\ln(c_{it})$ is normally distributed in a large sample with a mean of $X_{it}\hat{\beta}$ and a variance of $X_{it}\hat{\theta}$. Further details of this formulation can be found in Chaudhuri (2003) and Khandker (2006).

In using the data on household consumption expenditure, one can calculate the food vulnerability index of a household as defined by equation (4A.2), which gives its probability of being in extreme poverty based on its current characteristics. First, this requires the estimation of a household consumption function, based on all household-level and local area characteristics. Next, the squared residuals are regressed against the same household-level and area characteristics to get the estimated variance. Finally, the vulnerability index is computed as the right-hand side of equation (4A.2). It may be noted that the vulnerability index, thus calculated, varies from 0 to 1, where 0 indicates nonvulnerability and 1 indicates maximum vulnerability. From this broad spectrum of probabilities, vulnerable households are identified by setting a cutoff value of the index, which requires some judgment. Following a common practice, the cut-off value is set at 0.5 in the present exercise. A household is considered to be vulnerable if its vulnerability index is higher than 0.5 and nonvulnerable otherwise.

The data from the Household Income and Expenditure Survey, as discussed in chapter 3 in this book, can be used to estimate the household consumption function and the implied vulnerability index. For this estimation, household per capita consumption expenditure (log form) is regressed against the household-level and village characteristics that can be obtained from the HIES data. The estimates are made separately for Rangpur and the rest of the country, and in each case, separately for the monga (seasonal hunger) season and for all other (non-monga) seasons combined. However, the variance of the error term is estimated by pulling together the estimates for both monga and non-monga seasons, implying that no distinction is made between the seasons in this regard.

The HIES of 2000 and 2005 can provide panel data for the two years at the upazila (subdistrict) level (because the upazila is the sampling unit for the survey) so that a fixed-effects regression model can be applied for estimating the consumption function. The use of the model makes it possible to eliminate any unobserved time-invariant common effects at the upazila level. The use of such upazila-level fixed-effects models in other contexts is further discussed in this chapter and in chapter 5 in this book.

Notes

1. Here we rely on the assumption of a perfect substitutability model of income and consumption with an active labor market to justify the instrumental variable method (cf. Singh, Squire, and Strauss 1986).

2. An upazila is a subdistrict consisting of 10–12 *unions*, while a union consists of 10–12 villages. In 2005, some upazilas were newly created and could not be matched with the 2000 data. Merging data at the upazila level over the two years results in a common set of 184 upazilas included in the upazila-level panel.

3. The ideal panel should be at the household level, meaning the same households were interviewed in different seasons over two years. To apply the upazila-level fixed-effects method, we first multiply an upazila dummy by a seasonal dummy to create an upazila-seasonal dummy. Because we have two seasons (monga and non-monga), the difference between these upazila-seasonal

dummies cancels out the seasonal-specific unobserved effect within an upazila (μ_{sj}). Because these upazila-seasonal dummies are also observed in two years, the difference between them in two years cancels out upazila-specific fixed effects (η_j).

4. As noted in chapter 3 of this book, there are four distinct agricultural seasons, but here the three non-monga seasons are collapsed into one.

5. The estimation of seasonal income from crop production was discussed in chapter 3 of this book. Nonseasonal crops such as sugar and tobacco, which are rather minor crops in Bangladesh, are not included in the estimates of seasonal crop income.

6. This particular interpretation of the value of the estimated coefficients of the income seasonality variable is derived from the semilogarithmic form of the equation in which the value of the coefficient represents the proportionate change in the dependent variable with respect to a unitary change in the explanatory variable.

7. The inclusion of a dummy for the monga season and another for the interaction of the monga dummy with a Rangpur dummy yielded no significant regression coefficients. This suggested that there were no significant effects of any income seasonality other than what was captured by the seasonality of crop income either for the entire country or for Rangpur in particular. For details of these exercises, see Khandker (2012).

8. This finding contradicts the findings of Paxson (1993) for Thailand and those of Jacoby and Skoufias (1998) for India.

9. The use of the instrumental variable method was also justified by the Hausman F test for endogeneity; see table 4.4.

10. See table 3.6 in chapter 3 in this book. For the estimates of instrumented incomes, see Khandker (2012).

11. The majority of informal loans (about 50 percent) are from relatives, friends, and neighbors. The rest of the lenders consist of informal moneylenders, landlords, shopkeepers, employers, and input suppliers.

References

Chaudhuri, Shubham. 2003. "Assessing Vulnerability to Poverty: Concepts, Empirical Methods, and Illustrative Examples." World Bank, Washington, DC.

Chaudhuri, Shubham, Jyotsna Jalan, and Asep Suryahadi. 2002. "Assessing Household Vulnerability to Poverty from Cross-Sectional Data: A Methodology and Estimates from Indonesia." Discussion Paper 0102-52, Department of Economics, Columbia University, New York.

Deaton, Angus. 1997. *Analysis of Household Surveys: A Microeconomic Approach to Development Policy.* Baltimore, MD: Johns Hopkins University Press.

Dercon, Stefan. 2002. "Income Risk, Coping Strategies, and Safety Nets." *World Bank Research Observer* 17 (2): 141–66.

de Waal, Alex. 1989. *Famine That Kills*. Oxford, U.K.: Clarendon.

Jacoby, Hanan G., and Emmanuel Skoufias. 1998. "Testing Theories of Consumption Behavior Using Information on Aggregate Shocks: Income Seasonality and Rainfall in Rural India." *American Journal of Agricultural Economics* 80 (1): 1–14.

Jalan, Joytsna, and Martin Ravallion. 1999. "Are the Poor Less Well Insured? Evidence on Vulnerability to Income Risk in Rural China." *Journal of Development Economics* 58 (1): 61–81.

Kazianga, Harounan, and Christopher Udry. 2006. "Consumption Smoothing? Livestock, Insurance, and Drought in Rural Burkina Faso." *Journal of Development Economics* 79 (2): 413–46.

Khandker, Shahidur R. 2006. "Coping with Flood: Role of Institutions in Bangladesh." *Agriculture Economics* 36 (2): 169–80.

———. 2012. "Seasonality of Income and Poverty in Bangladesh." *Journal of Development Economics* 97 (2): 244–56.

Paxson, Christina. 1993. "Consumption and Income Seasonality in Thailand." *Journal of Political Economy* 101 (1): 39–72.

Pritchett, Lant, Asep Suryahadi, and Sudarno Sumarto. 2000. "Quantifying Vulnerability to Poverty: A Proposed Measure, Applied to Indonesia." Policy Research Paper 2437, World Bank, Washington, DC.

Ravallion, Martin, and Shubham Chaudhuri. 1997. "Risk and Insurance in Village India." *Econometrica* 65 (1): 171–84.

Singh, Inderjit, Lyn Squire, and John Strauss. 1986. *Agricultural Household Models: Extensions, Applications, and Policy*. Baltimore, MD: Johns Hopkins University Press.

Strauss, John. 1986. "Does Better Nutrition Raise Farm Productivity?" *Journal of Political Economy* 94 (2): 297–320.

Strauss, John, and Duncan Thomas. 1995. "Human Resources: Empirical Modeling of Household and Family Decisions." In *Handbook of Development Economics*, vol. 3B, ed. Jere Behrman and T. N. Srinivasan, 1883–2024. Amsterdam: North-Holland.

CHAPTER 5

Effects of Policies and Programs

Some Preliminary Findings

In the previous chapters, we observed that the seasonality of poverty and food deprivation is a major concern among rural households across all regions in Bangladesh, but it is much more pronounced in Rangpur than in other regions. What can be done to mitigate seasonal deprivation as persistent and widespread as in Rangpur? The analyses of the underlying causes point to some policy approaches. The basic hypothesis is that because seasonal poverty adversely interacts with chronic poverty and because it represents aggregate shocks to which certain households are more vulnerable than others, the mitigating policies must be broad based as well as targeted. Thus, such broad-based policies could be, for example, infrastructural development programs that help promote income diversification and overall income growth. In contrast, targeted policies such as Food for Work (FFW) or other kinds of public food distribution or cash transfers could focus on the vulnerable households, particularly during the lean season. Other policies for creating income-earning opportunities for the poor, such as through the provision of microcredit, could both be targeted and have a broader and longer-term effect on poverty.

In this chapter, we examine some evidence of how policies and programs may help mitigate seasonal poverty and hunger. For this analysis, we use the data sources discussed in chapters 3 and 4 of this book—namely,

(a) the 2000 and 2005 rounds of the official Household Income and Expenditure Survey (HIES) and (b) the Institute of Microfinance's baseline survey of 2006 conducted in the Rangpur region. We also address related questions of why policies differ by region and what role is played by economic geography. Because seasonal hunger (or *monga*, as it is called in Rangpur) is determined by the interactions of the economic and agroecological factors that characterize a rural economy, we need to understand how certain regions such as Rangpur differ from other regions in access to public policies and programs. Previous chapters already observed that, compared with other regions, households in Rangpur are found to have less access to nonfarm sources of income, including remittances, and they are also disadvantaged by less access to formal credit, electricity, and other infrastructural facilities.

How Agroclimatic Factors Affect Public Policies and Poverty

The agroclimatic endowments and location factors characterizing a region may affect income, consumption, and poverty in more than one way. Besides having a direct effect on the livelihoods of the local people, these factors may perpetuate a region's economic disadvantage by indirect ways as well. The reason is these factors determine agricultural and other opportunities of a region, thereby affecting both public and private investments (Binswanger, Khandker, and Rosenzweig 1993). Thus, the fact that Rangpur has poorer agroclimatic endowments than do other regions may explain why investments in, say, roads, markets, irrigation, and banks are lower in Rangpur, which in turn adversely affect the incidence of poverty and its seasonality.

Figure 5.1 shows how the same agroclimatic endowments affect income, consumption, and poverty through various pathways and can thus perpetuate the disadvantage of an agroecologically vulnerable region like Rangpur. Figure 5.1 also shows that those agroclimatic factors affect income, consumption, and poverty directly as well as indirectly through influencing public investment and policies as well as private investment. Public investments also have an indirect reinforcing effect by influencing the returns to private investments. This indirect effect also creates a problem of estimating the effect of public policies and programs independently of the direct and indirect effects of the agroclimatic factors; we shall return to this problem of estimating policy effect in the next section.

It is important for policy makers to know the biases created by agroclimatic factors in the placement of public programs, such as for

**Figure 5.1   Pathways of How Agroclimatic Endowments Affect
Public Policies and Poverty**

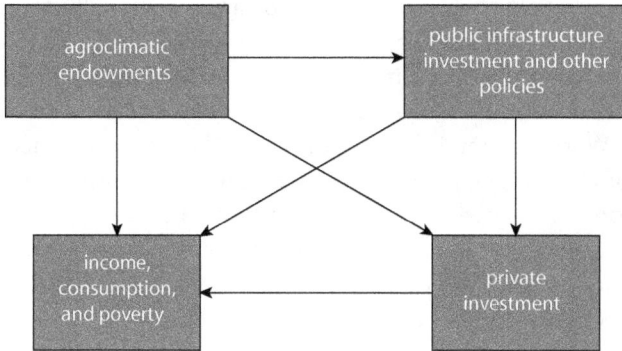

infrastructure development, service delivery, and poverty alleviation. The hypothesis is that the placement of these programs is not random but is influenced by agroclimatic and other local area endowments, which also affect the economic opportunities in a given locality, for example, an *upazila* (subdistrict) or a village. The better-endowed upazilas or villages are sometimes the likely targets (for example, public investments in roads may seek areas with better terrain and higher economic potential), whereas other public programs, such as those providing social safety nets for the poor, may target poorly endowed areas. Furthermore, local agroclimatic characteristics are also likely to be correlated with other potentially unobserved community features that could affect program placement, such as local political influence; in such a case, the distance of the village from the upazilas or district headquarters may be a good proxy variable (Binswanger, Khandker, and Rosenzweig 1993).

As discussed in chapter 4 of this book, the HIES data of 2000 and 2005 can provide upazila-level annual panel data for the two years. Thus, an upazila-level fixed-effects regression model was found appropriate for explaining the variation in the placement of policies and programs over this period. It may be noted that the use of the panel data makes it possible to estimate the effects of the observed upazila-level local characteristics (along with household characteristics) while eliminating those of the unobserved ones. For the estimation of the model, a distinction has to be made between the time-varying and time-invariant area characteristics (the latter interact with the year dummy so that their effects are not eliminated by differencing between the years).[1]

Table 5.1 presents these estimates. These results may be interpreted in many potential ways because the effects of the local area endowments—agroclimatic or otherwise—are found to vary substantially across different policy interventions. For example, the risk of flood potential had a statistically significant detrimental effect on the expansion of schools and financial institutions, but not on the expansion of electrification or Food for Work programs. Medium-high land areas experienced higher growth of electricity coverage but lower rates of expansion in the other interventions. Areas with excess rains attracted more schools but were disadvantaged with respect to expansion of the other interventions. As expected, a significant adverse relation was found between expansion in electrification and the remoteness of the village from the district headquarters.

Although we do not go into detailed interpretations of the above results, there is enough support for the hypothesis that program placement is not random, but it may be biased against agroecologically disadvantaged regions like Rangpur. This bias may explain in part why such regions cannot easily escape the trap of persistent seasonal and chronic poverty. A twofold policy approach may be needed to overcome such a poverty trap. First, the adverse effects of agroecological vulnerability may be mitigated to some extent by public policy measures, such as for flood protection or introduction of crop production technologies that are particularly suitable for such regions. Second, policy makers need to make a conscious effort to target the disadvantaged regions in the placement of programs for infrastructure development or for the provision of public services, including social safety nets.

Estimates of the Effect of Policies and Programs

Having established that agroclimatic factors matter in policy and program placements, we now estimate how income seasonality and poverty are affected by public policies and programs net of the effects of agroclimatic endowments. The aim is to determine the mechanisms through which a range of infrastructure and credit policies have affected growth in household income and its seasonal shares, and also whether these policies have led to a significant reduction of seasonal and chronic poverty.

As mentioned in the previous section, the joint determination of program placement and the outcomes of interest, such as household income and consumption, causes an estimation problem. To resolve this estimation bias, we again use the upazila-level panel data obtained from the

Table 5.1 Agroclimatic Effects on Placement of Programs and Policies

	Household has electricity (1 = yes, 0 = no)	Village has a primary school (1 = yes, 0 = no)	Village has an agricultural bank (1 = yes, 0 = no)	Village has Grameen Bank (1 = yes, 0 = no)	Village has FFW program (1 = yes, 0 = no)
Year (0 = 2000, 1 = 2005)	0.240**	-0.323	0.459	1.301**	0.446
	(0.082)	(0.280)	(0.343)	(0.356)	(0.425)
Village distance to district headquarters (km)	-0.003**	-0.001	0.001	-0.001	-0.001
	(0.001)	(0.002)	(0.005)	(0.003)	(0.005)
Average monthly rainfall during the season (mm)	-0.00002	-0.00002	-0.00003	0.00002	0.0001
	(0.0001)	(0.0001)	(0.0002)	(0.0002)	(0.0002)
Number of sunny months per year × year	-0.015*	0.096**	0.019	-0.056	-0.045
	(0.009)	(0.30)	(0.035)	(0.038)	(0.045)
Proportion of high land × year	-0.169**	-0.693**	-0.356	-0.543*	-0.652*
	(0.073)	(0.250)	(0.304)	(0.318)	(0.377)
Proportion of medium-high land × year	0.167*	-0.493*	-0.953**	-0.896**	-0.502
	(0.081)	(0.277)	(0.338)	(0.351)	(0.418)
Proportion of flood-prone area × year	0.060	-0.469**	-0.417**	-0.435**	0.095
	(0.048)	(0.163)	(0.200)	(0.207)	(0.25)
Excess rain per month (mm) × year	-0.00004*	0.002**	0.0002	-0.002*	-0.002
	(0.00002)	(0.0007)	(0.001)	(0.001)	(0.002)
R^2	0.038	0.168	0.045	0.079	0.261

Source: Khandker 2009.

Note: Figures in parentheses are robust standard errors. * and ** refer to a statistical significance of 10 percent and 5 percent or better, respectively. Number of observations is 7,640.
FFW = Food for Work; km = kilometer; mm = millimeter.

HIES of 2000 and 2005 to estimate a fixed-effects regression model. Household outcome variables are estimated by using household characteristics, such as their human and physical capital endowments along with access to public policies and programs, as explanatory variables, but excluding time-invariant agroclimatic area characteristics. This approach is equivalent to running a reduced-form equation in which income, consumption, or poverty is expressed as a function of all price and nonprice exogenous policy variables, such as public infrastructural and credit-related investments (for details, see Khandker 2009).

The regression results of consumption, income, and poverty equations showing the effect of public policies and programs are presented in table 5.2. The income and consumption equations are estimated in semilogarithmic form (that is, income and consumption are in the log form), whereas poverty estimates are derived from the probability of consumption's falling below the respective poverty thresholds of consumption. The results relating to the effects of household characteristics (such as the age of the household head or the ownership of land and other assets), though important, are not reported here because they are not of primary interest for this analysis. Overall, the results are fairly robust both in the statistical significance of the estimates and in the implied effect of policy interventions.

As noted in chapter 3 of this book, the definition of *moderate poverty* is based on the official poverty line, which includes the cost of a minimum food basket—also called the food poverty line—and an allowance for nonfood expenditures. *Extreme poverty*, in contrast, is defined by the household's total consumption expenditure on food and nonfood falling short of the food poverty line.

The results indicate a strong positive effect of human capital investments on household welfare. Each additional year of education for the head of household can be seen to increase total per capita expenditure by 2.4 percent and food consumption by 1.1 percent, thus reducing moderate poverty (by 2.5 percentage points) and extreme poverty (by 3.0 percentage points). Moreover, although per capita income is increased, its seasonality is reduced, presumably because education helps income diversification. Another finding is that those villages with a primary school are likely to have extreme poverty reduced by 4.3 percentage points. Although the presence of primary schools does not contribute to the educational attainments of the current workforce, it may be an indicator of the general educational level of the locality.

Table 5.2 Effects of Policies and Programs on Household Income, Consumption, and Poverty

Selected explanatory variables	Income estimates		Consumption estimates		Poverty estimates	
	Per capita total income	Crop income share	Total consumption	Food consumption	Moderate poverty	Extreme poverty
Household head's education (years)	0.025**	−0.001**	0.024**	0.011**	−0.025**	−0.030**
	(0.003)	(0.004)	(0.001)	(0.001)	(0.001)	(0.002)
Household with electricity (1 = yes, 0 = no)	0.228**	−0.008**	0.163**	0.081**	−0.146**	−0.184**
	(0.021)	(0.003)	(0.013)	(0.011)	(0.011)	(0.014)
Proportion of irrigated land in village	−0.035	0.031**	−0.011	0.031**	0.013	0.016
	(0.046)	(0.007)	(0.026)	(0.014)	(0.031)	(0.038)
Village with any primary school (1 = yes, 0 = no)	0.009	−0.003	0.036	0.074**	−0.036	−0.043
	(0.045)	(0.007)	(0.027)	(0.024)	(0.027)	(0.033)
Village with Grameen Bank (1 = yes, 0 = no)	0.011	0.012**	0.044**	−0.001	−0.045**	−0.053**
	(0.035)	(0.005)	(0.020)	(0.017)	(0.021)	(0.025)
Village with FFW program (1 = yes, 0 = no)	−0.023	−0.010**	0.069**	0.075**	−0.073**	−0.081**
	(0.027)	(0.004)	(0.016)	(0.014)	(0.017)	(0.019)
Village with VGF program (1 = yes, 0 = no)	0.066**	−0.001	0.027*	0.044**	−0.029*	−0.034
	(0.024)	(0.003)	(0.014)	(0.013)	(0.015)	(0.018)
R^2	0.253	0.165	0.371	0.249	—	—
Number of observations	7,640	7,640	7,640	7,640	7,640	7,640

Source: Khandker 2009.

Note: Estimated from a fixed-effects regression model using upazila-level panel data of 2000 and 2005. Regressions include other household variables (for example, household head's gender, age, education, and land and nonland assets) and time-varying community-level variables (for example, prices of consumer goods and daily wage). Income and consumption are in the log form. Figures in parentheses are robust standard errors. * and ** refer to a statistical significance of 10% and 5% or better, respectively. Crop income refers to seasonal crops. FFW = Food for Work; VGF = Vulnerable Group Feeding.

The results above, along with those regarding the effects of land and nonland assets (not shown in table 5.2) suggest that a lack of human and physical capital is a major source of both structural and seasonal poverty. Between land and nonland assets, the latter have stronger positive effects on consumption and negative effects on poverty. For example, a 1.0 percent increase in the size of a landholding reduces extreme poverty by 3.2 percentage points, whereas a similar increase in nonland assets reduces extreme poverty by 12.8 percentage points. Nonland assets also help reduce income seasonality. Therefore, a policy that stipulates asset transfers to the poor as a way to mitigate monga is likely to have more beneficial effects if it focuses on transfer of assets other than land. This outcome should also be true for programs like microcredit that encourage asset accumulation by the poor.

The estimates in table 5.2 also show that electrification has the expected substantial positive effects on consumption and, hence, negative effects on poverty and seasonal food deprivation. Households with electricity are likely to have their per capita total consumption increased by 16.3 percent, moderate poverty reduced by 14.6 percentage points, and extreme poverty by 18.4 percentage points. Electricity connection provides opportunities for expansion of both farm and nonfarm income, which ultimately helps increase consumption and thus reduces poverty and seasonal deprivation.

The provision of irrigated land in the village is found to enhance food consumption by 3.1 percent. However, it also increases the share of income from crop production, thus contributing to income seasonality. This result is expected because the contribution of irrigation is realized through increased crop production. This is a reminder of the fact that income seasonality by itself does not lead to adverse outcomes like seasonal hunger; much will depend on whether the seasonality of income arises from improved crop production technology that contributes to the overall prosperity of the local economy or from lack of diversification of the rural economy in an economically depressed locality.

Public investments on physical infrastructure, such as rural electrification and irrigation, can thus have substantive payoffs in poverty reduction. Rural road expansion is another public investment that may have beneficial effects on poverty. However, the HIES data do not provide information on rural roads. But given that the expansion of rural electrification or access to Grameen Bank is likely to follow rural road expansion, the effects of these interventions may capture in part the effect of roads.

Another important finding is that although the presence of agricultural banks does not seem to have any significant effect on consumption and poverty (not shown in table 5.2), microcredit programs can have significant beneficial effects. Thus, Grameen Bank's presence in the village is found to increase total consumption (by 4.4 percent) and hence reduce both moderate poverty (by 4.5 percentage points) and extreme poverty (by 5.3 percentage points). These estimates are similar to those of Khandker (2005), who estimated the effect of microcredit on village-level poverty using household-level panel data.

Among the social safety-net programs, the FFW program contributed substantially to overall per capita total consumption (by 6.9 percent) and food consumption (by 7.5 percent), with a consequent reduction of moderate poverty (by 7.3 percentage points) and extreme poverty (by 8.1 percentage points). Moreover, the extent of income seasonality is also reduced. Thus, the FFW program seems to be appropriate for addressing seasonality in both income and consumption as well as for containing seasonal and overall poverty. The Vulnerable Group Feeding (VGF) program also increases per capita total consumption and food consumption by 2.7 percent and 4.4 percent, respectively. This increase in turn reduces moderate poverty and extreme poverty by 2.9 and 3.4 percentage points, respectively.[2]

Do some of these programs have a particularly beneficial effect on consumption and poverty during the lean season? To demonstrate whether this was the case, the study obtained regression results by using a monga dummy variable that interacts with program variables, such as Grameen Bank, FFW, and VGF (results are not shown here). The results support that access to Grameen Bank and FFW during the monga season contributes substantially to both food expenditure and total consumption per capita. Even though these beneficial outcomes are estimated on an annual basis, the results suggest that access to these interventions during the monga season can have an added beneficial effect.

The implications of the findings discussed above can be put into a policy framework as shown in table 5.3.

Seasonal Hunger in Rangpur: Determining Factors and Policy Effects

The findings in the previous section do not directly address the problem of monga in Rangpur. Can the public programs and policies discussed earlier be expected to work as well in Rangpur as in other parts of the

Table 5.3   Policy Framework to Reduce Poverty

Policy variable	Action	Effect or outcome	
		Extreme poverty	Moderate poverty
Household head's education (mean = 2.76 years)	Increase years of schooling of household head by one year	Reduction by 3 percentage points	Reduction by 2.5 percentage points
Household with electricity (mean = 24 percentage points)	Increase electricity access of household by 10 percentage points	Reduction by 0.9 percentage point	Reduction by 1.4 percentage points
Proportion of irrigated land in the village (mean = 61 percentage points)	Increase proportion of irrigated land in the village by 10 percentage points	—	—
Village with any primary school (mean = 89 percentage points)	Increase number of villages having primary school by 10 percentage points	—	—
Village with Grameen Bank (mean = 18 percentage points)	Increase number of villages having Grameen Bank by 10 percentage points	Reduction by 0.5 percentage point	Reduction by 0.5 percentage point
Village with VGF program (mean = 62 percentage points)	Increase number of villages having VGF program by 10 percentage points	Reduction by 0.3 percentage point	Reduction by 0.3 percentage point
Village with FFW program (mean = 40 percentage points)	Increase number of villages having FFW program by 10 percentage points	Reduction by 0.8 percentage point	Reduction by 0.7 percentage point

Source: Based on the regression results reported in table 5.2.
Note: — = not statistically significant effect; FFW = Food for Work; VGF = Vulnerable Group Feeding.

country? Answering this question is important for designing policies for mitigating monga. For example, if microcredit indeed helps reduce the severity of food deprivation, the microcredit programs need to be strengthened in lagging regions like Rangpur. This section uses the Institute of Microfinance baseline survey data to determine what factors underlie the phenomenon of monga and what policies and programs could be effective in reducing its extent and severity.

Using the reported food deprivation status of the households during monga, we can construct an ordering of outcome as follows: 1 = household suffers starvation during monga, 2 = household rations meals during monga, and 3 = household has full meals during monga. This ordering represents a measure of severity of seasonal food deprivation. Because this outcome variable is an ordered variable (meaning outcome 3 is better than outcome 2, and outcome 2 is better than outcome 1), an ordered logit model is suitable for estimation purposes.[3]

If i denotes the individual ordered values of an outcome (for example, starvation, meal rationing, and so forth), then the probability of a given observation in an ordered logit model is given by

$$p_{ij} = P(y_j = i) = P(k_{i-1} < x_j \beta + u \le k_i)$$

$$= \frac{1}{1 + \exp(-k_i + x_j \beta)} - \frac{1}{1 + \exp(-k_{i-1} + x_j \beta)}, \tag{5.1}$$

where k_0 is defined as $-\infty$ and k_k is defined as $+\infty$, x is a set of explanatory variables (including policy variables, such as microcredit or safety-net programs), and β is the parameter to be estimated. However, for the purpose of our analysis, we are interested more in the change in the probability of an outcome with respect to a change in explanatory variables (marginal effect) than in the probability itself.

The estimation of the above ordered logit model with cross-sectional data involves the problem of endogeneity of policy interventions, such as microcredit and safety-net programs. However, we have used the fixed-effects method with the *union*-level data to control for any unobserved *union*-level heterogeneity (a *union* is the lowest administrative unit, below *upazila* or subdistrict, and contains about 10 to 12 villages). The estimated equation also included district-level rainfall information as an additional control. Nonetheless, because we cannot control for program endogeneity (owing to lack of suitable instrumental variables or panel data at the household level), we investigated the correlation of the residuals of the estimates of equation (5.1) with the respective policy variables. For each of the policy variables representing the presence of Grameen Bank and the VGF program, the correlation was found to be negative but statistically insignificant. That is, if any bias remains because of endogeneity of village-level program placement, the effects of policy variables using the union-level fixed-effects method are, at worst, underestimated.

Table 5.4 presents ordered logit estimates (the first column) and the derived estimates of marginal effects of the explanatory variables for the three outcomes considered (in the second, third, and fourth columns). As

Table 5.4 Determinants of Food Consumption Status During Monga in Greater Rangpur

Explanatory variables	Ordered logit estimates of food deprivation	Marginal effects on			Means of explanatory variables
		Starvation	Meal rationing	Full meals	
Household head's age (years)	-0.006**	0.002**	-0.002**	-0.0001**	39.98
	(0.0003)	(0.0001)	(0.0001)	(0.00001)	(12.68)
Dependency ratio	-0.017	0.004	-0.004	-0.0003	0.63
	(0.017)	(0.004)	(0.004)	(0.0003)	(0.21)
Log of land asset (decimal)	0.241**	-0.060**	0.056**	0.005**	8.20
	(0.003)	(0.001)	(0.001)	(0.0001)	(12.59)
Household head who is self-employed	0.143**	-0.036**	0.033**	0.003**	0.16
	(0.011)	(0.003)	(0.003)	(0.0002)	(0.37)
Household head who is wage employed	-0.099**	0.025**	-0.023**	-0.002**	0.54
	(0.008)	(0.002)	(0.002)	(0.0002)	(0.50)
Household with agricultural asset	0.208**	-0.052**	0.048**	0.004**	0.49
	(0.008)	(0.002)	(0.002)	(0.0002)	(0.50)
Household with nonagricultural asset	0.156**	-0.039**	0.036**	0.003**	0.13
	(0.011)	(0.003)	(0.002)	(0.0002)	(0.34)
Household with cash savings	0.148**	-0.037**	0.034**	0.003**	0.34
	(0.007)	(0.002)	(0.002)	(0.0002)	(0.47)

Household with a cow	0.126**	−0.031**	0.029**	0.003**	0.26
	(0.008)	(0.002)	(0.002)	(0.0002)	(0.44)
Village with safety-net programs	0.074**	−0.018**	0.017**	0.001**	0.10
	(0.011)	(0.003)	(0.003)	(0.0002)	(0.16)
Village with microcredit programs	0.384**	−0.095**	0.089**	0.006**	0.97
	(0.022)	(0.005)	(0.005)	(0.00003)	(0.18)
Average yearly rainfall in district (mm)	0.073**	−0.018**	0.017**	0.001**	198.54
	(0.007)	(0.002)	(0.002)	(0.0001)	(6.62)
Pseudo R^2	0.206				
Log likelihood	−322,393.4				
Mean value of an outcome		0.473	0.483	0.044	
Number of observations	480,918				

Source: Institute of Microfinance survey, 2006.

Note: Regression additionally includes union dummies to control for unobserved union-level effects. The estimates in the first column (that is, the ordered logit estimates of food deprivation) are the estimated right-hand side of equation (5.1), from which the coefficients of the subsequent columns are derived; these coefficients give marginal effects of the explanatory variables on the dependent variables. Figures in parentheses are standard errors except for the last column, where they are standard deviations. ** refer to a statistical significance of 5 percent or better; mm = millimeter.

the results show, the probability of starvation during monga is higher for households headed by older rather than younger individuals. As expected, landholding reduces the probability of starvation by raising the chances of either consumption rationing or full meals. The probability of starvation is lower with self-employment and higher with wage employment, suggesting that self-employed households are better off than wage-employed households as a whole. Again, as expected, households with more assets (either agricultural or nonagricultural) and cash savings are likely to be better able to avoid starvation during monga.

The results also largely support the earlier findings obtained from the analysis of the HIES data. There is, for example, a further confirmation of the finding suggesting that the probability of hunger is very much context specific and is partially determined by agroclimatic and location factors. Thus, favorable rainfall is found to help reduce the incidence of hunger. More important, the results confirm that even after netting out the influence of unobserved agroclimatic and location factors, most of the policies identified here do indeed help reduce seasonal hunger among the poor households in Rangpur.

A transfer of land or nonagricultural asset is likely to reduce seasonal hunger. A 10 percent increase in the household's landholding, for example, reduces the probability of starvation by almost 6 percent. Similarly, an income transfer during the monga season, which is equivalent to having cash savings, is expected to reduce the extent of hunger during monga. The case of transferring an asset, such as a cow, is similar. Providing livestock is a form of poverty intervention recently undertaken by some nongovernmental organizations in the monga-prone areas in Rangpur. Microcredit programs are also found to reduce the incidence of seasonal hunger. For example, the households in villages with microcredit programs have about a 10 percent lower chance of undergoing starvation. In contrast, the presence of a safety-net program in the village is expected to reduce the incidence of starvation by about 2 percent.

Concluding Remarks

The results of the statistical exercises reported in this chapter show that policies and programs matter in alleviating food deprivation and its seasonality. It is generally agreed that economic growth is necessary to reduce poverty and food insecurity by large numbers and in a sustained manner. But as discussed in the previous chapters, economic growth alone—not even when it leads to poverty reduction—is sufficient to combat the problem of food insecurity and seasonal hunger. Both global experience and that of Bangladesh discussed in the previous chapters testify to that fact. For that reason, it is important to look for a set of policies that can effectively address the interlocking problems of poverty, food insecurity, and seasonality.

Because of data limitations, the effects of only a limited range of policy interventions could be examined here. Nevertheless, the results show the effectiveness of policies, in varying degrees, in a number of areas: improving the production environment (such as through provision of electricity or irrigation); enhancing the human capital and asset base of households; and providing targeted safety nets, including microcredit. Most of these interventions are found to be effective even in reducing the extreme forms of food deprivation like starvation during monga in Rangpur.

The results are particularly important in shedding some light on the effectiveness of microcredit, given the ongoing debates surrounding the subject. The results for Rangpur show that the likelihood of poor households experiencing starvation during monga is reduced by 10 percent by the presence of microcredit programs in a village, whereas the results derived from the countrywide surveys show that the incidence of extreme poverty is reduced by more than 5 percentage points among households living in a village with a branch of Grameen Bank. The safety-net programs are also found to have favorable effects both on countrywide prevalence of extreme poverty and on the incidence of starvation during monga in Rangpur, although in the latter case, the effect is found to be rather small. For the safety-net programs to have any substantial effect on seasonal hunger, their coverage and the size of the benefits transferred need to be enhanced while sharpening their focus toward the most vulnerable individuals or households.

The areas with adverse economic geography and agroecological vulnerability, such as Rangpur, are doubly disadvantaged because public investments and other development programs may neglect these areas, which in turn may also discourage private investments. An underdeveloped region like Rangpur needs an area development plan that would promote investments in infrastructure and human capital and thus provide greater and more diversified income-earning opportunities.

Although the estimated effect of none of the interventions seems large enough, their combined effects clearly could make a big difference. We may therefore conclude that if the policies had been integrated and coordinated, the monga situation in Rangpur could have been much better, as in other regions of Bangladesh. Policy makers need to be aware that monga is not only a seasonal phenomenon but also an outcome of extreme and endemic poverty. The range of policies therefore needs to include those aimed at addressing the structural factors underlying endemic poverty along with seasonally sensitive policies, including short-term safety-net measures.

Notes

1. It may be noted that the distance of the village from the district headquarters can change because of the creation of new districts.

2. The VGF program, administered by the government, provides food to a select number of households in a community that is affected by disasters or during a period when acquiring food is difficult for beneficiary households. Priority is given to households that are low income, lack agricultural land or other productive assets, include day laborers, or are headed by women. In a normal year, a distressed household receives two to three months of food rations, with no work or labor participation required.

3. We considered estimating a binomial logit or probit equation separately for household starvation and for general household food deprivation (by combining starvation and meal rationing). However, a test for IIA (independence of irrelevant alternatives) rejects both null hypotheses that (a) starvation and meal rationing can be combined (against full meals) and (b) meal rationing and full meals can be combined (against starvation). So we supposed that these categories are independent or mutually exclusive and decided to estimate an ordered logit model, assuming an underlying order among these three categories.

References

Binswanger, Hans, Shahidur Khandker, and Mark Rosenzweig. 1993. "How Infrastructure and Financial Institutions Affect Agricultural Output and Investment in India." *Journal of Development Economics* 41 (2): 337–66.

Khandker, Shahidur R. 2005. "Microfinance and Poverty: Evidence Using Panel Data from Bangladesh." *World Bank Economic Review* 19 (2): 263–86.

———. 2009. "Poverty and Income Seasonality in Bangladesh." Policy Research Working Paper 4923, World Bank, Washington, DC.

CHAPTER 6

The Role of Seasonal Migration

Seasonal migration is a widely practiced household strategy for coping with agricultural seasonality in various parts of the developing world.[1] Seasonal migration needs to be distinguished from long-term or permanent migration. For our analysis, we look at short-term migration of household workers, which is often repetitive, related to the annual agricultural cycle. These characteristics of seasonal migrants also exclude workers who may decide to migrate during the lean months but do so on a long-term basis and not as part of an annual cycle. Seasonal migration has thus been aptly called "seasonal labor circulation" in the African context (Chambers, Longhurst, and Pacey 1981, 210–14).

As discussed in chapter 4 in this volume, seasonal migration was found to be the single most important coping mechanism adopted in response to *monga* (seasonal hunger) by poor households in the Rangpur region. Of the nearly half million poor households covered by the Institute of Microfinance (InM) baseline survey of 2006, about 35 percent reported having resorted to migration during the monga season. The InM follow-up survey of 2008 found considerable out-migration among the workers of the region in the non-monga seasons as well; furthermore, most of the migration was found to be seasonal or temporary.

National-level data also clearly show the exceptionally high levels of interdistrict out-migration from the Rangpur region. The findings of the official Agricultural Sample Survey 2005 are particularly revealing. Of all the country's agricultural workers who worked in agricultural and nonagricultural jobs outside their home districts, those originating from the five districts in Rangpur accounted for nearly one-half and one-quarter, respectively, although the region accounted for only 11 percent of the country's population (see BBS 2010, 268).[2] Although the nature of migration is unknown, most of the migration captured in such a survey is likely to be temporary or seasonal. It may also be noted that, compared with other regions, overseas migration is relatively rare in the Rangpur region. Temporary overseas migration from Bangladesh, especially to countries in the Middle East, has increasingly become an important feature of the country's economy; workers' remittances currently account for about 10 percent of gross national income.[3]

This chapter examines the issue of seasonal migration within the context of mitigating seasonal food deprivation. In doing so, we mainly use the huge data set of the 2006 InM baseline survey of 480,918 poor households in the Rangpur region. We ask the following questions: Is seasonal migration a viable strategy to mitigate seasonal hardships? Does seasonal starvation prompt seasonal migration? Who migrates, and what are the determinants of seasonal migration? What effect does it have on consumption-smoothing behavior and on overall household food security?

Understanding the Phenomenon of Seasonal Migration

Most of the literature on internal migration focuses on permanent rural-to-urban migration; much less is known about temporary migration as a coping strategy to mitigate seasonal hunger and poverty. However, the standard theory of internal migration remains a valid framework of analysis, namely, that an individual's decision to migrate is a utility maximization process involving the perceived benefits and costs arising from migration. In other words, migration is the result of individuals and households weighing the utility that is attainable under different migration regimes against that of not migrating.

It follows that incentives for migration may arise from both household-specific conditions and variations in economic opportunities across regions. Thus, much of the internal migration—whether from rural to urban areas or from one region of the country to another—is explained by higher labor demand, often reflected in higher wage rates, in the destination areas than in the local areas. In the absence of suitable employment or livelihood opportunities in the local areas, internal migration is most often a viable option with expectations of higher wages, better employment alternatives, and factors that maximize family employment in the destination areas (Srivastava 2005).

Although the utility-maximizing behavior may provide an overall framework for explaining migration, households' actual decision making regarding migration will depend on how they perceive the benefits and costs. Besides labor market conditions in the sending and receiving areas, household-specific characteristics also matter. For seasonal and temporary migration, the availability of an extra family worker (usually male) may help, because the remaining adult members can care for the family. The decision to migrate also depends on knowledge about jobs in the destination market and the ease of transition to a distant environment, both of which depend in turn on the extent of social networks that the households can access.[4] There are also potential costs of migration related to transport and relocation. The willingness to migrate will thus depend on whether the earning possibilities elsewhere relative to those available locally are regarded as adequate in relation to the cost of moving.

Another important element in the decision to migrate is the perception of risks. Uncertainties may exist regarding the income-earning opportunities in the destination areas, which may be reduced to some extent depending on a household's networking ability. Poor households, particularly those depending on income from agricultural wage labor, also face considerable uncertainty regarding their employment prospects in the local market during the lean season. As discussed in the earlier chapters in this volume, a household's perception regarding future risk of seasonal hunger can be an important factor in its choice of coping strategies, including seasonal migration. As an alternative to the income-maximizing model of migration, it has even been suggested that migration could be a household strategy to minimize risk to income and consumption in an imperfect market (Stark and Taylor 1989).

The proximate causes of the high prevalence of seasonal migration in Rangpur are clear. The relatively high incidence of landlessness in the region combined with lack of opportunities in nonfarm employment creates a large pool of landless agricultural workers.[5] They are the workers who are worst hit by the seasonal dip in the demand for agricultural labor. As noted earlier, wage employment in the farm sector drops sharply during the monga season in Rangpur (see figure 3.15 in chapter 3 in this volume). In the absence of enough demand for wage labor in the nonfarm sector, these workers have little alternative but to seek employment elsewhere. Apart from the seasonal factors, the generally high incidence of poverty in the region and the persistently large gap in the wage rates of agricultural labor between the region and the rest of the country create conditions favorable to interregional migration.

Is seasonal migration as observed among the poor households in Rangpur a strategy to maximize income or to avoid starvation? Because the decision to migrate is made by weighing the perceived benefits against costs, it is difficult to distinguish conceptually between distress-pushed or income-pulled migration. Thus, seasonal migration can be seen as both a strategy to augment income and a means of minimizing seasonal hardships. However, some judgment may still be made regarding the relative strengths of the push-pull forces. The fact that so many poor households opt for seasonal migration during the monga season suggests that it is a major means of coping with seasonal food deprivation.

It is also possible to gain insights from the perceptions of the households themselves. In the InM 2008 follow-up survey, about three-fourths of the households with migrant workers cited the prospect of hunger as the cause of migration, whereas the rest mainly mentioned earning opportunities elsewhere as the reason. The same survey showed that most out-migration in Rangpur takes place in the monga season and thus seems to be induced by lack of local employment rather than peak-season labor demand in labor-receiving regions. The seasonal migration in Rangpur is thus unlike what is sometimes called "labor circulation" in the context of some African countries, where the timing of labor demand in the sending and receiving regions complement each other (see Chambers, Longhurst, and Pacey 1981, 212).

It does not follow, however, that those who are most vulnerable to food insecurity will necessarily decide to migrate. They may lack not only the means to cover the financial costs of migration but also the access to the networks that minimize the risk related to migration outcome. In contrast, the relatively better off among the poor households may have sufficient means and access to labor market networks to be able to overcome the barriers to migration; they may thus decide to migrate for a better chance of maximizing their family's well-being. Consequently, no clear-cut way exists to profile the households that will resort to seasonal migration. By the same token, it is not easy to distinguish between the cause and the effect of migration by simply comparing the migrating and nonmigrating households with respect to their household characteristics and their well-being indicators, like the food deprivation status. These issues will be addressed later in this chapter.

Although households base decisions about migration on their cost-benefit calculations, large-scale seasonal out-migration affects the local economy in other ways as well. The seasonal slack in the local labor markets will be reduced. In addition, migrants' remittances may help stimulate the local economy (Afsar 2005; Deshingkar 2005; Oberai, Prasad, and Sardana 1989). Thus, nonmigrant households also stand to gain.

Patterns of Migration in Rangpur during Monga

The InM baseline survey data on 480,918 households drawn from the five districts of the Rangpur region can be used to analyze the pattern and effect of seasonal migration.[6] These households represented roughly the bottom 60 percent of the rural households in the region. Although some 36 percent of the households were found to have adopted seasonal migration as a coping strategy during the monga of 2006, there were considerable variations among the five districts (see table 4.6 in chapter 4 in this volume). The notable aspect of these variations is the scant systematic relationship between the rate of seasonal migration and the extent of seasonal food deprivation. Although Nilphamari district had the lowest incidence of starvation (26 percent) as well as the lowest rate of migration (25 percent), the Rangpur district also had a relatively low rate of migration (27 percent) in spite of having one of the worst records for the incidence of starvation (56 percent). The explanation may lie in the fact that many potential migrants in the Rangpur district may be able to find off-farm employment in the nearby regional city of Rangpur without having to move from their home. Lalmonirhat district had the highest rate of migration (50 percent), but it had an incidence of starvation similar to the regional average.

It may be interesting to see how the migration pattern varies depending on the other coping mechanisms that households adopt (see table 6.1). Among the survey households that did not adopt any other coping mechanisms (51 percent of the sample), 32 percent resorted to migration; about 16 percent of the sample households adopted migration as their only coping mechanism. The estimates also suggest that about 7 percent of the sample households adopted migration while also accessing support from social safety-net programs as their only other coping mechanism, whereas about 3 percent combined migration with borrowing only.

Table 6.1 Rate of Migration during Monga by Households' Other Coping Mechanisms

percent

Households' other coping mechanisms	Gaibandha district	Kurigram district	Lalmonirhat district	Nilphamari district	Rangpur district	Rangpur region
No other coping mechanism (51.2)	33.0	38.8	44.4	21.0	21.1	32.1
Asset or advance labor or crop sale only (6.5)	39.8	49.8	57.0	41.4	38.3	45.7
Borrowing only (8.2)	45.1	50.8	58.0	25.5	34.4	37.8
Support from SNPs only (20.7)	40.5	40.0	39.6	23.8	28.5	34.5
Multiple coping mechanisms (13.4)	49.7	57.9	66.2	32.2	42.9	47.3

Source: Khandker, Khalily, and Samad 2010.

Note: Number of observations is 480,918. Figures in parentheses are sample shares in respective coping mechanism groups. SNP = social safety-net program.

The migration rate was quite high (45.7 percent) among those house-holds that resorted to the sale of assets or the advance sale of labor or crops as their only other coping mechanism. For these households, the decision to migrate seems to have been made under distress, but they constituted only a small share (6.5 percent) of all households. The migra-tion rate was highest (47.3 percent) among the households that adopted multiple coping mechanisms (13.4 percent of the sample), making this group seem particularly vulnerable. This pattern is generally consistent across districts. Thus, migration is most prevalent among households that must adopt a wide range of coping strategies; but they still may be better off during monga than households with rather limited coping options. Overall, this pattern is a scenario of distress adaptation.

How does the migration pattern vary by the food consumption status of the households? Table 6.2 shows a household's migration rate by its food deprivation pattern during the monga period. It is not surprising that the migration rate is higher among household groups with a greater degree of seasonal hardship. For example, 28.7 percent of households that enjoy full meals migrate during the monga season, compared with 35.2 percent among the meal-rationed and 37.5 percent among the starving households. This pattern holds for all districts except Rangpur, where the migration rate is highest among the households that have full meals during the monga period. Migration may possibly have helped these households avoid food deprivation during the monga season. We will investigate this speculation later in this chapter.

Examining the relationship between food deprivation and migration from the opposite perspective raises questions: How does starvation status vary between the household groups with and without migrant workers? Is there a variation in this pattern between monga and non-monga periods? Table 6.3 provides possible answers to these questions by showing the distribution of households by food deprivation status during different periods broken out by migrant and nonmigrant households. Besides monga and non-monga periods, we can also classify the households according to their food deprivation status on an overall or year-round basis in the fol-lowing way: starvation households experience starvation during any period of the year (that is, during either the monga or the non-monga period); meal-rationing households have to ration meals during at least one period but they avoid starvation in all periods; and the remaining households have full meals during both monga and non-monga periods.

Table 6.3 indicates that the incidence of starvation is higher among the migrant households than among the nonmigrant households. This outcome

Table 6.2 Migration by Households' Food Consumption Status during Monga

percent

Food consumption status during monga	Gaibandha district	Kurigram district	Lalmonirhat district	Nilphamari district	Rangpur district	Rangpur region
Starvation (47.2)	39.6	41.7	52.5	25.3	25.5	37.5
Food rationing (48.3)	35.9	42.0	48.9	24.6	29.3	35.2
Full meals (4.4)	31.3	38.9	39.7	24.2	38.6	28.7

Source: Khandker, Khalily, and Samad 2010.

Note: Figures in parentheses are sample shares in respective food consumption groups. Number of observations is 480,918.

**Table 6.3   Distribution of Migrant and Nonmigrant Households
by Their Food Consumption Status in Different Periods**
percentage of sample households

Period	Migrant households			Nonmigrant households		
	Starvation	*Meal rationing*	*Full meals*	*Starvation*	*Meal rationing*	*Full meals*
Monga period	49.2	47.3	3.5	46.2	48.8	5.0
Non-monga period	7.3	53.7	39.0	9.2	49.3	41.5
Year round	51.7	45.5	2.8	49.4	46.3	4.3

Source: Khandker, Khalily, and Samad 2011. Year-round outcomes are defined in the text.
Note: Number of observations is 480,918.

suggests perhaps that the prospect of seasonal hardship prompted the households to migrate. One could also hypothesize that had the households not migrated, their seasonal hardship would have been even worse. Support for this hypothesis will be explored later in this chapter.

At this stage, it may be noted that merely by looking at the association of seasonal deprivation and seasonal migration, one cannot easily determine what causes what, that is, the direction of causality. Does seasonal deprivation pull the trigger, or does seasonal migration determine the extent of seasonal starvation? Both are likely to be true to some extent. For policy-making purposes, it is important to determine if seasonal migration reduces seasonal hardship. At any point in time, one can observe the confounding influences of all possible factors causing seasonal migration as well as seasonal deprivation. So, the simultaneous effects of these factors on seasonal migration and seasonal hardship must be untangled to assess the effectiveness of seasonal migration as a monga-coping mechanism. But first, we consider the determinants of seasonal migration.

Determinants of Seasonal Migration

As discussed, the decision to migrate will depend on the perceived benefits that the household expects to derive from such migration. We observe from the InM baseline survey data whether any member of a household had migrated over the previous monga season. The decision to migrate (m) is a discrete binomial choice variable (1,0) that depends on the perceived net benefits that the household expects to derive from such migration. In other words, the perceived net utility (the algebraic sum of utilities from migration and nonmigration) must be positive for the household to migrate. This net perceived utility for household i can be expressed as

$$u_i^* = \beta x_i + \varepsilon_i, \tag{6.1}$$

where u_i is perceived utility, x_i is a vector of household and community characteristics, β is a vector of parameters to be estimated, and ε is the random error term. For migrant households, $u_i^* > 0$. This perceived utility (u_i^*) is an unobserved or latent variable, and what we observe is a household's migration decision, m_i, so that, $m_i = 1$ if $u_i^* > 0$, and $m_i = 0$ otherwise. Because of the binomial nature of the migration decision, a probit model is used to estimate it, which is given as

$$prob\,(m = 1) = \int_{-\infty}^{\beta x} \phi(t)\,dt = \Phi(\beta x), \tag{6.2}$$

where ϕ and Φ are normal density distribution function and cumulative normal distribution function, respectively.

Both household- and community-level factors are likely to influence the decision to migrate during the monga season. Among the household factors, we consider household assets of different types, dependency ratio, and age of the household head. The community-level variables include the village's access to microfinance institutions and to safety-net programs, the village-level unemployment rate, and whether the village is located in *char* area.[7] The community factors also include interactions of household land asset with three community-and district-level variables: whether the village is located in char area, district-level data on rainfall, and the proportion of high land.[8] We also include union dummies to control for the role of unobserved area characteristics.[9] However, we do not use food deprivation status as an explanatory variable because it is also likely to be an outcome of the decision to migrate.[10]

The results of equation (6.2) showing the effects of different factors on the probability of migration are reported in table 6.4. With an increase in the household head's age, the probability of migration declines. Intuitively, this decline is expected because younger people are better able, more energetic, and more willing to take risks and are also more likely to be a working member alongside the household head. Similar findings were reported by Mora and Taylor (2005). A large number of dependents (captured by a high dependency ratio) make households more vulnerable to food deprivation, and thus, the migration rate is likely to rise as the dependency ratio rises.

Table 6.4   Major Determinants of Seasonal Migration during Monga

Explanatory variables	Marginal effects on migration probability
Household characteristics	
Household head's age (years)	−0.006**
	(0.001)
Dependency ratio	0.081**
	(0.020)
Log of land asset (decimal)	−0.086**
	(0.028)
Self-employed household head	−0.034**
	(0.008)
Wage-employed household head	0.081**
	(0.005)
Agricultural asset	0.073**
	(0.010)
Nonagricultural asset	−0.029**
	(0.008)
Cash savings	0.009*
	(0.005)
Livestock asset (cattle)	0.004
	(0.004)
Village characteristics	
Access to a safety net program	0.007
	(0.016)
Access to microcredit programs	−0.075**
	(0.034)
Village-level unemployment rate	0.074**
	(0.036)
Village located in char area	0.181**
	(0.026)
Others	
Village located in char area × log of land asset (decimal)	−0.009*
	(0.005)
Proportion of high land in district × log of land asset (decimal)	−0.006
	(0.023)
Average yearly rainfall in district (mm) × log of land asset (decimal)	−0.0005
	(0.0003)
Pseudo R^2	0.180
Number of observations	480,918

Source: Khandker, Khalily, and Samad 2011.
Note: Regression additionally includes union dummies to control for unobserved effects of union. Figures in parentheses are robust standard errors. * and ** refer to a statistical significance of 10 percent and 5 percent or better, respectively; mm = millimeter.

We find an inverse relationship between migration and landownership, suggesting that households with less landholding have a higher tendency to migrate. This finding is corroborated by a number of studies showing that as the value of family landholdings increases, the probability of migration decreases (Durand, Parrado, and Massey 1996; Garip 2006; Mora and Taylor 2005; Stark and Taylor 1989). We would expect this outcome if household landownership and land quality increase the productivity of the family labor.

The status of the household head's employment also matters, as does the type of employment. As shown in chapter 3 in this volume, the demand for agricultural wage labor takes a sharp dip during the monga period. In contrast, self-employment in the farm sector is subject to a much milder seasonal decline, whereas employment in the nonfarm sector—both self-employment and wage employment—remains almost stable year round (see figure 3.15 in chapter 3). Because agricultural wage laborers constitute the bulk of the rural labor force in the Rangpur region, their lack of employment and income-earning opportunities in the monga season seems to be the major reason for the migration flows. The results presented in table 6.4 appear to confirm this. Thus, those with wage employment have a high probability of migration, whereas self-employment reduces the chance of migration. Similarly, household ownership of nonagricultural assets can have a negative effect on the chance of migration by providing opportunities for self-employment.

For obvious reasons, overall village-level unemployment increases the rate of out-migration. For example, a 10 percent increase in the unemployment rate increases the probability of migration by 0.7 percent. Living in char area increases vulnerability and insecurity, and thus increases the probability of making seasonal migration. Char area residents are 18 percent more likely to migrate during the monga period than their counterpart mainland population.

The social safety-net programs (such as old-age pensions and Vulnerable Group Feeding) do not have a significant effect on seasonal migration. In contrast, access to microcredit programs is found to have a strong negative effect on seasonal migration. The presence of microcredit programs in a village reduces the chance of seasonal migration by nearly 8 percent. This finding suggests that people participating in microcredit programs to generate off-farm income and employment are less likely to feel threatened during the lean season and hence are less likely to migrate.

Interestingly, this finding regarding the effect of microcredit on seasonal migration apparently differs from that of a recent study based on a randomized experiment conducted in the Rangpur region (Chowdhury, Mobarak, and Bryan 2009). By offering a cash or credit incentive for migration through random selection, the study found that the migration rate increased from 34 percent in control villages to 57 percent in treatment villages. The food intakes of the migrant households were found to increase as a result of migration, and more interesting, the migration rate in treatment areas continued to be significantly higher even after the inducement was removed.

That study suggests that seasonal migration can be potentially beneficial even for those who cannot migrate because of the cost and the risk involved (that is, spending money for migration but not finding suitable employment, while the family left behind is threatened by starvation). It is, therefore, no wonder that the response to the cash or credit incentive for migration can be high, particularly if some risk-reducing mechanism exists. These findings are not, however, necessarily inconsistent with ours. Although conventional microcredit used for income-generating activities that are not subject to seasonality may discourage migration, other forms of credit or financial assistance may help households overcome the barriers to migration. The two types of credit can in fact be part of complementary strategies for mitigating seasonal hunger.

Does Seasonal Migration Help Mitigate Food Deprivation?

As discussed earlier, seasonal migration is determined by a host of factors that are also likely to influence the extent of seasonal food deprivation. These factors include household and community characteristics (such as the household head's age, household land and nonland assets, the demographic and occupational characteristics of the household, the availability of government and nongovernment safety-net mechanisms in the community, and local area agroclimatic characteristics). Together, these factors simultaneously affect a household's income-earning prospects without migration, the decision to migrate, and the likely gain from migration. The empirical challenge is to separate these effects to assess the net gains accrued because of migration.

To solve this problem of estimation, we use an endogenous switching regression method as proposed by Maddala (1983) to control for the endogeneity of the decision to migrate.[11] The details of the estimation methodology are given in the annex of this chapter. We divide all sample households into migrant and nonmigrant groups and estimate equations for food deprivation status for each household group by using various household and community characteristics. By switching the estimated parameters between the equations for the two groups, we can then also estimate the counterfactuals, that is, what would have been the food deprivation status of the migrants had they decided not to migrate (and similarly for the nonmigrants had they decided to migrate). However, to take care of the problem of endogeneity of the decision to migrate, we run the outcome equations after controlling for the selection biases distinguishing the two groups.[12] The effect of migration can then be estimated by taking the differences of these "conditional" outcomes with and without migration. Although this estimate can be made for both migrant and nonmigrant groups, for the latter group, the estimated effect of migration is of course in the nature of a counterfactual.

Table 6.5 reports the estimates of potential benefits of migration using the counterfactual evaluation approach outlined above. The results clearly show that seasonal migration lowers a household's hardship with regard to food deprivation for both migrant and nonmigrant households—for the latter, in a counterfactual scenario. This outcome is true for both the monga and the non-monga period and for the year-round effect. For extreme hardship (starvation), the expected or potential benefit is higher for nonmigrant households than for migrant households. For example, migration is found to lower the prevalence of starvation during the

Table 6.5   Effects of Seasonal Migration on Household Hardship

Household types by seasonal migration	Extreme hardship (starvation)	All hardships (starvation and food rationing)
Monga period		
Migrants	−0.081**	−0.018**
	(0.0002)	(0.0001)
Nonmigrants	−0.015**	−0.016**
	(0.002)	(0.0004)
Non-monga period		
Migrants	−0.051**	−0.031**
	(0.0001)	(0.0002)
Nonmigrants	−0.040**	−0.002**
	(0.0001)	(0.0001)
Year round		
Migrants	−0.051**	−0.020**
	(0.0002)	(0.0001)
Nonmigrants	−0.005**	−0.028**
	(0.0001)	(0.0004)

Source: Khandker, Khalily, and Samad 2011.

Notes: Year-round outcomes are defined in the text in the context of table 6.3. Figures in parentheses are robust standard errors. ** refers to a statistical significance of 5 percent or better.

monga period by 8.1 percentage points for migrant households and potentially by 1.5 percentage points for nonmigrant households. However, when both starvation and food rationing are considered, the migrant households gain (a 1.8 percentage point reduction) only slightly over the nonmigrant households (a 1.6 percentage point reduction). As for the year-round hardships, the reduction in the extreme hardship of migrant households is over ten times that of the nonmigrant households, whereas it is less for general hardship.

An apparently unexpected aspect of the results regarding the beneficial effects of migration during the monga season is that these effects are in some cases found to be more pronounced in the non-monga season than in the monga season in averting food deprivation. If one considers that the prevalence of both forms of food deprivation is far lower in the non-monga season than in the monga season, the seasonal contrasts in the accrued benefits become all the more striking.

Instead of being a puzzle, however, these results can in fact provide more insights into the phenomenon of seasonal migration in Rangpur. As discussed earlier, the lack of local employment opportunities, especially for wage labor, is the main driving force behind seasonal migration. But the immediate beneficial effects of such migration may be limited by lack of facilities for remitting money, particularly for migrants who find jobs in distant places.[13] Rather, many of the gains to the household may be realized after the migrant worker returns with his or her earnings. One would also expect that these gains would be more visible in the immediate post-monga period. This interpretation of the results is particularly plausible because the InM baseline survey was carried out in the immediate post-monga season; information was collected for that season and the preceding monga season.[14] The policy conclusion is that scope exists for enhancing the benefits of migration in mitigating monga by facilitating remittance facilities.

In the interpretation of these results, a few further points may be noted. First, because of the broad classification and the subjective nature of food deprivation status used in the InM survey, the significance of these results perhaps lies more in their qualitative rather than quantitative implications. Second, the counterfactual results show that migration could have benefited the nonmigrant households as well, and the reduction of seasonal starvation would have been even higher for them compared with those who actually migrated. The question then remains why more people do not migrate to avoid starvation. The explanations are likely to lie in the barriers to migration, such as the costs and risks involved, lack of social networking needed for such migration, and inadequate spatial integration of labor markets. Finally, the estimated benefits from seasonal migration reflect the household-level effect of migration under the existing labor market situation, and thus they do not fully capture the welfare gains of the local economy arising from migration on such a large scale. Nonmigrants stand to gain from the greater likelihood of finding employment locally and also from any beneficial effects of inward remittances.

Concluding Remarks

One of the major coping strategies observed in greater Rangpur during monga is seasonal migration. Among the poor households of the region covered in the 2006 InM baseline survey, about 173,000 opted for sending one or more of their household members to work elsewhere during the monga season of that year.[15] A sharp dip in local labor demand coupled with the generally high levels of impoverishment seems to be the major driving force behind seasonal migration on such a large scale.

More than half the households that opted for migration had to resort to other monga-coping mechanisms as well. The government social safety-net programs do not seem to have a strong role in keeping seasonal migration in check, perhaps because of their limited coverage and the inadequate support that is provided. The fact that many of the migrant households have to adopt multiple coping strategies, including borrowing, sale of assets, and advance sale of labor and crops, points to the particular vulnerability of these households. Even then, migration may give the households a better chance of reducing the extent of seasonal and year-round hunger compared with those that have limited coping options and that lack the means to migrate.

Seasonal migration is found to have a beneficial effect on household welfare by reducing the extent of seasonal food deprivation. More interesting, access to outside jobs during the lean period can alleviate households' food insecurity even to a larger extent than in other seasons, particularly immediately after monga when migrant workers return with their earnings. This finding suggests that the beneficial effect of migration in alleviating monga can be enhanced by improving the facilities for remitting money, such as through use of the recently introduced money transfers through mobile phones.

Our results also show (by simulating a counterfactual) that the non-migrant households would have benefited too had they migrated, although the reduction of seasonal starvation would not have been as high as that for migrant households. Evidently, not all monga-vulnerable households have the necessary networking ability or the financial means for migration. Policy measures may therefore be aimed at easing the barriers to migration. Although access to microcredit appears to work as an alternative to seasonal migration for the households, special schemes for providing credit or cash incentives are found to encourage seasonal migration and increase household welfare. Facilitating migration through such schemes may enable households to avoid resorting to such extreme measures as borrowing from moneylenders or selling assets to bear the cost of migration.

Although seasonal migration can have beneficial effects on the migrating households as well as on the local economy as a whole, apparently it is not enough to mitigate seasonal hunger. Efforts to facilitate seasonal migration should not therefore divert attention from the need to invest more and create more employment opportunities in the areas of outmigration, so that labor does not have to move on such a large scale. These policy approaches should not be regarded as alternatives but as a part of a coordinated strategy for eradicating seasonal hunger in vulnerable areas, such as Rangpur.

Annex 6A: Endogenous Switching Regression Method for Estimation of Gains from Seasonal Migration

To estimate the effect of seasonal migration on food deprivation of the poor households in Rangpur, we use an endogenous switching regression method as proposed by Maddala (1983). This method can control for endogeneity of the decision to migrate so as to measure the one-way causal effect of migration on a household's food deprivation status. We use the cross-sectional data from the Institute of Microfinance baseline survey of 2006 covering nearly half a million poor households in Rangpur. The huge size of the data set is particularly suitable for the implementation of this estimation model. This model is described below.

Let us assume that m_i denotes household i's decision to undertake seasonal migration ($m_i = 1$ when a household migrates, 0 when it does not), which is determined by the following selection model:

$$\text{if } \gamma Z_i + u_i > 0, \text{ then } m_i = 1, \tag{6A.1}$$

$$\text{and if } \gamma Z_i + u_i \leq 0, \text{ then } m_i = 0, \tag{6A.2}$$

where Z_i is a vector of household and village characteristics that determines a household's decision to migrate during the monga season; γ is the parameter to be estimated; and u_i is the error term. Let us further assume that the outcome (for example, seasonal food deprivation) equations of migrant and nonmigrant households are given by

$$C_{1i} = \beta_1 X_{1i} + \varepsilon_{1i}, \text{ when a household migrates } (m_i = 1) \text{ and} \qquad (6A.3)$$

$$C_{0i} = \beta_0 X_{0i} + \varepsilon_{0i}, \text{ when a household does not migrate } (m_i = 0), \qquad (6A.4)$$

where X_{1i} and X_{0i} are vectors of household and village characteristics that determine a household's food consumption when the household migrates and when it does not, respectively; β_1 and β_0 are parameters to be estimated; and ε_1 and ε_0 are the error terms. The outcome equations include all the X variables that were used in the probit equation for the decision to migrate, including the dummy variables for *union* (a collection of 10–12 villages) to control for any local-level heterogeneity.

The error terms u_i, ε_1, and ε_0 are assumed to have a trivariate normal distribution with mean vector zero and covariance matrix

$$\Omega = \begin{bmatrix} \sigma_1^2 & \sigma_{01} & \sigma_{1u} \\ & \sigma_0^2 & \sigma_{0u} \\ & & \sigma_u^2 \end{bmatrix},$$

where σ_u^2, σ_1^2, and σ_0^2, are the variances of u_i, ε_1, and ε_0, respectively; and σ_{1u}, σ_{0u}, and σ_{01} are covariances of ε_1 and u_i, ε_0 and u_i, and ε_0 and ε_1, respectively. The same signs of ρ_1 and ρ_0 indicate that the unobserved factors that influence a household's probability of migrating also affect its seasonal food deprivation the same way, whereas opposite signs of ρ_1 and ρ_0 indicate that unobserved factors have opposite effects in the probability of migration and the food deprivation status of the household. In our case, both ρ_1 and ρ_0 are found to have positive signs, which means that the unobserved factors influencing a household's migration decision also adversely affect its food consumption status. And this correlation is much stronger for the migrant households, demonstrating that seasonal migration and seasonal food deprivation are strongly correlated.

The next step is to find the direct effects of migration on household outcomes. In a switching regression model, outcome equations are run after controlling for a household's selection bias. Following the derivation of Lokshin and Sajaia (2004), we can construct the following terms:

$yc_{1\_1i} = E(y_{1i} \mid s = 1, x_{1i}) = x_{1i} \beta_1 + \sigma_1 \rho_1 \phi(\gamma Z_i)/\Phi(\gamma Z_i)$

= Conditional expected value of outcome of a migrant household with migration;

$yc_{0\_1i} = E(y_{0i} \mid s = 1, x_{1i}) = x_{1i} \beta_0 + \sigma_0 \rho_0 \phi(\gamma Z_i)/\Phi(\gamma Z_i)$

= Conditional expected value of outcome of a migrant household without migration (counterfactual);

$yc_{0\_0i} = E(y_{0i} \mid s = 0, x_{0i}) = x_{0i} \beta_0 + \sigma_0 \rho_0 \phi(\gamma Z_i)/[1 - \Phi(\gamma Z_i)]$

= Conditional expected value of outcome of a nonmigrant household without migration; and

$yc_{1\_0i} = E(y_{1i} \mid s = 0, x_{0i}) = x_{0i} \beta_1 + \sigma_1 \rho_1 \phi(\gamma Z_i)/[1 - \Phi(\gamma Z_i)]$

= Conditional expected value of outcome of a nonmigrant household with migration (counterfactual).

Here, ϕ and Φ are a normal density distribution function and a cumulative normal distribution function, respectively.

Using the calculations above, we construct the effects of seasonal migration on household outcomes in the following way:

$yc_{\_1i} = yc_{1\_1i} - yc_{0\_1i}$ = Expected outcome of a migrant household – expected outcome of a migrant household if it had not chosen to migrate (counterfactual)

= Gain in outcome of a migrant household from migration; and

$yc_{\_0i} = yc_{1\_0i} - yc_{0\_0i}$ = Expected outcome of a nonmigrant household had it chosen to migrate (counterfactual) – expected outcome of a nonmigrant household

= Gain in outcome of a nonmigrant household that would have accrued from migration.

Notes

1. For discussions on various kinds of internal migrations in the countries in Sub-Saharan Africa, see, for example, Amin (1974) and Gould and Prothero (1975).

2. The population estimate is from the population census of 2001.

3. Some pilot projects have been initiated recently to encourage overseas migration from the Rangpur region as part of efforts to alleviate monga.

4. For example, a study on Vietnam shows that, among other factors, social networks matter considerably in deciding who will migrate (see Brauw and Harigaya 2007). The same study also shows that seasonal migration plays an important role in the improvement of living standards.

5. The breakdown by district of various national-level censuses and surveys shows that the proportion of landless households and the proportion of the workforce engaged in agriculture are considerably higher in Rangpur compared with the national average; see, for example, the figures cited in Elahi and Ara (2008, table 2.11).

6. Throughout this chapter, the term *household migration* is used to refer to the physical migration of one or more capable members, as opposed to that of the whole family.

7. *Char* areas are land formed from river sediment. Tens of millions of poor people throughout Bangladesh with no other place to move live in such areas.

8. A *high land area*, according to the definition of the Bangladesh Agricultural Research Council, is where the floodwater level remains below 3 feet.

9. A *union* is a collection of 10–12 villages. We could have used a village-level fixed-effects method instead of a union-level fixed-effects estimate, in which case we would have lost the village-level explanatory variables.

10. Unfortunately, the InM baseline survey has no information about the areas to which these poor households migrate. Hence, there is no variable representing the demand side of the destination labor markets.

11. Alternatively, if we had appropriate instrumental variables to identify a migration equation (such as labor market conditions and networks related to the destination markets), we could follow a two-stage Heckman selection method to estimate the effect of seasonal migration.

12. For this calculation, the parameters of a selection model regarding the migration decision must be estimated first.

13. This lack of facilities for remitting money may indeed be the case for a large majority of seasonal migrants from Rangpur, many of whom are found to travel to such distant places as the northeastern district of Sylhet. Unfortunately, the InM baseline survey has no information about the destinations of seasonal migrants or about the way they remit money.

14. Moreover, this interpretation does not preclude the role of the prospect of hunger behind the decision to migrate. Households that are most vulnerable to starvation during monga are also likely to experience food deprivation, although to a lesser degree, during other seasons.

15. Although the InM baseline survey involved a complete enumeration of poor households in the survey villages, not all villages were covered.

References

Afsar, Rita. 2005. "Bangladesh: Internal Migration and Pro-Poor Policy." Paper presented at the Regional Conference on Migration and Development of Asia, Lanzhou, China, March 14–16.

Amin, Samir, ed. 1974. *Modern Migration in Western Africa*. London: Oxford University Press.

BBS (Bangladesh Bureau of Statistics). 2010. *Yearbook of Agricultural Statistics in Bangladesh 2009*. Dhaka: BBS, Government of Bangladesh.

Brauw, Alan De, and Tomoko Harigaya. 2007. "Seasonal Migration and Improving Living Standard in Vietnam." *American Journal of Agricultural Economics* 89 (2): 430–47.

Chambers, Robert, Richard Longhurst, and Arnold Pacey. 1981. *Seasonal Dimensions to Rural Poverty*. London: Frances Pinter.

Chowdhury, Shyamal, Ahmed Mushfiq Mobarak, and Gharad Bryan. 2009. "Migrating Away from a Seasonal Famine: A Randomized Intervention in Bangladesh." Human Development Research Paper 2009/41, United Nations Development Programme, New York.

Deshingkar, Priya. 2005. "Maximizing the Benefits of Internal Migration for Development." In *Migration, Development, and Poverty Reduction in Asia*, 23–53. Geneva: International Organization for Migration.

Durand, Jorge, Emilio A. Parrado, and Douglas S. Massey. 1996. "Migradollars and Development: A Reconsideration of the Mexican Case." *International Migration Review* 30 (2): 423–44.

Elahi, K. Maudood, and Iffat Ara. 2008. *Understanding the Monga in Northern Bangladesh*. Dhaka: Academic Press and Publishers Library.

Garip, Filiz. 2006. "Social and Economic Determinants of Migration and Remittances: An Analysis of 22 Thai Villages." Princeton University, Princeton, NJ.

Gould, William Taylor Sporkie, and Ralph Mansell Prothero. 1975. "Space and Time in African Population Mobility." In *People on the Move: Studies on Internal Migration*, ed. Leszek A. Kosinski and Ralph Mansell Prothero, 39–49. London: Methuen.

Khandker, Shahidur R., M. A. Baqui Khalily, and Hussain A. Samad. 2010. "Seasonal Migration and Mitigating Income Seasonality in Northwest Bangladesh." Working Paper 5, Institute of Microfinance, Dhaka.

Khandker, Shahidur R., M. A. Baqui Khalily, and Hussain A. Samad. 2011. "Seasonal Migration to Mitigate Income Seasonality: Evidence from Bangladesh." *Journal of Development Studies*, 2011, 1–21, iFirst article: http://www.tandfonline.com/doi/abs/10.1080/00220388.2011.561325.

Lokshin, Michael, and Zurab Sajaia. 2004. "Maximum Likelihood Estimation of Endogenous Switching Regression Models." *Stata Journal* 4 (3): 282–89.

Maddala, George S. 1983. *Limited-Dependent Qualitative Variables in Econometrics.* Cambridge, U.K.: Cambridge University Press.

Mora, Jorge, and J. Edward Taylor. 2005. "Determinants of Migration, Destination, and Sector Choice: Disentangling Individual, Household, and Community Effects." In *International Migration, Remittances, and the Brain Drain,* ed. Çaglar Özden and Maurice Schiff, 21–51. New York: Palgrave Macmillan.

Oberai, A. S., Pradhan H. Prasad, and M. G. Sardana. 1989. *Determinants and Consequences of Internal Migration in India: Studies in Bihar, Kerala, and Uttar Pradesh.* Delhi: Oxford University Press.

Srivastava, Ravi. 2005. "India: Internal Migration Links with Poverty and Development." In *Migration, Development, and Poverty Reduction in Asia,* 109–26. Geneva: International Organization for Migration.

Stark, Oded, and J. Edward Taylor. 1989. "Relative Deprivation and International Migration." *Demography* 26 (1): 1–14.

CHAPTER 7

Effectiveness of Social Safety-Net Programs

All over the world, various social safety-net programs are used to safeguard the economic security of poor and vulnerable groups. The welfare impact of these programs largely depends on their effectiveness and on adequate coverage, which in turn, are determined by administrative capacity, fund availability, and the design of the programs in relation to the needs of the vulnerable population. Although there is extensive literature on these various aspects of safety-net programs, not much is known about their effectiveness, particularly in mitigating seasonal poverty and hunger. In Bangladesh, the role of the safety-net programs is well recognized by the government and nongovernmental organizations (NGOs), given the high incidence of poverty, food insecurity, and the recurrence of climate-related shocks. In this chapter, we focus particularly on the seasonal dimensions of the possible welfare effects of safety-net programs.

The discussions and debates on social safety nets commonly revolve around several issues. There are the *protection* and *promotion* aspects of safety nets; the former aspect is concerned with preventing a decline in living conditions and averting the impact of shocks, while the latter is about lifting the vulnerable from endemic and persistent deprivation (Dréze and Sen 1989; Ravallion, van de Walle, and Gautam 1995). A related argument is that social safety nets should be designed to address the causes of poverty, not simply its symptoms (Holzmann and Grosh 2008). Another issue concerns targeting and the selection of beneficiaries, such as through universal social benefit systems, some actual or proxy criteria, or self-selection mechanisms (Ahmed et al. 2009; Narayan and Zaman 2009, chap. 9). Social protection and safety-net programs are also variously categorized by their objectives and delivery mechanisms: income transfers through cash, food-related programs, price subsidies, programs related to human capital development, public works programs, microcredit and informal insurance programs, and emergency assistance (Babu 2003). There are a priori legitimate concerns of public welfare behind these various types of programs, but their effectiveness in achieving the desired goals remains a matter of empirical assessment.

As a globally recognized strategy for alleviating extreme poverty, safety-net programs may be designed specifically for alleviating seasonal hardships. In a recent study of four African countries, for example, Devereux (2009) examines how a variety of social protection experiments have had different degrees of success in tackling seasonal distress.[1] Besides providing livelihood support generally, seasonally oriented safety-net programs can enhance the welfare of the poor by providing a less costly consumption-smoothing mechanism relative to alternative desperate measures (for example, Chetty and Looney 2006). But this approach depends on the timing of such seasonal or short-term programs. For example, with regard to decisions about the timing of seasonal public works programs, such as Food for Work (FFW), there may be balancing considerations of providing employment during the slack season (which is usually the late rainy season for rain-fed rice cultivation) and undertaking earthwork for infrastructure building (for which the dry season is more suitable).

The interlocking of endemic poverty and its seasonality, as discussed in the previous chapters, also has a bearing on the effectiveness of safety-net programs. Compared with short-run emergency type programs, long-term programs may be more oriented toward lifting households from endemic and persistent poverty (the promotion aspect of safety nets mentioned above), and eradicating such poverty is also an effective way of dealing with seasonal poverty in a sustainable way.[2] That orientation should not, however, detract attention from the programs that have direct counterseasonal effect. It may often be more cost-effective to address seasonal deprivation directly through seasonally oriented programs than through assistance in building new year-round livelihood strategies. Moreover, by providing protection particularly at times of severe seasonal distress, safety net programs can help the poor to better manage risks and thus make better livelihood choices (Holzmann and Grosh 2008). For poor households, seasonally oriented safety net programs can be a mechanism for both consumption smoothing and risk management.

Salient Features of Social Safety Net Programs in Bangladesh

Bangladesh has a long history of extensive social safety net provisions. Safety net programs have proliferated over time, which reflects an increasing recognition of the welfare responsibilities of the state. Beyond providing a minimum level of protection against frequent natural calamities, these programs have come to be seen as part of a sustainable antipoverty strategy. Consequently, emphasis has shifted from food rations and postdisaster relief to programs incorporating mainstream social and developmental concerns. The erosion of informal safety nets caused by the decay of the extended family system must also be taken into account.

The characteristics of the major safety net programs in Bangladesh (those with the largest budgetary allocations as of 2009–10) are given in table 7.1.[3] These programs may be divided into those that (a) provide allowances to people with special needs (for example, old age pensions or allowances for destitute women), (b) provide employment in public works (for example, FFW), (c) promote human development (for example, stipends to primary school students and Vulnerable Group Development (VGD) for poor women), and (d) provide food security or emergency assistance (for example, Vulnerable Group Feeding (VGF) and Test Relief). The programs may also be distinguished by their protection versus promotion characteristics, which in turn, are related to the criteria of entry and exit. The school stipend program and VGD are the only ones with a strategy for graduating the beneficiaries from their programs.

Another characteristic of the programs that is particularly relevant for this analysis is whether they are of a seasonal or temporary nature as distinct from the long-term or year-round programs. Of the nine programs listed in table 7.1, all except the first four provide seasonal or short-term benefits and account for nearly two-thirds of the total budgetary allocations for the nine programs taken together. The proportion may not be very different if allocations are considered for all government safety net programs (PPRC and UNDP 2011). The predominance of short-term programs does not, however, necessarily mean that there is

Table 7.1   Major Safety-Net Programs in Bangladesh, 2009–10

Program	Beneficiary and coverage	Allocation (Tk, million)	Requirement	Cash or in kind	Details
Primary Education Stipend Project (PESP)	Households; 5.2 million rural poor students	5,748.4	Schooling	Cash	Formerly known as Food for Education (FFE); promotion of primary education for students of rural poor households
Old Age Allowance	Old-age individuals unable to work; 2.3 million	8,100.0	No work requirement	Cash	Reduction of vulnerability of old-age people having no pension income in poor households in nonmunicipal areas; Tk 250 per month
Allowances for Widowed, Deserted, and Destitute Women	Destitute women; 0.9 million	3,312.0	No work requirement	Cash	Tk 250 per month
Vulnerable Group Development (VGD)	Women capable of income-generating activities; 0.75 million	5,951.7	No work requirement; skill training	Food grain	Provision of skill training to poor women for undertaking income-generating activities; 30 kg of wheat per month in 30-month cycles
Vulnerable Group Feeding (VGF)	Households; 7.5 million in 2008–09	10,971.7	No work requirement	Food grain	Addressing of seasonal distress and postdisaster needs of the poor; coverage that can vary from year to year; 10 kg of rice per month for three months

Program	Beneficiaries	Allocation	Work requirement	Transfer	Description
Food for Work (FFW)	Individuals able to work; 3.6 million person-months (1 million beneficiaries)	9,276.6	Work	Food grain	Reduction of food vulnerability of the poor through employment mostly in rural infrastructure development projects; seasonal program; payment based on workdays
Test Relief	Individuals able to work; 3.8 person-months (5 million beneficiaries in 2008–09)	8,978.5	Work	Food grain	Reduction of food vulnerability and seasonal distress of the poor in rural areas through employment in activities such as cleaning of ponds and bushes and minor infrastructure repair
Gratuitous Relief	Households; 6.4 million in 2008–09	1,652.2	No work requirement	Food grain	Way that government provides immediate relief to disaster areas; 10 kg of wheat/rice per person given once
Rural Employment and Road Maintenance Program (RERMP)	Women able to work; 0.7 million person-months; 0.5 million beneficiaries	1,850.0	Work	Cash	Rural public work program built on the experiences of the previous Road Maintenance Project (RMP); payment based on a daily rate basis
Employment Generation Program for the Poorest (EGPP)	Individuals able to work; 4.5 million person-months (2.0 million beneficiaries)	10,761.1	Work	Cash	A 100-day employment guarantee scheme in the lean seasons initiated in 2008–09: 60 days in October–December and 40 days in March–May; wage rate of Tk 100 per day

Sources: PPRC and UNDP 2011; various government documents. Allocations are according to the Revised Budget of 2009–10.

Note: kg = kilogram; person-month = equivalent of one person working for 30 days.

enough scope for seasonal targeting of safety nets. Except for VGF, the other seasonal programs involve some type of public works, mostly earthwork. Unfortunately, the lean season preceding the harvesting of *aman* (the late-monsoon rice crop), which coincides with the late rainy season, is not often suitable for earthwork; as a result, the safety-net programs involving public works are often undertaken in the dry season after the harvesting of the aman crop.

The above dilemma in the timing for the safety-net programs based on public works is evident from the design of the newly introduced 100-day employment guarantee scheme, Employment Generation Program for the Poorest (table 7.1). This scheme has a declared objective of providing employment in the lean seasons for 60 days during October to December and for 40 days during March to May. The latter period falls within the dry season and is also an agricultural lean period (preceding the *boro* rice harvest), although it lacks the same intensity of distress observed during the pre-aman lean season. The former period, however, only partly coincides with the *monga* (seasonal hunger) period toward the end of the monsoon rains and the regular annual floods; otherwise, it coincides with the aman harvesting season when there is usually no dearth of employment.

In the year-round programs, the benefits are to be paid at regular intervals. It is not known whether this actually happens. If there are irregularities in payments, such as those caused by bureaucratic delays, the effect on seasonality may go either way in mitigating seasonality. Because these programs are not directly aimed at having a counterseasonal effect, they should at least ensure that payments are not delayed during the seasons of stress. Deliberately adding a seasonal dimension to the programs, for example, in terms of the larger amounts of benefits provided during the lean seasons, could be a further step.

The coverage of the social safety-net system is fairly large in Bangladesh and has expanded rapidly in recent years. The VGF program alone, for example, had 7.5 million beneficiaries in 2009–10 who received short-term food rations under the program (table 7.1). The program's implementation mainly in rural areas suggests that nearly one-quarter of all rural households benefited from the program in that time frame.[4] One problem, however, is that the benefits may be distributed too thinly to have much effect on the levels of poverty. The other problem is that the actual number of beneficiaries and the amounts of benefits may be much smaller than shown on paper because of leakages of various kinds.

The information regarding the coverage of safety nets is also available from the data of the Household Income and Expenditure Survey (HIES). According to the HIES data of 2005 and 2010, the number of households countrywide benefiting from at least one safety-net program increased from 13 percent to nearly 25 percent between those years. Among rural households, the coverage rate is even higher.[5] The increase in the estimated coverage may to some extent be explained by the fact that in 2010, the HIES collected information on a larger number of programs than in 2005, but most of the additional programs included in the 2010 HIES were either insignificant in coverage or had gained in importance only in the intervening periods.

With the increasing coverage and diversification of safety-net programs, total public spending on these programs has also increased in recent years. The total budgetary allocation for safety nets increased from nearly 1 percent of gross domestic product in the 1990s to about 2 percent in 2009–10.[6] Even then, the amount of benefits received per beneficiary household remains very small. For example, according to the data from the 2010 HIES, the monthly benefits in taka received per beneficiary household are only about 7 percent of the national poverty line (in terms of household monthly consumption expenditure) of that year.[7] Moreover, the estimated monthly amount of benefits refers to the periods of program participation only. Although the same beneficiary households are found to participate in a number of safety-net programs in a year, the HIES data cannot show much about the average annualized value of the benefits per household.[8] There are, however, certain specialized subprograms, such as those within the purview of the VGD, that transfer more substantial amounts of benefits (Ahmed et al. 2009).

The increased public spending on safety nets has resulted mainly from the multiplication of programs and not from increases in the amounts of real benefits per beneficiary in each program. There are currently as many as 30 major safety-net programs and nearly as many minor ones (PPRC and UNDP 2011). New programs have been devised partly in response to the genuine needs of poor people at risk, but political competition resulting in a kind of populist tokenism has also been a factor. A program, once introduced, has rarely been rolled back, even if the benefits are so thinly distributed as to barely justify the cost of administration.

Another area of concern is that a sizable share of the benefits goes to the nonpoor, and there are many forms of leakages resulting in the beneficiaries receiving less than that shown on paper. The safety-net programs based on public works have a self-targeting mechanism because of the kind of employment offered, but even these programs suffer from problems of underpayment of wages, overreporting of work done, and the existence of so-called ghost workers. According to the 2005 HEIS data, more than 40 percent of the beneficiaries of safety-net programs were nonpoor (that is, they belonged to the top three quintiles) (Narayan and Zaman 2009). Similar results were obtained from the 2000 HIES as well (World Bank and ADB 2003, 78–79). Given the resource constraint faced by the government in the provision of safety nets, these targeting errors along with resource leakages pose a serious problem.

A weak link in channeling safety-net resources to the poor appears to be the process by which the government allocates resources across regions. For example, the data from the 2005 HIES show that although the coverage of safety-net programs varies significantly by region, the variations are not in accordance with the regions' poverty levels (Narayan and Zaman 2009, 282). The low coverage of relatively poor regions also translates into low coverage among the poor. Studies based on data from the earlier rounds of HIES in 1995 and 2000 provide an even more revealing analysis of the targeting differentials in terms of poor and non-poor participants. To the extent that the programs have pro-poor targeting (that is, the poor benefit more than the nonpoor), this outcome is found to be due to the pro-poor targeting *within* rather than *across* villages (Ravallion 2000; World Bank and ADB 2003). It is noteworthy that in all these programs, while beneficiary selection is fairly decentralized, the allocations are made at higher administrative levels.

The Special Case of Monga in Rangpur

Until a few years ago, the Rangpur region had not received any special attention in the allocation of safety-net resources (or in other public poverty alleviation measures). This is hardly surprising, given the general lack of sensitivity in these allocations with respect to poverty prevalence, as discussed earlier. But increased public awareness of monga, helped in part by media activism, seems to have changed the situation to some extent. The objective of monga eradication has become part of the government's strategy for dealing with food insecurity; this objective has featured prominently in the government's Poverty Reduction Strategy Paper prepared in 2005 and in the most recent Five-Year Plan (2010–15).

The data from the 2010 HIES suggest that the increased public attention given to monga may have begun to be translated into increased safety-net coverage in Rangpur. Thus, the proportion of households covered by at least one safety-net program was found to be about 34 percent in the Rangpur region compared with the previously cited national-level figure of 25 percent (BBS 2011, 74–75).[9] However, the incidence of multiple membership seems to be lower in Rangpur, and the average monthly benefits per beneficiary household are also lower (by about 20 percent) compared with those for the country as a whole.[10] In fact, the Rangpur region still falls slightly behind the rest of the country in the coverage of programs with year-round benefits, such as allowances for old people and destitute women. However, the higher overall safety-net coverage in Rangpur seems to be largely explained by programs with extremely small short-term or one-time benefits (mainly, Gratuitous Relief). The expanded coverage of safety nets in Rangpur may thus have been driven in part by the kind of populist tokenism discussed earlier.

The programs that have responded most proactively to the call for monga mitigation are those administered by NGOs and microfinance institutions (MFIs), often with support from foreign donors and sometimes in partnership with the government. Most of these programs provide livelihood support to the ultrapoor through a variety of means, such as through asset transfer, cash for work, skill training, health care provision, and flexible microcredit on easy terms outside the regular microcredit programs. Some of the programs were introduced specifically for the monga-prone areas, such as the Chars Livelihood Programme, which is implemented jointly by NGOs and the local government in the *char* (reclaimed river islands) areas of Rangpur and some adjacent districts. Other such projects, designed as countrywide programs to help the ultrapoor, are now specially targeting hunger-prone areas such as Rangpur. One example is the IGVGD–TUP (Income Gerneration for Vulnerable Group Development–Targeting the Ultra-Poor Programme), which is a partnership among the government, the Bangladesh Rural Advancement Committee (BRAC), and the United Nations World Food Programme (Matin and Hulme 2003).[11]

Similarly, the Palli Karma-Sahayak Foundation (PKSF) introduced an Ultra-Poor Program to be implemented by its partner NGOs and MFIs alongside their regular microcredit programs. As mentioned in the introductory chapter, PKSF subsequently started a special microcredit program specifically targeted to the monga-affected extreme poor of the Rangpur region. The effect of this program will, however, be discussed separately in chapter 8 in this volume. The rest of this chapter examines the patterns of access to safety nets and their effect on the basis of data from the Institute of Microfinance (InM) baseline survey.

InM Survey Findings on Social Safety Nets in Rangpur

The discussions in the earlier chapters clearly show that the social safety-net support is quite inadequate to mitigate the extreme situation of poverty and deprivation that exists in the Rangpur region, particularly during the monga period. The data from the InM baseline survey of 2006 can be further analyzed to provide insight into the role of the safety nets with respect to their coverage, targeting, timing, and effect. The information on safety nets was gathered in this survey according to two aspects: (a) whether the households were cardholder members of particular government safety-net programs (namely, VGD or VGF, Old Age Allowance, and FFW or Test Relief) regardless of whether they actually received any benefits during that monga season; and (b) whether the households received support, such as cash, food, clothing, building materials for houses, or livestock, during monga from the government or NGOs.

As discussed in chapter 4 in this volume, nearly one-third of the households reported receiving some support from government and nongovernmental sources during the monga season (see table 4.6 in chapter 4 in this volume and table 7.2). This coverage may be compared with that of 15 percent among rural households as found in the 2005 HIES. In making this comparison, however, one should remember that the estimate of coverage in the InM survey, which covered households approximately in the bottom three quintiles, would not be representative of all rural households. Even then, the coverage among the sample households seems to be on the higher side compared with the national estimate. This means that by the time of the InM survey, Rangpur had already started to attract

Table 7.2   Distribution of Poor Households by Participation in Government Safety-Net Program and Incidence of Starvation during Monga in Greater Rangpur Region, 2006

percent

Safety-net programs	Gaibandha district	Kurigram district	Lalmonirhat district	Nilphamari district	Rangpur district	Rangpur region
VGD and VGF	5.84	1.69	11.32	1.67	11.84	6.30
Old Age Allowance	1.71	1.22	3.20	1.88	2.62	2.05
FFW and Test Relief	1.45	1.49	0	4.52	2.23	1.63
Starvation during monga	57.62	48.47	47.95	26.16	56.34	47.27
Number of observations	120,426	128,987	102,866	56,772	71,867	480,918

Source: Institute of Microfinance baseline survey, 2006.
Note: FFW = Food for Work; VGD = Vulnerable Group Development; VGF = Vulnerable Group Feeding.

attention for the placement of safety nets. The important question is what amount of such support per beneficiary household is adequate to make any significant effect.

The above figure of safety-net coverage among survey households includes the beneficiaries of the NGO support programs, which have proliferated in the region in recent years. As for some of the main government-run safety-net programs mentioned above, these programs together covered only about 10 percent of the survey households. For these programs, this estimate of coverage would appear to be unusually low when compared with the national average for *all* rural households, such as estimated from the 2005 HIES, or as suggested by the allocations in the national budgets (Narayan and Zaman 2009; World Bank and ADB 2003). Thus, as of 2006, Rangpur seems to have remained disadvantaged in the placement of some of the major safety-net programs, as well as being specially targeted as an area vulnerable to food insecurity. Although some safety-net programs, especially those of NGOs, may have responded early to the call for the monga mitigation campaign, many major government programs failed to do so.

The coverage of the government's safety-net programs was not found to be equitably distributed even within the Rangpur region (table 7.2). Thus, the coverage of all the programs was less than the regional average in the Gaibandha district, although it was one of the districts worst affected by monga. Again, the severity of monga in both Kurigram and Lalmonirhat districts was about the same as in the region as a whole; yet less than 2 percent of the households in Kurigram were cardholders of VGD or VGF compared with the regional average of more than 6 percent, while Lalmonirhat had the highest coverage of these programs (11 percent).

Among the districts, Nilphamari had the lowest incidence of starvation during monga but had the highest proportion of households benefiting from FFW or Test Relief (the public works programs that are meant to be offered on the basis of need assessment for a particular area). However, for the Rangpur district, the relatively severe incidence of monga was matched by higher-than-average coverage of the programs, but this advantage might be due to its proximity to the regional city of Rangpur. These anomalies in area distribution of the programs should not, however, detract attention from the fact that the coverage of the programs was generally far from adequate, given the extent of the seasonal distress. According to the observed extent of food deprivation during monga, a large number of extremely vulnerable households appear to have been left out of the social safety-net system.

Membership in the government safety-net programs mentioned above does not necessarily guarantee receipt of support during the monga season. The data available from the InM baseline survey do not directly provide information regarding this receipt. But we can get some idea by looking at whether the households with membership in those selected government programs actually received support from *any* government or NGO programs during the monga season (table 7.3). For this analysis, the safety-net programs are grouped as short term (FFW and Test Relief) and long term (VGD and VGF and Old Age Allowance). This grouping is not entirely satisfactory, however, because VGF is actually a short-term program but is lumped together in the InM survey with VGD, which is a long-term program.

The estimates in table 7.3 show that, among the households receiving support during monga (31.6 percent), only about one-third were members of the government-run safety-net programs noted above, suggesting that the remaining households received support from the programs run by NGOs (and other relatively minor government programs). Moreover, about one-third of the members of the long-term or year-round government programs and one-half of the members of short-term programs did not receive safety-net support from *any* sources during monga. This means that even higher proportions of these households did not receive support during monga from those selected government programs in which they reported participation, because some of them are likely to have received support from other sources, mainly NGOs. The suggestion is that not all short-term programs are targeted to the monga season and that the payments of benefits even under the year-round programs may sometimes skip the monga season. The programs do not thus appear to be seasonally sensitive.

Next, this section examines how the meal consumption status of households varies by membership in the safety-net programs (table 7.4). No distinction is made between short-term and long-term programs or between those households that actually received support during monga and those that did not.[12] Moreover, such a comparison of the meal consumption status cannot convey much about the effect of the safety-net programs, because the selection of beneficiaries for the programs cannot be assumed to be independent of household characteristics. These endogeneity issues regarding impact estimation will be addressed later in this chapter. For the time being, it can be noted that the proportion of households experiencing starvation during monga is found to be higher among participant households (about 50 percent) compared with their

Table 7.3 Distribution of Households by Membership in Selected Government Safety-Net Programs and Actual Receipt of Support during Monga

Whether or not support received during monga	Members of long-term programs only (%)	Members of short-term programs only (%)	Members of both types of programs (%)	Nonmembers (%)	All (%)	Number of observations
Support received during monga	5.3	0.7	0.1	25.5	31.6	328,601
Support not received during monga	2.7	0.8	0	67.9	71.4	152,317
Total	8.0	1.5	0.1	90.4	100.0	480,918
Number of observations	38,476	7,143	695	434,604	480,918	

Source: Khandker, Khaleque, and Samad 2011.

Note: Long-term programs are Vulnerable Group Development, Vulnerable Group Feeding, and Old Age Allowance, whereas Test Relief and Food for Work are short-term programs.

Table 7.4 Meal Consumption Status during Monga and Non-monga Periods among Members and Nonmembers of Selected Government Safety-Net Programs

Period	Starvation		Meal rationing		Full meal	
	Members	Nonmembers	Members	Nonmembers	Members	Nonmembers
Monga	49.9	46.1	46.1	49.3	4.0	4.6
	(0.002)**		(0.002)**		(0.0006)**	
Non-monga	7.3	9.2	53.6	49.6	39.2	41.3
	(0.0009)**		(0.002)**		(0.002)**	

Source: Institute of Microfinance baseline survey, 2006.

Note: The safety-net programs include those in table 7.2. Figures in parentheses are standard errors of the difference. ** refers to a significance level of 5 percent of better.

counterpart nonparticipants (about 46 percent). Thus, whatever may be the extent of the beneficial effect of these programs, they seem to target the relatively more vulnerable among the generally poor households.[13] This is at least one positive aspect of these programs despite their inadequate coverage and inequitable area targeting discussed earlier.

Further insights regarding safety-net support can be gained by looking at the patterns of monga coping mechanisms adopted by the households. Table 7.5 shows the distribution of households by type of coping mechanism for households that received safety-net support and those that did not. Unlike the previous tables, here the recipients of safety-net support include those who actually received such support during the monga period from the government or NGOs. The striking feature of these estimates is that the beneficiaries of safety nets adopted each of the coping mechanisms in larger proportions compared with the rest of the households. It is clear that because of the small support from safety nets, the vulnerable households had to combine other coping methods to mitigate monga.

Seasonal migration was by far the most commonly adopted coping mechanism among both groups of households: 39 percent among the beneficiaries of safety nets and 35 percent among the others. Safety nets may in fact help seasonal migration by providing some support to the households in the absence of their working members. However, the more remarkable aspect of these estimates is that the incidence of the so-called

Table 7.5   Coping Mechanisms Adopted during Monga by Recipients and Nonrecipients of Safety-Net Benefits

percent

Coping mechanism	Among recipients of safety-net benefits	Among nonrecipients of safety-net benefits
Advance sale of labor	6.0	3.6
Advance sale of crop	0.5	0.5
Sale of asset	14.5	9.9
Out-migration	38.6	34.8
Borrowing from informal sources	15.9	10.7
Borrowing from formal or semi-formal sources	6.5	5.5
Any coping mechanism	57.2	49.1
Number of observations	152,317	328,601

Source: Khandker, Khaleque, and Samad 2011.
Note: Safety-net benefits are those actually received during monga from the government or from nongovernment organizations.

erosive coping mechanisms, such as asset sale or advance labor sale, was also higher among the beneficiaries of safety nets compared with others. This suggests that the extent of safety-net support was not adequate enough even to avoid the coping mechanisms that are adopted only under severe distress. In the absence of such support, the situation of the households could have been, of course, even more desperate. This finding also suggests that the households that received the safety-net benefits seem to be relatively more vulnerable among the entire sample of poor households. This corroborates the earlier finding regarding the targeting of the government safety-net programs.

Determinants of Access to Safety Nets

This section examines various factors that might determine whether or not a household would receive safety-net benefits. One important criterion used to identify the extreme poor in Bangladesh is the size of land-holding—namely, households that have fewer than 50 decimals (half an acre) of land are the extreme poor. When this criterion is applied to the InM baseline survey, more than 98 percent of the sample households are included. However, with regard to receiving the benefits of the safety-net programs during the monga period, less than one-third of the sample households actually received such benefits. This may have less to do with targeting efficiency than with the fact that safety-net resources are mea-ger; there is simply not enough to provide for all who deserve them. Nevertheless, it may be worthwhile to examine whether, even among the extreme poor, some households are more likely than others to access safety-net benefits.

Because of the binomial nature of whether or not a household received safety-net benefits (s), the probability of receiving such benefits may be estimated by a probit model as given by

$$prob(s = 1) = \int_{-\infty}^{\beta x} \phi(t)dt = \Phi(\beta x), \tag{7.1}$$

where ϕ and Φ are the normal density distribution function and cumulative normal distribution function, respectively; x is a vector of household and community characteristics; and β is the vector of parameters that needs to be determined. Both household and village characteristics are likely to affect the receipt of safety-net benefits during the monga season.

Among the determining factors at the household level, we consider household assets of different types, such as dependency ratio, age of the household head, nature of employment, and so on. The community-level variables include village access to microcredit and the village-level unemployment rate.[14] Moreover, some area characteristics are included that can affect households' vulnerability to monga and the outreach of safety-net resources to them, namely, the average yearly rainfall at the *upazila* level and the proportion of high land in the upazila, as well as if the village is in a char area.[15] Finally, we control for local (*union* level) unobserved area characteristics that may influence the probability of receiving safety-net benefits during the monga season.

The probit results of equation (7.1) are reported in table 7.6. The table also presents the descriptive statistics of the major explanatory variables used in the regression. In the interpretation of the implications of the results, a few caveats should be kept in mind. The exercise is based on the information on all safety-net support received during monga, whether from the government or NGOs. Lumping together all the safety-net programs is problematic in that the various programs are targeted to households with varying characteristics because of the specific objectives of the programs. Moreover, the targeting of government programs may be influenced by factors that may not apply to NGO programs. Also, there is likely to be some degree of randomness in beneficiary selection when the coverage of the programs falls far short of the numbers of households in need of support. It is remarkable that in spite of these caveats, the statistical exercise yields a number of results that are both meaningful and statistically significant.

Household-level variables such as the age and employment status of the household head and the ownership of nonagricultural assets are found to matter in terms of accessing social safety-net support. For example, a household with a self-employed head is less likely to receive safety-net benefits, while wage employment has the opposite effect. The self-employment status of the household head reduces the probability of receiving safety-net benefits during monga by about 10 percent. With regard to ownership of assets, owning nonagricultural assets lowers the likelihood of receiving safety-net benefits by 3 percent. As discussed in earlier chapters, the households with a wage-employed head are generally more vulnerable to starvation during monga compared with those with a self-employed head, and self-employment, particularly in the nonfarm sector, can have beneficial counterseasonal effects on the livelihoods of the poor.[16] The above results thus suggest that the targeting of

Table 7.6   Probit Estimates of Receipt of Safety-Net Support during Monga

Explanatory variables	Marginal effects	Mean of explanatory variables
Age of household head (years)	0.021**	40.0
	(0.001)	(12.7)
Age of household head squared	−0.0002**	40.0
	(0.00001)	(12.7)
Dependency ratio	0.031	0.63
	(0.024)	(0.21)
Log of land asset (decimal)	0.296	8.20
	(0.182)	(12.59)
Self-employed household head	−0.103**	0.16
	(0.007)	(0.37)
Wage-employed household head	0.012**	0.54
	(0.005)	(0.50)
Household with agricultural asset	−0.017	0.49
	(0.013)	(0.50)
Household with nonagricultural asset	−0.030**	0.13
	(0.013)	(0.34)
Household with cash savings	0.049**	0.34
	(0.010)	(0.47)
Household with livestock	0.015	0.26
	(0.010)	(0.44)
Village with microcredit programs	−0.003	0.97
	(0.030)	(0.18)
Village-level unemployment rate	0.115**	0.30
	(0.033)	(0.24)
Proportion of high lands in upazila	0.465**	0.81
	(0.137)	(0.08)
Average annual rainfall in upazila (mm)	0.018**	198.55
	(0.002)	(6.62)
Village located in char area	−0.005	0.19
	(0.024)	(0.39)
Proportion of high lands in upazila × Log land asset (decimals)	−0.017**	—
	(0.007)	
Average annual rainfall in upazila (mm) × Log land asset (decimals)	−0.006**	—
	(0.001)	
Village located in char area × Log land asset (decimals)	−0.009**	—
	(0.001)	
Pseudo R^2	0.050	
Log likelihood	−285,258.5	
Number of observations	480,918	

Source: Khandker, Khaleque, and Samad 2011.

Notes: Regression additionally includes union dummies to control for unobserved union-level effects. Figures in parentheses are standard deviations for the column of mean of variables and standard errors for the column of marginal effects. ** refers to a statistical significance of 5 percent or better; mm = millimeter; — = not applicable.

the safety-net programs was generally in conformity with the risks of food insecurity during monga.

In terms of area characteristics, households from a village with a high unemployment rate are found more likely to receive support than those from a village with a low unemployment rate. The results are, however, less encouraging when one views targeting with respect to other area characteristics. Thus, areas with higher rainfall as well as areas with more high lands (both characteristics indicate better agricultural opportunities) are likely to receive more benefits compared with other areas. Also, the vulnerability of households living in the adverse agroecological conditions of the char land does not seem to influence decisions about targeting of support during monga. However, once the safety-net programs are in place—whether in high land areas, areas with high rainfall, or char land—the chance of receiving safety-net benefits decreases with an increase in the size of land owned by a household (as can be seen from the regression coefficients of the interaction of land asset with the respective area characteristic). These findings, therefore, further confirm that safety-net programs perform rather poorly in targeting vulnerable areas, but once the villages have access to such programs, the relatively more vulnerable among the poor households are likely to benefit more.

Evaluating the Effect of Social Safety Nets on Seasonal Hunger

The findings so far give some idea about the relative situation of households that received safety-net benefits compared with those that did not and about the possible determining factors in accessing such benefits. However, these findings cannot indicate the extent to which safety-net programs were effective in lowering food deprivation for the households that received the benefits. For a determination of the effect of safety-net programs, it is important to control for a host of other factors (both observed and unobserved) that determine households' food deprivation. Moreover, among the sample households, access to safety-net benefits is not randomly given, but depends on many factors, including both household and area characteristics. These same factors are also important in determining a household's situation regarding food deprivation. The estimation of the program effect must therefore tackle the problem of joint dependence of households' food deprivation and access to safety nets on the same factors, both observed and unobserved.

To solve the problem of estimating the net effect of the safety-net benefits after controlling for simultaneous determination of receiving such benefits, we use an endogenous switching regression method as proposed by Maddala (1983) and extended by Lokshin and Sajaia (2004).[17] The details of this estimation methodology were discussed in chapter 6 in this volume, while the effect of migration on households' food deprivation was estimated and need not be repeated here (see annex to chapter 6).

Essentially, all sample households are divided into those that received safety-net benefits during monga and those that did not, and then equations are estimated for food deprivation status for each household group by using various household and community characteristics. By switching the estimated parameters between the equations for the two groups, we can then estimate the counterfactuals, that is, what would have been the food deprivation status of the beneficiary households if they had no access to safety nets (and, similarly for the nonbeneficiaries if they could have accessed safety net benefits)? However, as a control for the endogeneity of access to safety-nets, the outcome equations are run after controlling for the selection biases distinguishing the two groups.[18] The effect of safety nets can then be estimated by differencing these "conditional" outcomes with and without the receipt of the benefits. This can be done for both beneficiary and nonbeneficiary groups, but for the latter group, the estimated effect of safety nets is, of course, in the nature of a counterfactual.

Table 7.7 reports the estimates of the potential benefits of safety-net programs. The benefits are shown in terms of the reduction in the probability of experiencing different extents of food deprivation, in the monga and the non-monga periods and year round. As in the previous chapters, the year-round or overall food deprivation status is defined in the following way: starvation means experiencing starvation during any period of the year (that is, during either the monga or the non-monga period); meal rationing means having to ration meals during at least one period, but avoiding starvation in all periods; and the rest of the households have full meals during both monga and non-monga periods.

The results clearly show that safety-net benefits lower the seasonal hardship for both recipient and nonrecipient households. The expected reduction in starvation during monga for recipient households is 4.4 percentage points (which are actually accrued to them), and for non-recipient households, it is 2.5 percentage points (which would have accrued to them had they received safety-net benefits). Moreover, general food deprivation (for example, starvation or food rationing) during the monga period declines by 3.9 percentage points for the recipient

Table 7.7   Effect of Receipt of Support during Monga on Household Food Deprivation

Household type	Extreme hardship (starvation)	All hardships (starvation or food rationing)
During monga period		
Recipients of support during monga	−0.044**	−0.039**
	(0.0002)	(0.0001)
Nonrecipients of support during	−0.025**	−0.052**
monga	(0.0001)	(0.00003)
During non-monga period		
Recipients of support during monga	−0.044**	−0.030**
	(0.0002)	(0.0001)
Nonrecipients of support during	−0.032**	−0.011**
monga	(0.0001)	(0.0002)
Year round or overall		
Recipients of support during monga	−0.038**	−0.015**
	(0.0002)	(0.0002)
Nonrecipients of support during	−0.024**	−0.045**
monga	(0.0001)	(0.00003)

Source: Khandker, Khaleque, and Samad 2011.
Note: Results are based on the switching regression method discussed in the text. The year-round/overall status is as defined in the earlier discussions. Figures in parentheses are robust standard errors. ** refers to a statistical significance of 5 percent or bettter. The number of observations is 480,918.

households and 5.2 percentage points for nonrecipient households as a result of receiving safety-net benefits.

A noteworthy aspect of the results is that the accrued benefit to recipient households is higher than that for nonrecipient households with regard to avoiding extreme hardship or starvation. But for general food deprivation, nonrecipients would likely have benefited more had they received such benefits. This points to the underlying differences between the recipient and nonrecipient households. However, regardless of the household types, benefits of safety-net programs on seasonal food deprivation have been unequivocally established in this exercise.

In extending the analysis to estimation of the potential effects on non-monga outcomes, we find that the receipt of safety-net benefits during the monga season has a beneficial effect for other seasons as well. This finding could have alternative explanations. Although the exercise is based on safety-net benefits received during the monga season only, there may be a positive spillover effect during other seasons. More plausibly, the positive non-monga effect may arise from the fact that the households that receive safety-net benefits during monga are also more likely than others to receive such benefits in non-monga seasons. This is obviously the case for the cardholder members of the year-round programs. Whatever may be the case, the results show that safety-net programs can have beneficial effects on both transitory and year-round food deprivation.

Concluding Remarks

Bangladesh has a fairly large and elaborate social safety-net system aimed at safeguarding the economic security of the poor and vulnerable groups. This chapter has examined in particular the seasonal dimensions of the effect of safety-net programs.

An important consideration in this respect is an appropriate balance between short-term seasonally oriented programs and long-term or year-round programs Although a predominant part of the existing safety-net system in Bangladesh consists of short-term programs, this does not mean that the system has an effective counterseasonal impact. For decisions about the timing of seasonal public works programs, such as FFW, there may be balancing considerations of providing employment during the pre-aman lean season (which partly coincides with the late rainy season and annual floods) and undertaking earthwork for infrastructure building (for which the dry season is more suitable). But more disconcerting is the survey finding from Rangpur that the payments of benefits even under the year-round programs may sometimes skip the monga season, thus betraying a lack of sensitivity to seasonal distress.

Another area of concern is that, along with various forms of resource leakages, a sizable share of the benefits goes to the nonpoor. Yet another weak link in channeling safety-net resources to the poor appears to be the process used by the government to allocate resources across regions, which corresponds poorly with the regional variations in poverty levels. To the extent that the programs have pro-poor targeting (that is, the poor benefit more than the nonpoor), this outcome is found to be due to pro-poor targeting *within* rather than *across* villages. The analysis of survey data from Rangpur confirms that safety-net programs perform rather poorly in targeting vulnerable areas. However, when villages have access to such programs, the relatively more vulnerable among the poor households are likely to benefit more.

Further insights into targeting and the effect of safety nets among the poor households in Rangpur can be gained when the households are divided into those that received safety net benefits during the monga season and those that did not. Compared with nonbeneficiaries, the beneficiary households were worse off in experiencing starvation during monga and had to resort more often to various coping mechanisms, including those adopted only under extreme distress. Thus, although the more vulnerable among the poor may have been targeted, the amount of support was clearly inadequate to lift these households out of extreme seasonal distress. Moreover, judged simply by the observed extent of food deprivation during monga, a large number of extremely vulnerable households were apparently overlooked by the social safety-net system.

Political competition, driven by the creation of public awareness, seems to have played a role in shaping the government's social safety-net system. Despite the general lack of sensitivity in the safety-net allocations with respect to poverty prevalence, the increased public attention given to monga in recent years may have translated into increased safety-net coverage in the Rangpur region. However, this increase in coverage may be explained in part by programs with extremely small short-term or one-time benefits. This aspect may reflect a kind of populist tokenism in the provision of safety-net benefits.

In spite of the limitations, the safety-net programs do have a positive effect on mitigating monga, as found in the statistical exercises. Moreover, there are both seasonal and year-round beneficial effects. It may be correct to argue therefore that these programs need to be expanded in coverage, made more cost-effective, and designed to be more sensitive to seasonal needs.

Notes

1. These programs include a "productivity enhancing safety net" in Ghana in the 1980s designed to promote household food security and reduce seasonal hunger gap; Food for Work and Vulnerable Group Feeding programs in Namibia in the 1990s; emergency cash transfers in Malawi in the mid-2000s in response to localized crop failures; and the "household extension packages" and cash transfers to cover a hunger gap of four to six months in Ethiopia in the mid-2000s (see also Devereux, Vatila, and Swan 2008).

2. There are differing opinions regarding how far social safety-net programs can be effective in alleviating not only transitory poverty but also persistent poverty; see, for example, Devereux (2002) and Ravallion, van de Walle, and Gautam (1995).

3. Another major safety-net program with relatively large budget allocations is Open Market Sales under which rice is sold to the urban poor at subsidized prices, but the program is not included here because of its urban orientation.

4. This amount is based on the estimated total population of 146 million of which 75 percent was rural with an average household size of 4.5 persons.

5. According to the 2005 HIES, the coverage rate was 15 percent of households in rural areas compared with 5 percent in urban areas (Narayan and Zaman 2009, 280).

6. This estimate excludes programs that cannot appropriately be called safety nets, although these are designated so in the government budget. The universal stipend program for female secondary students is an example (see PPRC and UNDP 2011, annex 4 and other annexes).

7. Amounts are estimated from the data reported in BBS (2011, 74).

8. According to 2010 HIES data, the proportions of beneficiary households in the thirty listed safety-net programs add up to nearly three times the proportion of households receiving benefits from at least one program, suggesting widespread prevalence of multiple program membership (see BBS 2011, 75).

9. Because a new administrative division has recently been created from the Rangpur region, the published results of the 2010 HIES, unlike those of the previous rounds, have separate information on this region in the regional breakdowns of the results.

10. As discussed earlier, the comparison of net monthly benefits received during the program period is not very meaningful without information regarding the duration of the year for which the benefits were received.

11. TUP is a BRAC program, and IGVGD is a particular variety of VGD program with emphasis on training for income generation.

12. This is not an entirely satisfactory comparison because the nonparticipants include those who received safety-net benefits from programs other than those listed here.

13. This result would be so if it is assumed that at worst, there would be no perceptible program effect on household food consumption status.

14. Village-level unemployment rate has been defined by the proportion of households in the village whose heads are unemployed.

15. Upazila is a subdistrict. The high land is defined by the Bangladesh Agricultural Research Council in relation to the annual flood water level. Char areas are islands and land fragments formed by river sediments, which are then inhabited by destitute people who have no other place to live.

16. See chapter 5 in this volume for the findings regarding the determining factors behind food deprivation during monga in Rangpur; see also figure 3.15 in chapter 3 in this volume for the patterns of seasonality of various types of employment.

17. Alternatively, if appropriate instrumental variables could be identified that would directly affect households' receipt of safety-net benefits, but not the

outcomes regarding food deprivation, a two-stage Heckman selection method could be used to estimate the effect of the safety nets.

18. For this exercise, the parameters of a selection model regarding participation in safety-net programs must first be estimated. The results of the entire exercise show that the outcome variable (a household's starvation status) is indeed affected by the endogeneity bias; hence, there is justification for controlling for the unobserved factors that influence a household's probability of receiving safety-net benefits in the first place.

References

Ahmed, Akhter, Agnes R. Quisumbing, Mahbuba Nasreen, John F. Hoddinott, and Elizabeth Bryan. 2009. *Comparing Food and Cash Transfers to the Ultra Poor in Bangladesh*. Research Monograph 163, Washington, DC: International Food Policy Research Institute.

Babu, Suresh Chandra. 2003. "Social Safety Nets for Poverty Reduction in South Asia–Global Experiences." *Sri Lankan Journal of Agricultural Economics* 5 (1): 1–8.

BBS (Bangladesh Bureau of Statistics). 2011. *Preliminary Report on Household Income and Expenditure Survey 2010*. Dhaka: BBS, Government of Bangladesh.

Chetty, Raj, and Adam Looney. 2006. "Consumption Smoothing and the Welfare Consequences of Social Insurance in Developing Economies." *Journal of Public Economics* 90 (12): 2351–56.

Devereux, Stephen. 2002. "Can Safety Nets Reduce Chronic Poverty?" *Development Policy Review* 20 (5): 657–75.

———. 2009. "Seasonality and Social Protection in Africa," FAC Working paper SP07, Future Agricultures Consortium, University of Sussex, Brighton, U.K.

Devereux, Stephen, Bapu Vatila, and Samuel Swan. 2008. *Seasons of Hunger: Fighting Cycles of Quiet Starvation among the World's Rural Poor*. London: Pluto Press.

Drèze, Jean, and Amartya Sen. 1989. *Hunger and Public Action*. Oxford, U.K.: Clarendon Press.

Holzmann, Robert, and Margaret Grosh. 2008. "Social Protection for the Poorest: The Position and Experience of the World Bank." Washington, DC, World Bank.

IMF (International Monetary Fund). 2005. "Bangladesh: Unlocking the Potential—National Strategy for Accelerated Poverty Reduction." IMF Country Report 05/410, IMF, Washington, DC.

Khandker, Shahidur R., M. Abdul Khaleque, and Hussain A. Samad. 2011. "Can Safety Nets Alleviate Seasonal Deprivation? Evidence from

Northwest Bangladesh." Policy Research Working Paper 5865, World Bank, Washington, DC.

Lokshin, Michael, and Zurab Sajaia. 2004. "Maximum Likelihood Estimation of Endogenous Switching Regression Models." *Stata Journal* 4 (3): 282–89.

Maddala, George S. 1983. *Limited-Dependent Qualitative Variables in Econometrics.* Cambridge, U.K.: Cambridge University Press.

Matin, Imran, and David Hulme. 2003. "Programs for the Poorest: Learning from the IGVGD Program in Bangladesh." *World Development* 31 (3): 647–65.

Narayan, Ambar, and Hassan Zaman. 2009. *Breaking Down Poverty in Bangladesh.* Dhaka: University Press Limited.

PPRC (Power and Participation Research Centre) and UNDP (United Nations Development Programme). 2011. *Social Safety Nets in Bangladesh, Vol. 1: Review of Issues and Analytical Inventory*, Dhaka: PPRC and Dhaka.

Ravallion, Martin. 2000. "Monitoring Targeting Performance When Decentralized Allocations to the Poor Are Unobserved." *World Bank Economic Review* 14 (2): 331–45.

Ravallion, Martin, Dominique van de Walle, and Madhur Gautam. 1995. "Testing a Social Safety Net." *Journal of Public Economics* 57 (2): 175–99.

World Bank and ADB (Asian Development Bank). 2003. *Bangladesh Public Expenditure Review.* Washington, DC: World Bank.

CHAPTER 8

Microfinance to Tackle Seasonality

There is an increasing debate on the role of microfinance in development: Is microfinance a financial service or a social safety-net program? Those who believe microfinance is a business model offering financial services on a commercial basis do not want to give prominence to the social safety-net aspects of microfinance. Those who see the role of microfinance as being important in consumption smoothing and extreme poverty reduction argue that microfinance is a part of social protection strategies. Whatever the merits of this debate, microfinance has carved out its own market through a strategy that mitigates the moral hazards of lending by adopting innovative methods, such as group-based lending.[1] Microfinance is no doubt a financial service. Yet by simply targeting the poor—especially women, who are often excluded from regular financial institutions because of insufficient physical collateral—microfinance serves the underserved poor. Therefore, it has a role to play in poverty reduction by releasing a borrowing constraint in household resource allocation.

However, findings from several countries do not support the expected poverty reduction aspect of microfinance. But several other studies from a number of countries, including Bangladesh, demonstrate that microfinance reduces poverty. For example, a seven-year study carried out in Bangladesh suggests that even if gains from microfinance are not necessarily large, microcredit reduces extreme poverty more than moderate poverty (Khandker 2005).

Microfinance also helps stabilize income and consumption fluctuations, thereby playing a social safety-net service. For example, even if microfinance does not lend much to agriculture, the poor with microcredit support initiate income-earning activities mostly in the rural nonfarm sectors, which are subject to the same covariate risk affecting agricultural production. Research shows that households unable to smooth consumption because of income seasonality are more likely to participate in microcredit programs, which promote income-earning activities in rural nonfarm sectors that are less vulnerable to seasonality than those in the farming sector. In this way, borrowers are helped in smoothing consumption and thus reducing vulnerability to seasonal consumption. Pitt and Khandker (2002, 21) find that production credit helps smooth seasonal consumption by financing new productive activities whose "income flows and time demands do not seasonally co-vary with income generated by existing activities of households." Microfinance is seen to help households absorb shocks, such as the death of a family member or a natural disaster resulting in plummeting income and consumption. Microfinance therefore acts as a social protection scheme as well as a scheme for providing financial services to the poor.

This chapter focuses on the role of microfinance in addressing seasonality of income and poverty, including seasonal food deprivation. In recent years, microfinance has been criticized for not reaching a large percentage of the ultrapoor (Datta 2004; Webb, Coates, and Houser 2002).[2] In Bangladesh, despite the country's overwhelmingly large proportion of ultrapoor, microfinance reaches not more than 20 percent of that population (Khandker 1998, 2005). Similarly, microfinance has limited coverage in ecologically vulnerable areas, such as the northwest region of Bangladesh (Khandker 2009), where the incidence of poverty is high, much higher than in other regions.[3]

Questions then arise: Why don't the ultrapoor participate in microfinance? Why is a small share of the microfinance portfolio in areas such as the northwest region, which features pronounced income seasonality? Does income seasonality reinforce extreme poverty and, as a result, the limited coverage of microfinance in the seasonally pronounced northwest region? Is a microfinance program different from what is currently available needed to tackle both income seasonality and extreme poverty?

Addressing extreme poverty or pronounced seasonality of income is a formidable task for any institution, let alone a microfinance institution.

When poverty is already rampant, pronounced seasonality of income and consumption only makes poverty worse. Therefore, tackling both seasonality and poverty with a single intervention, such as microfinance, is a major challenge for policy makers. Yet a large body of literature shows that the observed seasonality in consumption is driven mainly by the seasonal variation in income and that lack of access to credit impedes consumption smoothing, often among the poor (Chaudhuri and Paxson 2002; Paxson 1993; Rosenzweig 1988; Rosenzweig and Wolpin 1993). However, if the risk is idiosyncratic (that is, specific to certain households), then local risk pooling or insurance is feasible, which becomes limited in the event of an aggregate shock (Townsend 1995). The development literature indicates that better access to institutional finance is a useful approach for better allocation of resources under seasonality of agriculture (Rosenzweig and Binswanger 1993).

If lack of access to credit causes households not to smooth consumption or allocate resources efficiently, then both seasonal and extreme poverty are caused, in part, by a lack of access to institutional credit. Introducing a microfinance program that targets the extreme poor and that is designed to tackle pronounced income seasonality is perhaps a way to make a dent in both seasonal and chronic poverty.

In recent years, with donor assistance and under government pressure, some microfinance institutions (MFIs) in Bangladesh have introduced a variety of programs to better handle seasonality and extreme poverty. In 2002, the Bangladesh Rural Advancement Committee (BRAC), Bangladesh's leading nongovernmental organization (NGO), launched a multidimensional microcredit program targeting the ultrapoor (Emran, Robano, and Smith 2009; Matin and Hulme 2003).[4] BRAC's ultrapoor program emphasizes both human and physical capital development through transferring assets and other means, such as skills-based training, before the ultrapoor graduate to become members of its regular microfinance program. Similar programs introduced by Grameen Bank target the ultrapoor, such as beggars. Many MFIs, including Grameen Bank, have introduced seasonal loans as part of their regular microfinance programs to address seasonality of income.

In 2006, the Palli Karma-Sahayak Foundation (PKSF), the country's premier wholesale MFI, introduced a major microfinance program—the Programmed Initiatives for Monga Eradication (PRIME).[5] PRIME's objective is to deal exclusively with the extreme poor, who are highly vulnerable to seasonal poverty, especially in the Rangpur region. PRIME offers the ultrapoor microcredit and other services on flexible terms.

This chapter addresses whether a program such as PRIME can achieve the goal of reducing both extreme poverty and seasonal poverty. More specifically, this chapter (a) evaluates the extent to which PRIME's flexible microfinance program is effective in reaching the ultrapoor and seasonally poor, (b) quantifies program benefits with respect to mitigating extreme and seasonal poverty, and (c) assesses the relative effectiveness of PRIME vis-à-vis regular microfinance in reducing extreme and seasonal poverty.

Why Choose PRIME to Tackle Seasonality of Income and Poverty?

As discussed in chapters 3 and 4 in this volume, those who suffer most from seasonal deprivation are mainly the extreme poor, who have few assets and scarce savings with which to smooth consumption during lean periods. Because they lack access to credit markets, they are unable to borrow against future income. Without well-functioning credit markets, households frequently attempt to smooth consumption during *monga* by drawing on informal credit market arrangements, known locally as *dadan*. Under these arrangements, laborers sell labor or farmers sell crops in advance on terms that are often severe. Households also employ traditional self-insurance methods of coping, such as use of buffer stock (livestock and grain storage), and mutual insurance, such as interfamily transfers. But for many households, these traditional methods of smoothing consumption are inadequate and inefficient.

As discussed in chapter 7 in this volume, government institutions use short-term measures, such as cash transfers, Food for Work programs, food coupons, and public works to manage monga. These safety-net measures have limited effects, which occur when variations in consumption are only transitory and idiosyncratic across households. But because monga is widespread and partly caused by structural factors, such as low productivity and lack of diversification of local economies, safety-net interventions are found to have limited success in containing monga on a sustained basis.

In addition, regular microfinance with group-based lending with a weekly repayment schedule as practiced by MFIs in Bangladesh appears to have limited scope in mitigating monga or seasonality of poverty on a sustained basis for several reasons. First, microfinance has an inherent bias against the ultrapoor, who are normally hit hard by seasonality of income and consumption. Second, the weekly repayment schedule conflicts with seasonality of income and employment, which also inhibits the ultrapoor's participation in microfinance. Third, activities generating seasonality of income often limit the ability of microcredit agencies to support new loans during lean seasons. Finally, group-based lending works well when income variations are idiosyncratic so that group members assist or insure each other through difficult times. But when seasonality is systematic, affecting everyone in a group, the ability of mutual insurance to provide help is severely curtailed, and the group as a whole has a greater incentive to collude on a strategy of default. Thus, regular microfinance is not well suited to addressing seasonality of income and poverty effectively. It is little wonder that microfinance has been less effective in reaching the extreme poor who are more seasonally poor and vulnerable than others living in a vulnerable region such as Rangpur.

To alleviate some of these concerns, the PKSF and its partners introduced PRIME as a pilot project in 2006 to address seasonal deprivation and ultrapoverty in Rangpur. Unlike regular microfinance, PRIME is a flexible microfinance program that includes both production and consumption loans and that specifically targets the ultrapoor. Unlike regular microfinance, PRIME has a flexible repayment schedule; a production loan can be used for consumption if needed; the interest rate is not more than 10 percent (compared with 20 percent for regular microfinance); and no fixed savings or weekly meetings are stipulated.

The target beneficiaries of PRIME are the ultrapoor, identified on the basis of a village census taken before the program intervention using the following criteria: (a) households have strictly fewer than 50 decimals of land, (b) household per capita monthly income does not exceed Tk 1,500 (US$25), and (c) one household member is a daily wage worker. The preprogram intervention data collected by the PKSF in 2006 reveals that, in listing the households for PRIME intervention, eligibility conditions were strictly enforced. PRIME is therefore worthy of a rigorous impact evaluation, which must determine whether the intervention is effective in mitigating seasonal deprivation and extreme poverty.

Table 8.1 shows the growth of membership, borrowers, and savings mobilized. Over a period of one and one-half years, PRIME mobilized 460,000 members, of which 90 percent were borrowers. About Tk 344.6 million was disbursed during October–December 2009, almost 15 percent of which was mobilized. PRIME achieved remarkable success in mobilizing the ultrapoor to engage in income-generating activities through microfinance in flexible terms.

In addition to flexible microfinance, PRIME offers year-round services to support income-generating activities, skills-based training, remittances,

Table 8.1   Distribution of PRIME Membership, Borrowers, Disbursement, and Savings

Time period	Membership	Disbursement (Tk, million)	Savings (Tk, million)	Savings (% of disbursement)
Up to June 2008	160,324 (71.73)	459.59	66.78	14.53
July–September 2008	189,555 (76.09)	115.92	21.31	18.38
October–December 2008	221,249 (79.52)	186.24	24.23	13.01
January–March 2009	301,788 (84.98)	343.20	33.73	9.83
April–June 2009	359,441 (87.39)	278.29	49.49	17.78
July–September 2009	403,512 (88.77)	246.71	43.27	17.54
October–December 2009	459,496 (90.14)	344.62	50.94	14.78

Source: PKSF.
Note: Figures in parentheses are percentage of borrowers among members. PRIME = Programmed Initiatives for Monga Eradication.

and primary health care (Khalily and Latif 2010). During the monga season, PRIME also provides emergency loans for consumption smoothing and cash for work related to local infrastructure development. However, PRIME does not offer consumption credit without either subsequent or prior production credit. Figure 8.1 shows the distribution of program inputs to PRIME participants in 2009. PRIME offers a number of services other than mobilizing loans and savings. As figure 8.1 shows, although half the PRIME members sought lending services (48.9 percent), its program activities included health services (40.7 percent) followed by skills-based training (7.5 percent), emergency loan services (2.2 percent), and remittance services (0.6 percent).

Important to the identification of appropriate policies is an understanding of the extent of the seasonal nature of poverty vis-à-vis chronic poverty. Although transient or seasonal poverty may be addressed by offering credit and bolstering safety nets that stabilize income and consumption, the roots of chronic poverty are deeper and must be addressed through long-term investments in human and physical capital (for example, Jalan and Ravallion 2000). Therefore, the evaluation of PRIME must examine whether the provision of credit, along with other nonfinancial services, is capable of addressing both the human and the physical capital

Figure 8.1   Distribution of Program Inputs to PRIME Participants, 2009

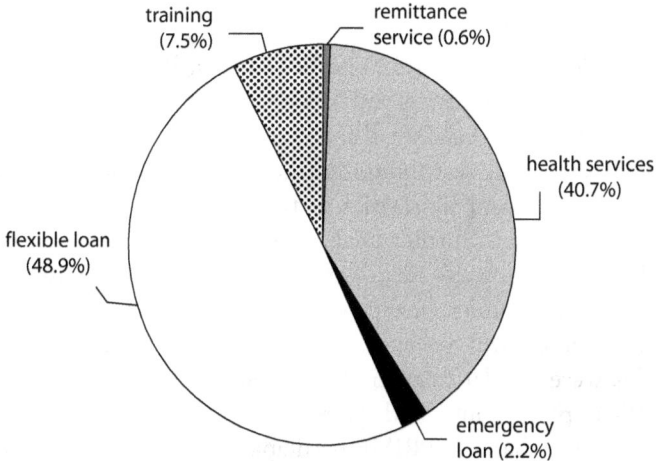

training
(7.5%)

remittance
service (0.6%)

health services
(40.7%)

flexible loan
(48.9%)

emergency
loan (2.2%)

Source: Authors' calculation based on InM follow-up survey 2008.
Note: PRIME = Programmed Initiatives for Monga Eradication.

needs of the ultrapoor for mitigating seasonal and extreme poverty in a sustainable way.

Does PRIME Handle Seasonality Better Than Regular Microfinance?

Between December 2008 and February 2009, the Institute of Microfinance (InM) administered a detailed survey that sampled target households to assess the effect of PRIME. A multistage cluster sampling technique was used to draw a random sample of 4,589 households from 16 *upazilas* (subdistricts that each comprise 10–12 *unions*), 61 unions (a union is a collection of 10–12 villages), and 271 villages from the total area that received the intervention. Interestingly, not all selected households that were eligible for the PRIME intervention participated in the second interview (two years after program intervention began). Moreover, some randomly sampled households from PRIME catchment villages participated in regular microfinance.

In addition to this sample survey of households, InM carried out a similar survey in areas of three districts that were targeted for the PRIME intervention by 2010 but had not received it by 2008–09. Of 11 upazilas in three districts, 4 were selected as control upazilas. Of the 40 villages in these four upazilas not yet covered under PRIME, 27 were selected, from which 618 PRIME-eligible households were randomly drawn on the basis of the village census. Thus, the total sample of households selected for the study was 5,207, of which 1,520 participated in PRIME, 1,718 participated in regular microfinance, and 1,968 did not participate in any program (for details, see Khandker, Khalily, and Samad 2010).

Table 8.2 shows the distribution of the 5,207 households by program participation status and by district in the greater Rangpur region. The sample distribution was further disaggregated by PRIME and non-PRIME areas. Three groups were identified by program participation status: PRIME-only, regular microfinance only, and nonparticipants (in PRIME, non-PRIME, or control villages).[6] In all areas, 33.0 percent of target households were regular microcredit program participants, 29.2 percent were PRIME participants, and 37.8 percent were nonparticipants. In PRIME areas, the shares of PRIME participants, regular microfinance participants, and nonparticipants were 33.2, 33.8, and 33.0 percent, respectively. In non-PRIME villages, 26.5 percent of the ultrapoor participated in regular microfinance, whereas 73.5 percent were nonparticipants.

Although Lalmonirhat received the earliest PRIME treatment, Kurigram had the highest percentage of PRIME participants, followed by Nilphamari, Lalmonirhat, Rangpur, and Gaibandha (table 8.2). Interestingly, Lalmonirhat has high participation in regular microfinance programs (36.9 percent), second only to Gaibandha.

Table 8.3 presents descriptive statistics of major outcomes by program participation status for the 2008–09 survey of 5,207 households. Of particular importance are the poverty and seasonal deprivation measures. Two measures of poverty (moderate and extreme) are calculated and presented in table 8.3 using the year-round consumption data. The extent of both dimensions of poverty is about the same for all three categories of households. For example, the share of moderate poverty is 86.1 percent among the regular microfinance participants, compared with 87.1 percent among PRIME participants and 89.2 percent among nonparticipants.

By contrast, among regular microcredit programs, 67.6 percent are extremely poor, compared with 67.5 percent among PRIME participants and 72.7 percent among nonparticipants; that is, among the targeted ultrapoor, participants in both regular and PRIME microcredit programs are slightly better off than nonparticipants.

As table 8.3 shows, the year-round subjective measure of food deprivation (either starvation or meal rationing) is 94.5 percent for all households, compared with 69.5 percent of extreme poverty among the same

Table 8.2 Household Participation Rates in Major Monga Intervention Programs

percent

Program type	Gaibandha district	Kurigram district	Lalmonirhat district	Nilphamari district	Rangpur district	All districts
PRIME area						
PRIME	28.7	39.7	31.9	36.3	29.9	33.2
Regular microfinance	37.2	30.0	36.9	25.5	35.5	33.8
Nonparticipants	34.1	30.3	31.2	38.2	34.6	33.0
Number of observations	1,257	1,135	1,015	490	692	4,589
Non-PRIME area						
PRIME	0	—	—	0	0	0
Regular microfinance	6.3	—	—	31.2	25.8	26.5
Nonparticipants	93.7	—	—	68.8	74.2	73.5
Number of observations	64	0	0	314	240	618
All areas						
PRIME	27.3	39.7	31.9	22.2	22.3	29.2
Regular microfinance	35.7	30.0	36.8	27.7	33.0	33.0
Nonparticipants	37.0	30.3	31.3	50.1	44.7	37.8
Number of observations	1,321	1,135	1,015	804	932	5,207

Source: Khandker, Khalily, and Samad 2010.

Note: PRIME = Programmed Initiatives for Monga Eradication; — = not applicable.

Table 8.3   Household-Level Outcome Indicators by Program Participation

Outcome indicator	PRIME	Regular MFIs	Nonparticipants	Whole sample
Year-round outcomes				
Male employment (hours/month)	168.0	183.6	154.0	167.9
Female employment (hours/month)	41.1	33.8	30.9	34.9
Total employment (hours/month)	209.2	217.4	184.9	202.8
Per capita income (Tk/month)	963.6	1,005.9	841.6	931.4
Current savings (Tk)	90.8	192.7	53.3	110.2
Per capita food expenditure (Tk/month)	654.7	656.3	638.5	649.1
Per capita total expenditure (Tk/month)	810.3	831.7	771.4	802.6
Moderate poverty head count	0.871	0.861	0.892	0.876
Extreme poverty head count	0.675	0.676	0.727	0.695
Household with year-round starvation	0.435	0.464	0.491	0.466
Household with year-round starvation or meal rationing	0.941	0.933	0.958	0.945
Seasonal outcomes				
Employment during monga period (days/month)	24.3	25.1	20.9	23.3
Employment during non-monga period (days/month)	27.1	27.6	23.5	25.9
Per capita food expenditure during monga (Tk/month)	510.2	516.1	498.3	507.6
Per capita food expenditure during non-monga (Tk/month)	702.9	703.1	685.3	696.3
Household had starvation during monga	0.428	0.453	0.483	0.457
Household had starvation or meal rationing during monga	0.938	0.924	0.954	0.940
Household had starvation during non-monga	0.022	0.019	0.022	0.021
Household had starvation or meal rationing during non-monga	0.733	0.739	0.820	0.768
Number of observations	1,520	1,717	1,970	5,207

Source: Khandker, Khalily, and Samad 2010.

Note: MFI = microfinance institution; PRIME = Programmed Initiatives for Monga Eradication.

households. A high correlation between these two measures of depriva-tion suggests that most households that are extremely poor are likely to starve or skip meals at certain times, on either a daily or a weekly basis.

Does PRIME Reach the Seasonal and Extreme Poor?

According to the InM survey, about 62 percent of the ultrapoor in the northwest region's five districts participate in some form of microfinance. Of these, 29 percent are PRIME participants, whereas 33 percent par-ticipate in regular microfinance. However, the annual growth rate of participation among the ultrapoor is much lower for regular microfinance (3.3 percent) than for PRIME (11.2 percent) (figure 8.2).[7]

Figure 8.2 shows the microcredit program participation rates in areas with PRIME and without PRIME. Participation in regular microfinance gradually increases over time in both PRIME and non-PRIME areas, but participation in regular microfinance is much higher in PRIME areas compared with non-PRIME areas. PRIME was introduced in areas that already had a higher rate of participation in regular microfinance among the ultrapoor. This finding is not surprising, given that PKSF's partner organizations, which introduced PRIME, were providers of regular

Figure 8.2   Cumulative Rate of Microcredit Program Participation by Year

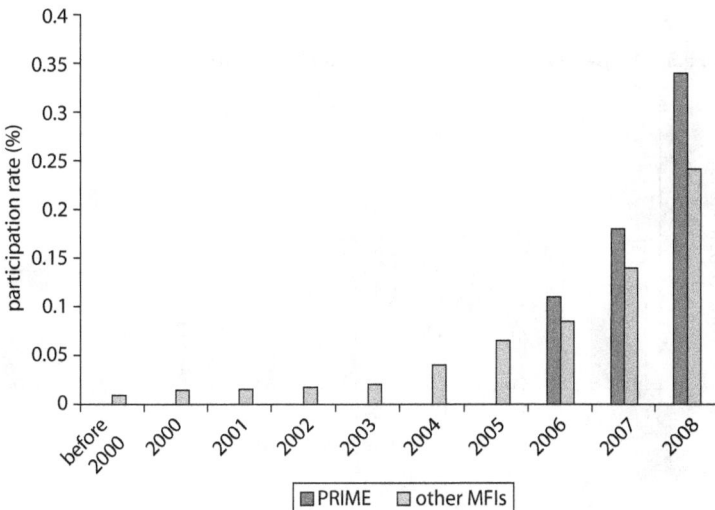

Source: Authors' calculation based on InM follow-up survey 2008.
Note: MFI = microfinance institution; PRIME = Programmed Initiatives for Monga Eradication.

microfinance before PRIME was introduced by PKSF. Because PKSF provides grants and loans on better, more flexible terms for PRIME than for
regular microfinance, the partner organizations understandably introduced PRIME initially in areas of their current operation. Higher participation rates of the ultrapoor with PRIME may also reflect greater demand
for PRIME services by the ultrapoor. The PRIME program is perhaps better designed than regular microfinance to reach the ultrapoor.

If we consider the distribution of ultrapoor participation by landholding,
we find that the participation rate among the landless (fewer than 5 decimals in landholdings) is slightly higher for PRIME than for regular microfinance (figure 8.3). Also, the participation rate among the ultrapoor in
regular microfinance is higher in PRIME than non-PRIME areas. For both
types of microfinance, the participation rate is about 25 percent to 30 percent among the households with more than 50 decimals in landholdings—
the official threshold for eligibility in most MFIs in Bangladesh.[8] For PRIME,
the eligibility criteria are defined not only by landholdings (ownership of
fewer than 50 decimals) but also by household members' selling of labor for
wages or household monthly incomes of less than Tk 1,500 (US$25).

The group with fewer than 50 decimals of landholdings represents
the bulk of microfinance participants (more than 93 percent of PRIME
and regular microfinance in PRIME areas) (figure 8.4). It appears that
PRIME is a well-targeted program that effectively reaches the ultrapoor
defined by landholdings.[9]

Figure 8.3   Microcredit Program Participation by Landholdings

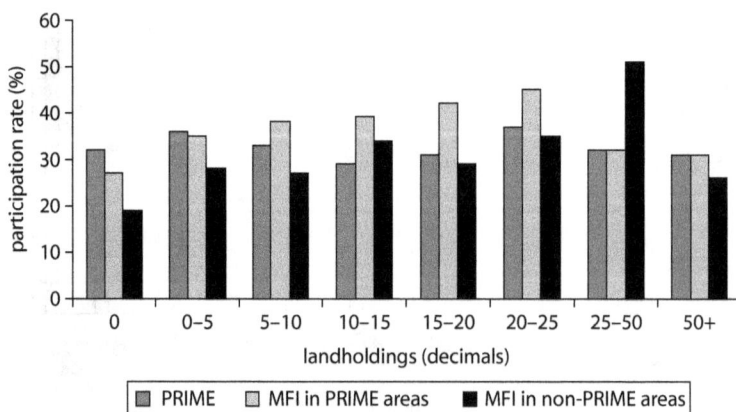

Source: Authors' calculation based on InM follow-up survey 2008.
Note: MFI = microfinance institution; PRIME = Programmed Initiatives for Monga Eradication.

Figure 8.4   Distribution of Total Microcredit Participation by Landholdings

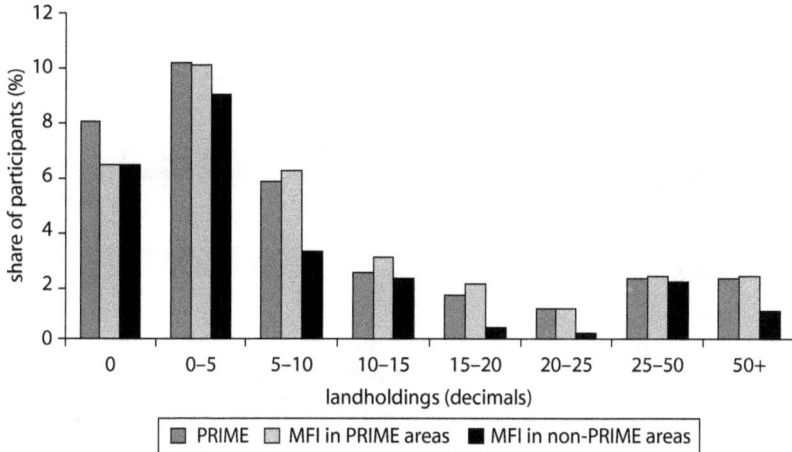

Source: Authors' calculation based on InM follow-up survey 2008.
Note: MFI = microfinance institution; PRIME = Programmed Initiatives for Monga Eradication.

Is PRIME also a well-designed program for reaching the seasonally poor who suffer from occasional starvation or experience meal rationing during the lean season? Because the baseline information on seasonal food deprivation was collected before PRIME was introduced, we can examine how households varied in program participation by their pre-PRIME participation status of food deprivation. Observation of household participation in PRIME and MFIs by meal consumption patterns during the monga period shows that, regardless of its meal-consumption pattern, a household is twice as likely to join PRIME as a regular microfinance program, which may be attributable to PRIME's focus on addressing immediate household needs during the lean season (figure 8.5).[10]

Although PRIME is a better tool than regular microfinance in reaching both the extreme poor and the seasonal poor, it is unclear whether the basic nature of seasonality in rural credit operation still exists with PRIME as well as with regular microfinance. To examine this basic fact, we present the seasonal loan disbursement of regular microfinance vis-à-vis PRIME supported by PKSF. Figure 8.6 shows the seasonal pattern of loans disbursed by the PKSF partners under regular microfinance, whereas figure 8.7 presents the seasonal distribution of loans advanced under PRIME administered only in Rangpur.

Figure 8.6 clearly shows a pronounced seasonality in microcredit operation of regular microfinance programs under PKSF. That is, the

Figure 8.5   Microcredit Program Participation Rate by Preintervention Food Consumption Status

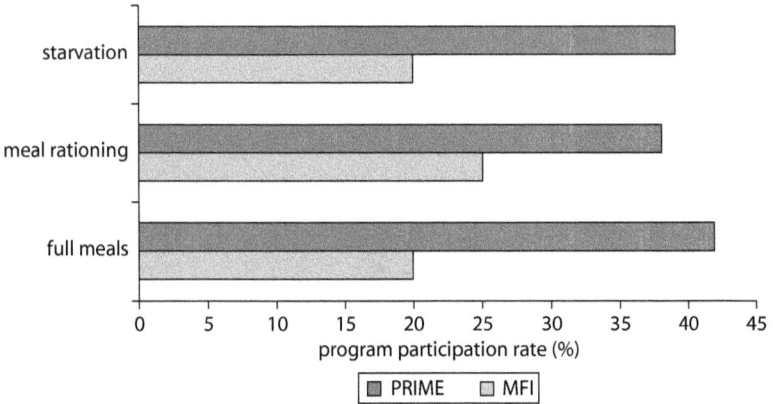

Source: Authors' calculation based on InM follow-up survey 2008.
Note: MFI = microfinance institution; PRIME = Programmed Initiatives for Monga Eradication.

Figure 8.6   Seasonal Pattern of Microcredit Disbursements under Regular Rural Microcredit Programs

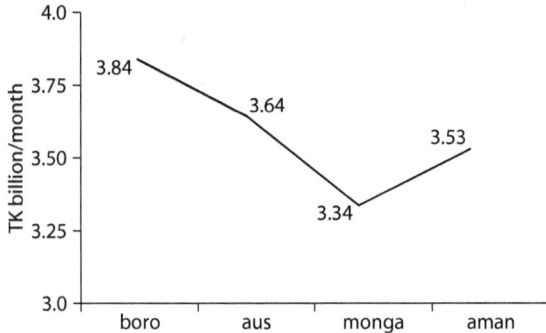

Source: Estimated from unpublished data of Palli Karma-Sahayak Foundation (PKSF).
Note: The seasons are boro (March–May), aus (June–August), monga (September–November), and aman (December–February). Figure shows five-year average from 2004/05 to 2008/09.

amount of disbursement is lowest during the monga season compared with other regions. This pattern is common for all areas of Bangladesh, including the Rangpur region. Interestingly, with the introduction of PRIME, the same seasonal patterns of actual loan disbursements (as shown in figure 8.7) indicate that PRIME is no different from regular

Figure 8.7   Seasonal Pattern of PRIME Disbursements, Rangpur Region

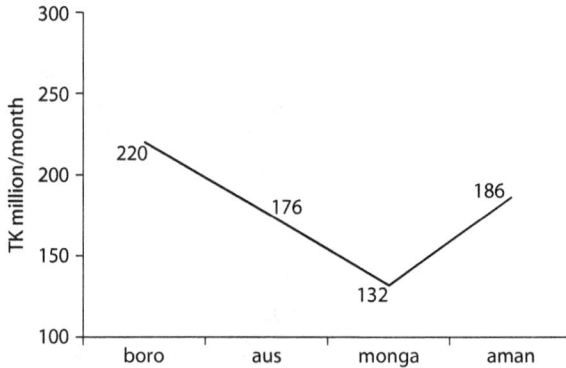

Source: Estimated from unpublished data of PKSF.
Note: The seasons are boro (March–May), aus (June–August), monga (September–November), and aman (December–February). Figure shows disbursement between March 2010 and February 2011.
PRIME = Programmed Initiatives for Monga Eradication.

microcredit in financing income-generating activities and it is not specially oriented toward meeting consumption loans (in which case, the seasonal pattern of PRIME operation would have been reversed). The fewer disbursements in the monga season may reflect fewer opportunities for starting income-generating activities in that season. The fact that there are fewer rather than more disbursements under PRIME during monga may reflect either demand-side (borrowers are not interested in taking out consumption loans) or supply-side (MFIs may ration disbursements because of their apprehension that loans may be used for consumption) lending. Whatever the case, PRIME has not proved to be primarily a vehicle for addressing seasonality of regular microcredit programs. Even with this limited scope of rural credit operation in rural areas, it is worth pursuing the relative effects of PRIME intervention vis-à-vis regular microcredit intervention in mitigating seasonal and chronic poverty.

What Determines Microcredit Program Participation?

Given the distribution of the three types of households presented in table 8.2 (PRIME, regular microfinance, and nonparticipants), we would like to identify the factors that determine the choice of participation in each of these mutually exclusive categories (1 = PRIME, 2 = regular microfinance, and 3 = nonparticipants). This determination is made by fitting a maximum-likelihood multinomial logit (MNL) model.[11]

The objective is to discover what factors (denoted by *x*) besides program availability help the ultrapoor decide to participate in one of the microfinance programs. The MNL results suggest that the explanatory variables (for example, age and gender of household head, education, landholdings, and other assets) are important in a household's decision to participate in one of the programs (table 8.4).

Participants in both PRIME and regular microfinance are relatively young. Education generally has a pronounced negative effect on participation in regular microfinance. However, educated males participate more in regular microfinance, whereas educated females do not participate in PRIME. Although land and nonland assets matter for participation in regular microfinance, they are irrelevant to PRIME participation. The

Table 8.4   Determinants of Program Participation (MNL Estimates Using Cross-Sectional Data)

Explanatory variable	PRIME	Regular microfinance
Education of household head (years)	−0.0003	−0.013**
	(0.0003)	(0.005)
Maximum education of adult males (years)	0.0003	0.011**
	(0.0003)	(0.005)
Maximum education of adult females (years)	−0.001**	0.001
	(0.0004)	(0.004)
Log land (decimals)	0.0001	0.012*
	(0.001)	(0.007)
Log nonland assets (Tk)	0.001	0.067**
	(0.0008)	(0.009)
Village has Grameen Bank	−0.005**	0.087**
	(0.002)	(0.023)
Village has other NGOs	0.005	0.302**
	(0.004)	(0.047)
Village has PRIME	0.360**	−0.012
	(0.022)	(0.020)
Village has safety-net programs	−0.0005	0.068
	(0.004)	(0.050)
Village is on *char* land	−0.002	−0.128**
	(0.002)	(0.022)
Proportion of high lands in *thana*	−0.032**	0.225
	(0.010)	(0.167)
Log likelihood		−5,076.11
Number of observations		5,202

Source: Khandker, Khalily, and Samad 2010.

Note: Coefficients are marginal impacts. Figures in parentheses are robust standard error. * and ** refer to a statistical significance of 10 percent and 5 percent or better, respectively; MNL = multinomial logit; NGO = nongovernmental organization; PRIME = Programmed Initiatives for Monga Eradication.

participation rate in regular microfinance is much lower in villages with larger populations and villages with higher male wages, reflecting a negative effect of a large local economy. These factors do not matter for PRIME participation, suggesting that PRIME is more pro-ultrapoor than is regular microfinance.

Village-level infrastructure, such as paved roads and electrification, positively influences a household's decision to participate in a microfinance program. However, better access to markets reduces the probability of PRIME participation among the ultrapoor, perhaps because of the availability of alternative employment opportunities. As expected, the presence of any type of microfinance program in a village influences the decision to participate. For example, the probability of participating in regular microfinance is 8.7 percent among the ultrapoor owing to Grameen Bank's presence, compared with 30.2 percent owing to the presence of NGOs. However, about 36 percent of the ultrapoor participate in PRIME because of a PRIME intervention. Thus, PRIME does better than regular microfinance in reaching the ultrapoor. Although Grameen Bank discourages participation in PRIME, NGO programs do not.

Agroclimatic and location-specific factors influence returns to public and private investments. It is little wonder that these factors affect the decision of the ultrapoor to join a microfinance program. Better agroclimatic conditions, such as more rainfall or greater extent of high lands, reduce the probability that the ultrapoor will join a microfinance program, perhaps because of the better alternatives available. Similarly, the probability of microfinance participation, especially regular microfinance, is much lower in *char* (reclaimed river islands) villages. Thus, regular microfinance programs are not well represented in such areas.

Does PRIME Alleviate Seasonal and Chronic Food Deprivation?

When randomized control data are unavailable, one alternative is to use a panel method at the household level to resolve the bias from unobserved characteristics influencing both program participation and the outcomes of interest. Panel analysis also helps control for common season-specific bias. For example, when we examine the incidence of starvation or meal rationing for a particular season, we may invariably introduce a common seasonal effect, such as seasonal preference that affects both the participation decision and the consumption. It is possible that a common seasonal shock could induce all households in an area to behave a certain way, independent of unobserved household heterogeneity, which would affect program participation. Household consumption may be completely independent of seasonal variations and still covary strongly with the lean season, simply because of common season-specific shocks. Resolving both sources of bias—unobserved household- and village-level heterogeneity and common seasonal effects—requires season-specific household panel data.

We have preintervention baseline information for the target and non-target households from the PRIME villages. However, the data have limited information on both explanatory variables and outcomes. Figure 8.8 presents the distribution of seasonal outcomes in 2005 and 2008 with the pre- and postintervention data.

In the baseline data, we have only subjective measures of food deprivation by season as outcomes.[12] In figure 8.8, we see that household welfare measured by food deprivation improves between 2005 and 2008. For example, the rate of occasional starvation during the lean (monga) season declined from 50.1 percent in 2005 to 45.2 percent in 2008, whereas the

Figure 8.8   Progress in Seasonal and Chronic Food Deprivation, 2005 and 2008

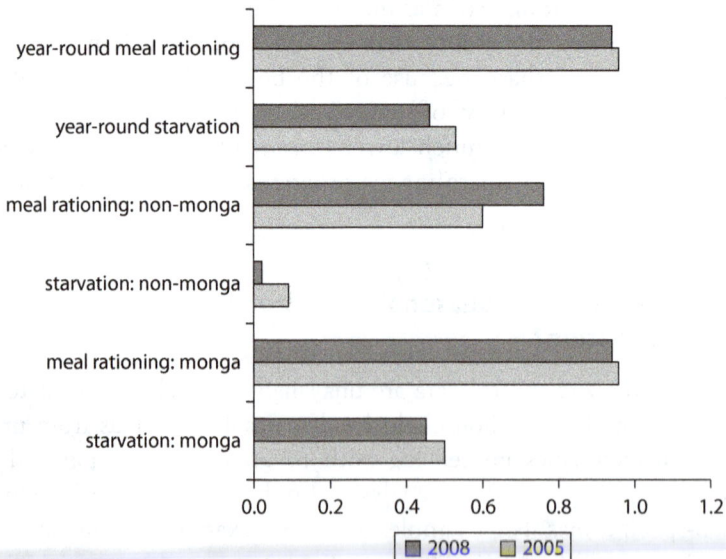

Source: Authors' calculation based on InM baseline and follow-up surveys, 2006 and 2008.

rate of occasional starvation during the non-monga season also decreased from 9.3 percent in 2005 to 2.3 percent in 2008. Year-round starvation similarly declined over this period.

Assuming that outcomes before and after program intervention are only for change in program participation status, we may rely on the difference-in-differences (DID) method that compares the difference of the changes in outcomes of PRIME participants with the changes of nonparticipants over 2005 and 2008. Table 8.5 provides the calculations. However, we find that none of the differences of outcomes of program participants over the nonparticipants is statistically significant. That is, there seem to be no statistically significant gains in the reduction in seasonal and chronic starvation by simply participating in a program such as PRIME.

However, the simple DID analysis does not control for changes in other exogenous variables affecting program participation and seasonal and chronic outcomes. To control for those changes, we propose to use a fixed-effects (FE) method to estimate the program effect (see the annex of this chapter for details). The FE results are presented in table 8.6. We find that PRIME reduces seasonal starvation by 5.5 percentage points during the lean season, compared with a 3.9 percentage point reduction as a result of the participation in regular microfinance.

Similarly, PRIME has a larger effect (7.2 percentage points) than regular microfinance programs (positive 3.5 percentage points which is statistically insignificant) on mitigating year-round starvation. But regular microfinance has a larger role than PRIME in mitigating food deprivation generally (that is, when starvation and meal rationing are combined). Because the incidence of meal rationing is much higher than that of occasional starvation, we conclude that regular microfinance has a relatively larger effect on reducing food rationing than starvation.[13]

Concluding Remarks

Microfinance is often criticized for not adequately addressing both seasonal and extreme poverty in Bangladesh and elsewhere. In response to such criticism, MFIs have introduced innovations in program design to address both concerns. In Bangladesh, one such program, designed and implemented by PKSF is the PRIME initiative. Begun in 2006, PRIME targets the northwest region's ultrapoor, who are most vulnerable to seasonality of income, employment, and consumption. The program essentially offers microfinance services on flexible terms. For example, PRIME

Table 8.5 PRIME Effects Using Difference-in-Difference (DID) Technique

Outcome variable (meal consumption pattern)	Participants		Nonparticipants		DID (effects)
	2005 (Y_P^0)	2008 (Y_P^1)	2005 (Y_{NP}^0)	2008 (Y_{NP}^1)	
Starvation during monga	0.475666	0.422936	0.507635	0.460542	–0.00564
Starvation or meal rationing during monga	0.475666	0.507339	0.458369	0.478111	0.011932
Starvation during non-monga	0.10101	0.019266	0.092193	0.023906	–0.01346
Starvation or meal rationing during non-monga	0.482094	0.695413	0.513973	0.742512	–0.01522
Year-round starvation	0.508257	0.429958	0.532546	0.471198	–0.01755
Year-round starvation or meal rationing	0.952294	0.933028	0.966878	0.943836	0.003775
Number of observations	1,492	3,025	1,492	3,025	4,517

Source: Authors' calculation based on InM baseline and follow-up surveys, 2006 and 2008.

Note: DID (difference-in-difference) = $\left[\left(Y_P^1 - Y_P^0\right) - \left(Y_{NP}^1 - Y_{NP}^0\right)\right]$. All the differences are statistically insignificant. PRIME = Programmed Initiatives for Monga Eradication.

Table 8.6   Program Effects Using Fixed-Effects Method

	p-weighted FE	
Meal consumption pattern	PRIME	Regular microfinance
Starvation during monga	−0.055**	0.039
	(0.025)	(0.025)
Starvation or meal rationing during monga	−0.002	−0.008**
	(0.002)	(0.003)
Starvation during non-monga	−0.009	−0.005
	(0.011)	(0.011)
Starvation or meal rationing during non-monga	−0.111**	−0.055*
	(0.028)	(0.028)
Year-round starvation	−0.072**	0.035
	(0.025)	(0.023)
Year-round starvation or meal rationing	−0.002	−0.004**
	(0.002)	(0.002)
Number of observations	4,517	

Source: Khandker, Khalily, and Samad 2010.
Note: Regression uses all explanatory variables listed in table 8.4. Figures in parentheses are robust standard errors.
* and ** refer to a statistical significance of 10 percent and 5 percent or better, respectively. FE = fixed-effects; PRIME = Programmed Initiatives for Monga Eradication.

provides consumption loans to address consumption seasonality, whereas regular MFIs offer seasonal production loans to deal with seasonality.

This chapter evaluates the effectiveness of PRIME, relative to regular microfinance, in tackling seasonal and extreme poverty in Bangladesh's northwest region. Our research suggests that microfinance generally has reached a large percentage of the ultrapoor and seasonal poor in recent years. It was found that about 62 percent of the ultrapoor participate in microfinance. In contrast, 59 percent of the ultrapoor who experience occasional starvation and 63 percent of the ultrapoor with meal rationing are beneficiaries of microfinance. The introduction of PRIME has only enhanced the ultrapoor's participation in microfinance. However, PRIME program placement and participation are not randomly given but are determined by a host of factors, including prior availability of a regular microfinance program.

Evaluating the program's effect thus requires correction for the non-random placement and participation of a microfinance program. An experimental evaluation design was beyond the scope of this chapter. Therefore, a quasi-experimental method was adopted to estimate the program's effect. The household FE method yields encouraging results for program participation.

Both PRIME and MFIs are found to reduce seasonal deprivation. PRIME reduces seasonal deprivation by 5.5 percentage points, compared with 3.9 percentage points with regular microfinance. However, PRIME is found to reduce seasonal deprivation more than year-round deprivation. Yet the relative impact estimates of alternative programs (PRIME versus MFI) are not statistically significant.

Do the results suggest that PRIME is just like a regular microfinance program? It should be noted that, despite PRIME's being a microfinance program, it is more popular than regular microfinance among the ultrapoor, perhaps because of its flexible design. This finding is evidenced by the higher PRIME participation rate among the ultrapoor in areas where both types of programs operate. Because PRIME has been in operation since only 2006, it is perhaps too early to say whether it equals or surpasses regular microfinance in tackling poverty and seasonality. It is also not possible to confirm whether PRIME or microfinance can simultaneously tackle seasonality and chronic poverty in an efficient way on a broader level.

Annex 8A: Household Fixed-Effects or Difference-in-Differences Method

With panel data available, we write the outcome equation as follows:

$$y_{ijst} = \alpha + x_{ijt}\beta + p_{ijt}\gamma + \mu_{ij} + \eta_j + \mu_s + \xi_{ijst}, \qquad (8A.1)$$

where y represents measures of starvation; x represents a vector of household and community characteristics affecting outcomes; p measures program participation status; t is year; and μ_{ij}, η_j, and μ_s are unobserved household, village, and season-specific fixed characteristics, respectively.

For the two-year period, if we take the difference of equation (8A.1) from the second to the first period, we eliminate the unobserved time-invariant household, village, and seasonal common fixed effects; that is,

$$\Delta y_{ijs} = \Delta x_{ij}\beta + \Delta p_{ij}\gamma + \Delta \xi_{ijs}, \qquad (8A.2)$$

where a fixed-effects method is used to estimate program effects on household outcomes. However, equation (8A.2) assumes that the selection bias is time invariant, in which case the changes in outcome for nonparticipants reveal the counterfactual outcome changes. Thus, the difference between the mean differences of participants and nonparticipants is the impact estimate. More formally, the FE compares treatment and comparison groups with respect to outcome changes over time relative to the outcomes observed for a preintervention baseline. The FE method allows for conditional dependence in the levels arising from additive time-invariant latent heterogeneity, after controlling for changes in exogenous variables affecting outcomes.

The household FE method may not produce consistent estimates if household-level unobservables are time varying. For example, the initial conditions may be important enough to influence the outcomes later such that the FE or difference-in-differences estimator is a biased estimate, because subsequent outcome changes are a function of initial conditions that also influenced program participation in the first place. In this case, the selection bias is not constant over time, introducing a violation of the assumptions of the FE method. It follows that controlling for the initial heterogeneity is critical to the creditability of the FE method.

Propensity-score matching is an obvious choice for cleaning out this initial heterogeneity before doing the differencing. If there is no observable heterogeneity in the differences (that is, it has been cleaned out by differencing), then there is no gain from matching on top of FE. Combining PSM for selecting the comparison group with FE can reduce (though probably not eliminate) the bias found in other evaluation methods, including single-difference matching. Because PSM optimally balances observed covariates between the treatment and comparison groups, it is the method of choice for selecting the comparison group in panel data studies. Obviously, one requires preintervention baseline information for the participants and nonparticipants, which fortunately is available for the Palli Karma-Sahayak Foundation credit intervention program.

Following Hirano, Imbens, and Ridder (2003), a weighted least-squares regression that weights nonparticipants according to their propensity score can yield a fully efficient estimator in the following regression:

$$\Delta y_{ijs} = \Delta x_{ij}\beta + \gamma T + \Delta \xi_{ijs},\qquad (8A.3)$$

where T = treatment status.

The weights to be used in the above regression are 1 for treated households and $p/(1 - p)$ for control observations, where p is the estimated p-score using the PSM method in the preprogram baseline data.

Notes

1. Besides covariate risk, rural lending is subject to problems of asymmetric information, incentive to repay, and enforcing loan contracts (Stiglitz 1990). Also, besides group-based lending, microfinance institutions adopt other innovative aspects to reduce the default cost of lending.

2. Although the terms *ultrapoor, extreme poor,* and *hardcore poor* are often used interchangeably, for targeting purposes, microfinance institutions specifically use the term *ultrapoor* on the basis of landholdings, income, and employment as defined in this chapter.

3. In 2005, only 12 percent of villages in the northwest region of Bangladesh had a Grameen Bank, compared with 34 percent in other regions of the country. It should be noted that the northwest region is the worst hit with regard to the negative consequences of extreme seasonality of agriculture.

4. Evaluations of such programs indicate that BRAC's ultrapoor program has desirable effects on the poor.

5. The term *monga* means seasonal food deprivation, as discussed in earlier chapters.

6. Although nonparticipants may include ineligible households from PRIME or control villages, they were not sampled in these surveys.

7. About 6.1 percent of PRIME participation came from those who had participated in regular microfinance. Of the 33 percent who participated in regular microfinance, about 14 percent participated before 2006 (the year PRIME was introduced); after 2006, the participation rate fell to 19 percent.

8. Only 6 percent of the participants were from this group in both types of programs.

9. We cannot say the same for regular microfinance programs, because we have incomplete data on participation that may contain households that are ineligible based on landholdings.

10. Households that were MFI members before the PRIME intervention (about 15 percent of panel households) were excluded from this figure to capture the behavior of new participants.

11. Formally, an MNL model expresses the relative probability of observing a particular value k of outcome Y compared with observing a base value as

$$\Pr(Y = k) = \exp\left(\sum_{i=0}^{p} x_i \beta_{ik}\right) \Big/ \sum_{m=1}^{r} \exp\left(\sum_{i=0}^{p} x_i \beta_{im}\right).$$

12. However, we found earlier that the qualitative measures of deprivation are good approximations of quantitative measures of deprivation.

13. It is possible that because of their longer-term operation, regular microfinance programs are more suited to handling the general hardship associated with meal rationing than PRIME is, which helps alleviate more acute forms of hardship (that is, starvation). We reran the same regression with two types of microfinance memberships: those started before PRIME and those after PRIME (that is, after 2006). We find that longer exposure to regular

microfinance has a greater effect on meal rationing than more recent regular microfinance, thus confirming our assumption.

References

Chaudhuri, Shubham, and Christina Paxson. 2002. "Smoothing Consumption under Income Seasonality: Buffer Stocks vs. Credit Markets." Discussion Paper 0102-54, Department of Economics, Columbia University, New York.

Datta, Dipankar. 2004. "Microcredit in Rural Bangladesh: Is It Reaching the Poor?" *Journal of Microfinance* 6 (1): 55–81.

Emran, Shahe, Virginia Robano, and Stephen C. Smith. 2009. "Assessing the Frontiers of Ultra-Poverty Reduction: Evidence from CFPR/TUP, an Innovative Program in Bangladesh." Department of Economics, George Washington University, Washington, DC.

Hirano, Keisuke, Guido Imbens, and Geert Ridder. 2003. "Efficient Estimation of Average Treatment Effects Using the Estimated Propensity Score." *Econometrica* 71 (4): 1161–89.

Jalan, Jyotsna, and Martin Ravallion. 2000. "Is Transient Poverty Different? Evidence for Rural China." *Journal of Development Studies* 36 (6): 82–99.

Khalily, M. A. Baqui, and Muhammad Abdul Latif. 2010. "Impact of PRIME Interventions on Monga Mitigation in Greater Rangpur Region in Bangladesh." Institute of Microfinance, Dhaka.

Khandker, Shahidur R. 1998. *Fighting Poverty with Microcredit: Experience in Bangladesh.* New York: Oxford University Press.

———. 2005. "Microfinance and Poverty: Evidence Using Panel Data from Bangladesh." *World Bank Economic Review* 19 (2): 263–86.

———. 2009. "Poverty and Income Seasonality in Bangladesh." Policy Research Working Paper 4923, World Bank, Washington, DC.

Khandker, Shahidur R., M. A. Baqui Khalily, and Hussain A. Samad. 2010. "Seasonal and Extreme Poverty in Bangladesh: Evaluating an Ultra-Poor Microcredit Project." Policy Research Working Paper number 5331, World Bank, Washington, DC.

Matin, Imran, and David Hulme. 2003. "Programs for the Poorest: Learning from the IGVGD Program in Bangladesh." *World Development* 31 (3): 647–65.

Paxson, Christina. 1993. "Consumption and Income Seasonality in Thailand." *Journal of Political Economy* 101 (1): 39–72.

Pitt, Mark, and Shahidur R. Khandker. 2002. "Credit Programmes for the Poor and Seasonality in Rural Bangladesh." *Journal of Development Studies* 39 (2): 1–24.

Rosenzweig, Mark. 1988. "Risk, Implicit Contracts, and the Family in Rural Areas of Low-Income Countries." *Economic Journal* 98 (393): 1148–70.

Rosenzweig, Mark, and Hans Binswanger. 1993. "Wealth, Weather Risk, and the Composition and Profitability of Agricultural Investments." *Economic Journal* 103 (416): 56–78.

Rosenzweig, Mark, and Kenneth Wolpin. 1993. "Credit Market Constraints, Consumption Smoothing, and the Accumulation of Durable Production Assets in Low-Income Countries: Investments in Bullocks in India." *Journal of Political Economy* 101 (2): 223–44.

Stiglitz, Joseph E. 1990, "Peer Monitoring and Credit Markets" *The World Bank Economic Review* 4(3): 351–66.

Townsend, Robert. 1995. "Consumption Insurance: An Evaluation of Risk-Bearing Systems in Low-Income Economies." *Journal of Economic Perspectives* 9 (3): 83–102.

Webb, Patrick, Jennifer Coates, and Robert Houser. 2002. "Does Microcredit Meet the Needs of All Poor Women? Constraints to Participation among Destitute Women in Bangladesh." Tufts Nutrition Discussion Paper 3, Tufts University, Boston, http://nutrition.tufts.edu.

CHAPTER 9

Overview, Policy Perspectives, and Emerging Issues

Seasonal hunger is often overlooked in discussions on food insecurity. Yet just as the problem of extreme poverty and food insecurity will likely remain persistent in large parts of the developing world, so too will its seasonal dimensions. In fact, it appears reasonable to argue that most of the world's acute hunger and undernutrition occur in the annual *hunger season*—the time of year when the previous year's harvest stocks have declined, food prices are high, wages are low, credit access is limited, and jobs are scarce. In economically depressed or ecologically vulnerable areas in particular, a crop failure or a poor harvest can easily magnify seasonal adversity into a disaster. Seasonal hunger has thus been aptly called the "father of famine," and controlling seasonal hunger is a step toward averting famine. Seasonality issues will also need renewed attention because of the rising new threat to global food security and livelihoods of the poor from climate changes and the associated extreme weather conditions that may make seasonal shocks more frequent, severe, and unpredictable.

One reason the discourses on food insecurity neglect seasonal hunger is that the official data collection system that annualizes poverty estimates does not include seasonality. A large percentage of the rural households that depend on agriculture for their livelihoods and are vulnerable to seasonal food insecurity may thus remain invisible to official poverty statistics. As such, they may be disregarded by policy makers if the causes of seasonal hunger differ from those that affect year-round poverty. The lack of data also makes it difficult to monitor the effect of whatever policies and programs are undertaken to address seasonality. Another reason for inaction is a lack of understanding of the complex cycle of poverty and its seasonality, each potentially reinforcing the other. To make matters worse, regions prone to severe seasonal hunger often fail to attract the investments that are necessary to raise the local economy's resilience through diversification and thus break the poverty-seasonality cycle.

Bangladesh has recently achieved considerable progress in reducing poverty and improving the food security of its people. With the country's sustained growth in food production and good record of disaster management, famines have almost become a phenomenon of the past. Yet a large number of people in rural areas still must deal with the annual problem of seasonal hunger. More than 70 percent of the country's nearly 150 million people live in the rural areas of Bangladesh, where life revolves around its so-called rice economy. Although the rural economy has become increasingly diversified with the growth of nonfarm activities, nearly 60 percent of the rural workers (and about half the country's entire workforce) are still employed in the agriculture sector. The country is also prone to floods and other natural disasters. In such a setting, one would expect to find regular occurrences of seasonality of income and consumption, which are only made worse by the natural calamities.

The Extent and Sources of Seasonal Hunger

Although seasonality of poverty and food deprivation is a common feature of rural livelihood in Bangladesh, it is more marked in the northwest region of Rangpur where the interlocking of seasonality and endemic poverty results in severe hunger. Rangpur is well known in the famine literature; it was among the worst-hit districts in the Great Bengal Famine of 1942–44 and was the epicenter of the 1974 famine in Bangladesh. The region has not only lagged other regions in poverty reduction, but also has remained particularly vulnerable to seasonal hunger, known locally as *monga*. Until recently, the phenomenon of monga was hardly mentioned, let alone given any special attention, in the government's plans and programs. But partly because of increased media attention, the subject has caught public interest and is now featured prominently in the government's poverty reduction efforts. The various recent initiatives undertaken to combat monga in Rangpur include (a) introducing new crop technology, (b) providing public works and other safety nets, (c) facilitating out-migration, (d) transferring assets to the poor along with providing skill-based training, and (e) introducing specially designed microcredit programs in addition to the regular ones. These policy interventions thus provide a test case of what works and what does not in combating seasonal hunger.

The baseline survey conducted by the Institute of Microfinance (InM) in 2006 covered nearly half a million poor households in the Rangpur region and has provided a unique wealth of information for analyzing the phenomenon of monga in the region. Both the extent and the seasonality of hunger become strikingly evident from the survey findings. Among the survey households, representing nearly the bottom 60 percent of all households, the incidence of starvation (that is, skipping meals from time to time) was found to rise from 10 percent in the non-monga seasons to a staggering 50 percent in the monga season. Moreover, nearly half the households had to ration food (that is, take half meals) during both the monga and non-monga periods. The households that undergo starvation during monga are also likely to experience food deprivation, though in a milder form, in non-monga seasons. And those that are exposed to starvation during a monga season expect to suffer hardship in the next monga season as well. Seasonal hunger is thus found to be both an aggregate shock and an extension of year-round poverty and food deprivation.

The severe and persistent seasonal hunger that is observed in Rangpur can hardly be caused unless there is a confluence of many adverse factors. These factors are generally a reflection of the agroecological vulnerability of the region along with its adverse economic geography. Some of the factors that put the region at a disadvantage compared with other regions of the country can be readily identified. Some proximate causes include (a) a generally high level of poverty, particularly extreme poverty; (b) low crop yields as a result of poor soil quality; (c) risk of floods and river erosion; (d) a high proportion of households that are landless and depend on income from daily wages; (e) low wage rates for both male and female agricultural day laborers; (f) livelihood vulnerability of the people living in *char* areas, consisting of island-like land fragments reclaimed from rivers; (g) low inflows of remittances from migrant family members; and (h) inadequate investments in infrastructure, including electricity, resulting in a lack of diversification of the rural economy.

The phenomenon of monga must also be understood in light of the famine history of the region. Although famine is epochal, monga is a recurrent phenomenon, and yet famine can be seen as the extreme manifestation of the monga phenomenon. The explanation for famines with regard to a food entitlement failure can thus be relevant in explaining seasonal hunger as well. For example, monga does not seem to be caused by a lack of food availability, but by the failure of the income-earning opportunities for the poor during a particular time of year. Moreover, as in the case of past famines in this region, the landless agricultural laborers are found to be most at risk.

But unlike with famines, failure of income-earning opportunities need not be accompanied by food price inflation to cause monga. Consequently, monga may remain unnoticed as a form of silent hunger, because the abnormal increases in food prices are what usually create public uproar and attract the attention of policy makers. This also explains why the government's interventions for food price stabilization as a means of ensuring food security have not worked to mitigate monga. However, poverty reduction generally, along with more integration of labor and food markets, is likely to have helped reduce the adverse effects of seasonality to some extent. This factor may explain why, since 1974, seasonal hunger in Rangpur has never taken on the proportions of a famine in spite of the much more severe intensity of floods and crop damage than happened in that year.

Although the seasonality in poverty and food deprivation is particularly pronounced in Rangpur, it is in fact observed all over rural Bangladesh. This finding is confirmed by the analysis of the data from the various rounds of the official Household Income and Expenditure Survey (HIES). Incidentally, this research shows that the incorporation of seasonal analysis in the official poverty statistics does not require additional data collection. The statistical exercises based on the HIES data show that seasonal food consumption is related to seasonal income at least as strongly as it is to year-round income. Seasonal poverty and hunger can thus be seen to result from the marked seasonality in agricultural income combined with the lack of poor households' capacity to smooth consumption year round, such as through savings, loans, or food storage. Combating seasonal hunger thus calls for reducing income seasonality through agricultural and rural diversification and enhancing the ability of poor households to insure against seasonality.

Poor households' inability to smooth consumption in the face of income seasonality raises several issues—both policy related and behavioral. Rural households use traditional risk management devices, such as local pooling of resources or mutual support provided by family or friends. Such community-based insurance is feasible when the risks are idiosyncratic (that is, particular to households), but it has limited use in the event of aggregate shocks, like seasonal ones. Even if the rural poor would like to save for precautionary reasons, the lack of appropriate financial institutions could prevent them from doing so. The unpredictability of the extent of seasonal stress may also explain inadequate self-insurance by poor households, either through savings or storage of grains. But even in the case of a predictable decline in income, it is difficult for a poor household that lives near subsistence to consciously fend off future hardship, whether one regards it as a lack of self-control or a "present bias" in decision making. In other words, immediate needs may compromise poor households' ability or willingness to smooth consumption. Therefore, seasonal hunger can be properly understood only in the context of the underlying endemic poverty.

The analysis of how poor households in Rangpur cope with seasonal hunger provides further insights into their livelihood strategies. The vast majority of them are found to adopt a variety of monga-coping mechanisms, including accessing social safety-net support provided by the government and by nongovernmental organizations. Most of the informal coping mechanisms—such as borrowing from moneylenders, sale of assets, or advance sale of labor—are adopted only under extreme distress at the risk of further hardship and erosion of income in the future. In spite of such widespread adoption of coping mechanisms, most of the poor households cannot avoid experiencing food deprivation of varying intensity during the monga season. The uncertainty regarding future seasonal distress also makes poor households opt for inefficient livelihood strategies, thus perpetuating the cycle of endemic poverty and its seasonality. Overall, the picture is thus one of grossly inadequate coping abilities of the monga-vulnerable households in Rangpur.

Seasonal Migration

One of the major coping strategies observed in the Rangpur region during monga is seasonal migration. Among the poor households of the region covered in the InM baseline survey of 2006, about 173,000 opted to send one or more of their household members to work elsewhere during the monga season of that year. A sharp dip in local labor demand coupled with the generally high levels of impoverishment seem to be the major driving forces behind seasonal migration on such a large scale. Both community-level and household characteristics can be important in determining the decision to migrate: households with younger working members, more wage workers compared with self-employed ones, more dependents, or fewer landholdings are more likely to migrate. Higher land productivity (reflected in better agroclimatic conditions) and lower village-level unemployment reduce the probability of migration.

Because of the simultaneity of factors affecting both a household's migration decision and the extent of its food deprivation, one cannot easily determine the direction of causality. When statistical techniques are used to deal with this endogeneity problem, seasonal migration is found to have a beneficial effect on household welfare by reducing the extent of both seasonal and year-round food deprivation. Yet the benefits should not be exaggerated. More than half the households that opted for migration had to resort to other monga-coping mechanisms as well. The fact that many of the migrant households must adopt multiple coping strategies—including borrowing, sale of assets, or advance sale of labor— points to their particular vulnerability. Even then, migration may give the households a better chance of reducing the extent of seasonal and year-round hunger compared with those who lack the necessary net-working capability or financial means to migrate.

Although seasonal migration can have beneficial effects on the migrating households, as well as on the local economy as a whole, it is evidently not enough to mitigate seasonal hunger. Therefore, efforts for facilitating seasonal migration should not divert attention from the need to invest in the local economy and create more employment opportunities, so that labor does not have to move on such a large scale. Interestingly, although access to microcredit seems to be an effective alternative to seasonal migration for households, special schemes for providing credit or cash incentives are found to encourage seasonal migration. There is also scope for promoting the kinds of migration that entail much larger gains to the households compared with seasonal migration. In spite of the widespread prevalence of seasonal migration in Rangpur, there is scarcely any out-migration from the region for overseas employment, or even for factory employment in the cities. Some initiatives have recently been undertaken for sending laborers from the region for overseas employment, though on a very limited scale. Another recently initiated project, supported by the World Bank, aims at providing training and housing facilities for female laborers from the Rangpur region for employment in the export-oriented garment factories located in the export processing zones.

Social Safety Nets

Bangladesh has a fairly large and elaborate social safety-net system aimed at safeguarding the economic security of the poor and vulnerable groups. These programs can potentially act as a kind of social insurance against seasonal poverty, but their effect may be limited by inappropriate targeting, resource leakages, and limited coverage dictated by fund constraints. This research has examined in particular the seasonal dimensions of the effect of safety-net programs.

An area of concern regarding the safety-net programs is that, along with various forms of resource leakages, a sizable share of the benefits goes to the nonpoor. Yet another weak link in channeling safety-net resources to the poor appears to be the process by which the government allocates resources across regions, which corresponds poorly with the regional variations in the poverty levels. In this regard, the analysis of survey data from Rangpur confirms the findings of other studies, namely, that safety-net programs target vulnerable areas rather poorly; but once villages have access to such programs, the relatively more vulnerable among the poor households are likely to benefit more. Even though the programs might have been well targeted within a village, the amount of support was found clearly inadequate to lift the beneficiary households out of extreme seasonal distress. Moreover, judged simply by the observed extent of food deprivation during monga, a large number of extremely vulnerable households must have been left out of the social safety-net system.

An important consideration regarding the role of safety nets in combating seasonal hunger is an appropriate balance between short-term seasonally oriented programs and long-term or year-round ones. In spite of the fact that a predominant part of the existing safety-net system in Bangladesh consists of short-term programs, the system does not necessarily have a beneficial counterseasonal effect. In deciding about the timing of seasonal public works programs like Food for Work, the government agencies may need to balance considerations of providing employment during the pre-*aman* lean season (which coincides in part with the late rainy season and annual floods) and undertaking earthwork for infrastructure building (for which the dry season is more suitable). However, more disconcerting is the survey finding from Rangpur that the payments of benefits even under the year-round programs may sometimes skip the monga season, thus betraying a lack of sensitivity to seasonal distress.

Political competition, driven by the creation of public awareness, seems to have played a role in shaping the government's social safety-net system. In spite of the general lack of sensitivity in the safety-net allocations with respect to poverty prevalence, the increased public attention given to monga in recent years seems to have been translated into increased safety-net coverage in the Rangpur region. However, this increase in coverage may be explained in part by programs with extremely small short-term or one-time benefits, which may reflect a kind of populist "tokenism" in the provision of such benefits. Overall, in spite of their limitations, the safety-net programs have a positive effect on mitigating monga, as found in the statistical exercises that control for the problem of endogeneity of program participation. Moreover, there are both seasonal and year-round beneficial effects. It will probably be correct to argue therefore that these programs need to be expanded in coverage, made more cost-effective, and designed to be more sensitive to the seasonal needs.

Microcredit for the Ultrapoor

The information on access to microcredit as part of village-level area characteristics is available from the two main sources of data for this research, the HIES and the InM baseline survey of poor households in Rangpur conducted in 2006–07. These data could therefore be used to estimate the effect of microcredit on both poverty levels in general and seasonal hunger in particular. The effect of microcredit on both counts was found to be positive and substantial (after controlling for the possible biases in program placement to the extent possible).

This research is, however, concerned less with the effect of regular microcredit than it is with the effect of a specially designed microcredit program for the ultrapoor in combating seasonal poverty. In fact, the InM baseline survey found coverage of regular microcredit programs among the poor households in Rangpur to be much too low compared with that in other regions of the country. This finding confirms the view that the ultrapoor households as well as the regional pockets of extreme poverty are bypassed by the regular microcredit programs. However, in 2006, as part of the new measures to combat monga, the Programmed Initiatives for Monga Eradication (PRIME) was introduced by the Palli Karma-Sahayak Foundation (PKSF), the country's premier wholesale microfinance institution. An assessment of this program's effect has been possible by use of the household panel data obtained from a follow-up survey of a subsample of the InM's baseline survey.

As a specially designed microcredit program, PRIME's objective is to deal exclusively with the extreme poor who are highly vulnerable to seasonal poverty in the Rangpur region. Several of PRIME's features distinguish it from regular microcredit programs: (a) interest rates are relatively low; (b) repayment is on more flexible terms; (c) loans can be used for consumption if so needed; (d) no fixed savings or weekly meetings are stipulated; and (e) loans are often combined with other benefits, like skills-based training, provision of health services, and facilitation of migration.[1]

The regular microcredit programs have not reached the ultrapoor—particularly those who are hit hard by seasonal poverty—for several reasons. The ultrapoor are generally considered less creditworthy than the moderate poor because of their lower capacity to engage in income-generating self-employment. The commonly practiced weekly repayment schedule is at odds with seasonality of income and employment. Many rural nonfarm activities are also linked to the agricultural cycle, often limiting the ability of microcredit agencies to support new loans during lean seasons.

Moreover, group-based lending works well when income variations are idiosyncratic so that group members assist or insure one another through difficult times. But when seasonality is systematic, affecting everyone in a group, the ability of mutual insurance is severely curtailed, and the group as a whole has a greater incentive to collude on a strategy of default. The PRIME initiative therefore represents an experiment in designing micro-credit programs in a way that suits the needs of the extreme poor who are vulnerable to seasonal poverty. This objective, of course, involves some subsidies, even if implicit—such as PKSF providing loans with easier terms to its partner microfinance institutions (MFIs) and probably also the MFIs themselves cross-subsidizing between PRIME and their regular microcredit programs.

With regard to mobilization of the ultrapoor into microcredit, PRIME has been a success. Within less than two years of its initiation in 2006–07, about 62 percent of the poor households in the Rangpur region were found to participate in some form of microfinance. Of these, 29 percent were PRIME participants, whereas 33 percent participated in regular microfinance. It is clear that the MFIs successfully reached the ultrapoor in Rangpur under the PRIME initiative in parallel to their already-existing regular microcredit programs in the region. The experience so far is that both types of programs have also been successful in attaining a loan recovery rate almost as high (over 95 percent) as that found in other parts of the country. Furthermore, PRIME appears to be better designed than regular microcredit programs in meeting the needs of the ultrapoor households.

How effective is PRIME in alleviating seasonal and chronic food deprivation? The answer is found by performing statistical exercises of impact assessment based on the household panel data from the InM's 2008 follow-up survey. The results show that PRIME reduces the probability of starvation during the monga season compared with a statistically insignificant effect of regular microfinance programs. For the non-monga season as well, PRIME has a larger effect in reducing the probability of food deprivation generally (that is, starvation and meal rationing combined) compared with regular microcredit programs. These results do not, however, tell us much about the longer-term effects of the two types of programs on asset accumulation and changes in households' net worth. It is possible that regular microfinance programs have longer-term benefits through asset accumulation, whereas PRIME alleviates more immediate and severe types of hardship, like starvation. These findings also suggest that microcredit programs can be variously designed to reflect their two very different characteristics: (a) a banking operation for the poor requiring financial viability and (b) a type of social safety-net program for the poor requiring subsidies or fund support.

Policy Effectiveness and Emerging Concerns

This research has shown that policies and programs matter in alleviating food deprivation and its seasonality. It is generally agreed that economic growth is necessary to reduce poverty and food insecurity for large numbers of households and in a sustained way. But economic growth alone—even when it leads to poverty reduction—may not be sufficient to deal with particular dimensions of food insecurity, such as seasonal hunger (child malnutrition is another such dimension). Both global experience and that of Bangladesh discussed in this book testify to that possibility. Therefore, it is important to look for a set of policies that can effectively address the interlocking problems of poverty, food insecurity, and seasonality.

Because of data limitations, the effects of only a limited range of policy interventions could be examined in this book. Nevertheless, the results show the effectiveness of policies, in varying degrees, in a number of areas: improving the production environment (such as through provision of electricity or irrigation); enhancing the human capital and asset base of households; and providing targeted safety nets, including microcredit.

Most of these interventions are found to be effective in reducing both extreme poverty and its seasonality, but a well-coordinated strategy is needed. Such a strategy requires a threefold approach: (a) combining seasonally oriented policies with those that are aimed at removing the underlying structural causes of endemic poverty, (b) reducing income seasonality through agricultural and rural diversification and enhancing the ability of poor households to insure against seasonality, and (c) helping the poor households cope with seasonal hunger so they can avoid using extreme coping measures under distress.

The beneficial effect of the various initiatives undertaken to combat monga in Rangpur is already visible. In addition to media reports and official assertions, the evidence on this effect comes from the InM's three-phase follow-up surveys conducted in 2008, 2009, and 2010 (figure 9.1). These surveys, the results of which are yet to be fully analyzed, covered a subsample of households from the 2006 baseline survey and as such are representative of the bottom 60 percent of the population of the region. The most remarkable finding is the sharp decline in the incidence of starvation during monga, from about 50 percent to only 6 percent. However, most of those escaping starvation still experience the less severe form of food deprivation (that is, half meals or meal rationing), and only 20 percent of households have full meals. Although these estimates indicate remarkable progress in reducing the extent of monga, there is little room for complacence.

Figure 9.1   Trends in Food Deprivation Status during Monga among Poor Households in the Rangpur Region, 2006–10

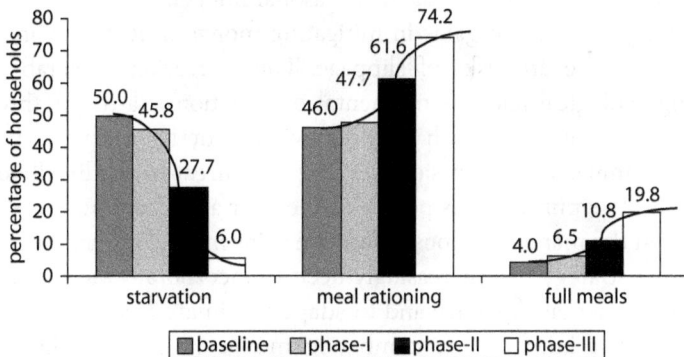

Sources: Institute of Microfinance surveys, 2006 (baseline), 2008 (Phase I), 2009 (Phase II), 2010 (Phase III).
Note: Based on panel data for 3,664 households.

The factors contributing to the observed reduction in the severity of monga need a more detailed analysis than has been possible in this book. The various measures are found to alleviate seasonal hunger in varying degrees. Together, their effect seems to have been greater than the separately estimated effect for each one, suggesting the existence of beneficial synergies and complementarities. Additionally, these findings need to be interpreted in two important contexts. First, the accelerated rate of overall poverty reduction in Bangladesh during this period—by nearly 2 percentage points annually according to the official head-count poverty estimates—is likely to have had a favorable effect on alleviating monga. Second, poverty reduction countrywide and the alleviation of monga in Rangpur have been possible in spite of the food price hikes of 2007–08, making these gains all the more remarkable.

An important intervention, the effect of which has not been analyzed here, is the recent introduction of some new rice varieties in the Rangpur region specifically to mitigate monga. These short-duration, high-yielding rice varieties mature in about 115 days (instead of 165 days in the case of prevalent high-yielding rice varieties) and can be grown in the *aman* season. Because these varieties can be harvested from early October onward, demand for agricultural labor is created precisely during the lean period of October–November; moreover, farmers gain a chance to grow another crop, like potatoes, vegetables, wheat, or maize, before starting the rice crop cycle again. By 2011, about one-fifth of all aman land in the Rangpur region had been switched to these rice varieties.[2] This success—which is due to the combined efforts of agricultural research institutions, nongovernmental organizations, and government agricultural extension services—highlights the important role that agricultural research and development can play in mitigating seasonal hunger.

Although the recent gains in mitigating monga in Rangpur are commendable, there are risks of slippage. The increasing vulnerability to looming ecological and environmental degradation is a major threat to these gains, many of which may be wiped out by a severe drought or flood. Similarly, river erosion is a constant threat to the livelihoods of people in Rangpur, whereas people in the char areas continue to eke out a living on the margin. To consolidate the gains made thus far, the monga-mitigating strategy will increasingly need to incorporate ways to address the environmental challenge and to adapt to climate change.

The recent initiatives in combating monga in Rangpur have been prompted by widespread public awareness, which in turn has been largely created by media reports and civic activism. It has been argued that the incentives in democracy are more effective in averting major economic disasters like famines than in addressing the problem of endemic hunger and poverty (Bardhan 1999; Drèze and Sen 1989; Sen 1981, 1983). The recent public action against monga is a testimony to the fact that political incentives in a democracy can be created for combating severe incidence of seasonal hunger as well, once the phenomenon catches public attention. However, a lack of similar awareness may have resulted in the neglect of other regions in Bangladesh that are vulnerable to seasonal poverty and hunger.

In the northern region of the country, the areas on the eastern bank of the Jamuna River in the Jamalpur district and on the western bank of the Jamuna River south of Rangpur and the *haor* (depressed land) areas in the other northern districts remain ecologically vulnerable poverty pockets. The southern coastal regions are increasingly facing threats to livelihoods from environmental degradation and climate change. This research has found that the areas with adverse agroecological environments tend to be doubly disadvantaged; these areas are particularly vulnerable to seasonal shocks and may be neglected by the public infrastructure investments and other development programs that help mitigate seasonality.

Although reliable poverty estimates are lacking, some districts in the southern and southwestern coastal regions of Bangladesh have already emerged as new ecologically vulnerable poverty pockets. Widespread damage to livelihoods in these areas is resulting from a combination of factors: (a) increasing intrusion of saline water caused by reduced river water flows resulting in reduced agricultural productivity; (b) waterlogging of vast land areas from siltation of riverbeds; (c) more frequent cyclones, including the two recent devastating ones, Sidr and Aila; and (d) the adverse geography reflected in poor infrastructure and remoteness to metropolitan centers.

The InM has recently carried out a baseline survey of some of the worst-affected coastal areas as part of the preparation to launch a special microcredit program similar to PRIME in Rangpur. The survey's preliminary findings are quite revealing: not only is the extent of food deprivation among the poor households severe, but there also is a very marked seasonality. However, the patterns of seasonal variations are quite different from those in other parts of the country, including Rangpur. The percentage of the poor households sampled that have full meals each day increases to about 70 percent during the September–November period from a low of less than 10 percent during the April–June period (InM 2011). Thus, the commonly observed seasonal pattern seems to be almost reversed.

This finding is hardly surprising. The dry season high-yielding *boro*, which is the major rice crop in most parts of Bangladesh, is almost non-existent in these coastal areas. Instead, the early rainy season low-yielding *aus* crop is grown in these areas along with the main aman crop. However, many households in these coastal areas depend for their livelihoods mainly on low-technology marine fishing, which has its distinct seasonality and is vulnerable to climate change. Thus, the pattern of hunger and seasonality in these emerging poverty pockets may differ from that of Rangpur and may call for different types of policy interventions. But some lessons are still to be drawn from the experience of Rangpur.

What are those general lessons? The sources of seasonal hunger are context specific, so that policies for addressing the problem need to be locally relevant, socially acceptable, and economically feasible. Each type of environment, being unique in some respect, will have its own priorities and will require its own mix of policies. Because of the multidimensional nature of the problem, these policies need to be harmonized within the general economic, social, and environmental policies of a country. No single cure exists for seasonal hunger; a country may need to implement an array of specific measures with the help of government agencies, non-governmental organizations, and international actors.[3] Meeting the emerging threats of climate change and environmental degradation will need even more innovative solutions. Ultimately, the challenge will be how to enhance the ability of the rural poor to cope with the increasing complexity and uncertainty linked to seasonality by making their livelihoods more flexible, adaptable, and resilient. This book addresses some of these questions using data from Bangladesh with the hope that the findings are relevant for policy makers from the governments and international agencies that fight poverty and hunger worldwide.

Notes

1. Initially, some type of "food or cash for work" employment was also made a component of the program, but this component was subsequently dropped as the government expanded such employment programs in the region.

2. These varieties include BRRI-33, BRRI-39, and BINA-7, which are adapted to local conditions for the aman season and have been developed to substitute for the currently popular BRRI-11.

3. See further policy discussions in Devereux, Sabates-Wheeler, and Longhurst (2012).

References

Bardhan, Pranab. 1999. "Democracy and Development: A Complex Relationship." In *Democracy's Value*, ed. Ian Shapiro and Casiano Hacker-Cordon. Cambridge: Cambridge University Press.

Devereux, Stephen, Rachel Sabates-Wheeler, and Richard Longhurst. 2012. *Seasonality, Rural Livelihoods, and Development*. London: Earthscan.

Drèze, Jean, and Amartya Sen. 1989. *Hunger and Public Action*. Oxford, U.K.: Clarendon Press.

InM (Institute of Microfinance). 2011. "PRIME Interventions in the Coastal Areas of South-West Bangladesh: A Baseline Survey." InM, Dhaka.

Sen, Amartya K. 1981. *Poverty and Famines: An Essay on Entitlement and Deprivation*. New York: Oxford University Press.

———. 1983. "Development: Which Way Now?" *Economic Journal* 93: 745–62.